REVIEW TEXT IN
LATIN THREE AND FOUR YEARS
(Prose and Poetry)

By CHARLES I. FREUNDLICH

Author of
Latin for the Grades, Books I, II, III
Latin First Year
Latin Two Years

Dedicated to serving

our nation's youth

When ordering this book, please specify:
either **N 334 P** *or*
REVIEW TEXT IN LATIN THREE AND FOUR YEARS

AMSCO SCHOOL PUBLICATIONS, Inc.
315 Hudson Street   **New York, N. Y. 10013**

ISBN 0-87720-558-2

PREFACE

This review text fills a longfelt need for a combined review of Latin prose and poetry studied in the third and fourth years of high school. All too often enrollments in the upper grades of Latin are too small to permit simultaneous classes in prose and poetry. By combining levels III and IV into one class, the teacher can alternate the course, teaching prose one year and poetry the next. This arrangement would insure an advanced Latin class, which would otherwise be dropped because of a paucity of numbers.

The book is divided into two sections. The first part (Three Years) deals with Latin prose, and contains a comprehensive review of all the forms and grammatical structures required for a proper understanding of prose authors, particularly Cicero. In addition to a section devoted to the life of Cicero, the book contains lessons on oratory, Roman government, Roman religion, prominent contemporaries of Cicero, places of interest, the calendar, etc.

The second part of the book (Four Years) treats of poetry in all its aspects, namely, poetical forms, poetical structures, versification, figures of speech, etc. There is also a section on the life and works of Vergil and Ovid, a list of familiar quotations from the *Aeneid*, and an outline of the entire twelve books of the *Aeneid*. Also included is a listing of important characters, deities, and geographical terms mentioned in the *Aeneid*.

Both parts of the book contain sections on word study and derivation, vocabularies, and guides to the College Board Achievement Test in Latin. Explanations are presented in simple, understandable terms, and are replete with illustrative examples. Exercises of all types are in abundance throughout the book.

Since this review text contains material suitable for both prose and poetry, this one book can be used to advantage by students for both their third and fourth years of Latin. It should prove exceedingly valuable as a supplement to any textbook used in level III or IV.

—C. I. F.

CONTENTS—THREE YEARS

Unit I—Verbs, Indicative Mood

Unit II—Imperatives, Infinitives, Participles, Gerund

Unit III—Subjunctive Mood

Unit IV—Nouns

Unit V—Adjectives and Numerals

Unit VI—Comparison

Unit VII—Pronouns

Unit XIII—Vocabularies

CONTENTS—FOUR YEARS

Unit XIV—Forms

Unit XV—Grammatical Structures

Unit XVI—Versification

Unit XVII—Figures of Speech

Unit XVIII—Quotations

Unit XIX—Word Study and Derivation

Unit XX—Culture

Unit XXI—Vocabulary

LATIN THREE YEARS

PROSE

(*Cicero*)

Unit I—Verbs, Indicative Mood

Lesson 1. PRESENT AND IMPERFECT TENSES

FIRST CONJUGATION

PRINCIPAL PARTS: **iūdicō, iūdicāre, iūdicāvī, iūdicātus**
STEMS: *present,* **iūdicā-**; *perfect,* **iūdicāv-**; *participial,* **iūdicāt-**

ACTIVE		PASSIVE	
		PRESENT	
I judge, am judging, do judge		*I am judged*	
iūdic**ō**	iūdicā**mus**	iūdic**or**	iūdicā**mur**
iūdicā**s**	iūdicā**tis**	iūdicā**ris** (**-re**)	iūdicā**minī**
iūdica**t**	iūdica**nt**	iūdicā**tur**	iūdica**ntur**
		IMPERFECT	
I was judging, judged		*I was judged*	
iūdicā**bam**	iūdicā**bāmus**	iūdicā**bar**	iūdicā**bāmur**
iūdicā**bās**	iūdicā**bātis**	iūdicā**bāris** (**-re**)	iūdicā**bāminī**
iūdicā**bat**	iūdicā**bant**	iūdicā**bātur**	iūdicā**bantur**

SECOND CONJUGATION

PRINCIPAL PARTS: **dēbeō, dēbēre, dēbuī, dēbitus**
STEMS: *present,* **dēbē-**; *perfect,* **dēbu-**; *participial,* **dēbit-**

ACTIVE		PASSIVE	
		PRESENT	
dēbe**ō**	dēbē**mus**	dēbe**or**	dēbē**mur**
dēbē**s**	dēbē**tis**	dēbē**ris** (**-re**)	dēbē**minī**
dēbe**t**	dēbe**nt**	dēbē**tur**	dēbe**ntur**
		IMPERFECT	
dēbē**bam**	dēbē**bāmus**	dēbē**bar**	dēbē**bāmur**
dēbē**bās**	dēbē**bātis**	dēbē**bāris** (**-re**)	dēbē**bāminī**
dēbē**bat**	dēbē**bant**	dēbē**bātur**	dēbē**bantur**

1

THIRD CONJUGATION

PRINCIPAL PARTS: **pellō, pellere, pepulī, pulsus**
STEMS: *present,* **pelle-;** *perfect,* **pepul-;** *participial,* **puls-**

ACTIVE		PASSIVE	
	PRESENT		
pell*ō*	pelli*mus*	pell*or*	pelli*mur*
pelli*s*	pelli*tis*	peller*is* (-*re*)	pelli*minī*
pelli*t*	pell*unt*	pelli*tur*	pell*untur*
	IMPERFECT		
pellē*bam*	pellē*bāmus*	pellē*bar*	pellē*bāmur*
pellē*bās*	pellē*bātis*	pellē*bāris* (-*re*)	pellē*bāminī*
pellē*bat*	pellē*bant*	pellē*bātur*	pellē*bantur*

-IŌ THIRD CONJUGATION

PRINCIPAL PARTS: **capiō, capere, cēpī, captus**
STEMS: *present,* **cape-;** *perfect,* **cēp-;** *participial,* **capt-**

ACTIVE		PASSIVE	
	PRESENT		
capi*ō*	capi*mus*	capi*or*	capi*mur*
capi*s*	capi*tis*	caper*is* (-*re*)	capi*minī*
capi*t*	capi*unt*	capi*tur*	capi*untur*
	IMPERFECT		
capiē*bam*	capiē*bāmus*	capiē*bar*	capiē*bāmur*
capiē*bās*	capiē*bātis*	capiē*bāris* (-*re*)	capiē*bāminī*
capiē*bat*	capiē*bant*	capiē*bātur*	capiē*bantur*

FOURTH CONJUGATION

PRINCIPAL PARTS: **sentiō, sentīre, sēnsī, sēnsus**
STEMS: *present*, **sentī-**; *perfect*, **sēns-**; *participial*, **sēns-**

ACTIVE		PASSIVE	
		PRESENT	
sentiō	sentīmus	sentior	sentīmur
sentīs	sentītis	sentīris (-re)	sentīminī
sentit	sentiunt	sentītur	sentiuntur
		IMPERFECT	
sentiēbam	sentiēbāmus	sentiēbar	sentiēbāmur
sentiēbās	sentiēbātis	sentiēbāris (-re)	sentiēbāminī
sentiēbat	sentiēbant	sentiēbātur	sentiēbantur

Note:
1. The personal endings of the present indicative, attached to the present stem, are:

ACTIVE		PASSIVE	
-ō	-mus	-r (-or)	-mur
-s	-tis	-ris (-re)	-minī
-t	-nt	-tur	-ntur

2. The endings of the imperfect indicative, attached to the present stem, are:

ACTIVE		PASSIVE	
-bam	-bāmus	-bar	-bāmur
-bās	-bātis	-bāris (-re)	-bāminī
-bat	-bant	-bātur	-bantur

3. In the active voice, the subject generally performs some action. In the passive voice, the subject is acted upon.

ACTIVE	PASSIVE
Cicerō ōrātiōnem **habet**.	Ōrātiō ā Cicerōne **habētur**.
Cicero is delivering a speech.	A speech is being delivered by Cicero.

WORKING VOCABULARY OF VERBS

First Conjugation

iūdicō, iūdicāre, iūdicāvī, iūdicātus, judge

cōgitō, think
coniūrō, conspire, plot
dubitō, doubt, hesitate
mandō, entrust
necō, kill
negō, say no, deny

postulō, demand
probō, approve
rēgnō, reign
vigilō, watch
vītō, avoid

Second Conjugation

dēbeō, dēbēre, dēbuī, dēbitus, owe

abhorreō, shrink from
cēnseō, decree
iaceō, lie

mereō, deserve
studeō, be eager for
valeō, be well

dēleō, dēlēre, dēlēvī, dēlētus, destroy
prōvideō, prōvidēre, prōvīdī, prōvīsus, foresee

Third Conjugation

cōgō, cōgere, coēgī, coāctus, collect, compel
crēdō, crēdere, crēdidī, crēditus, believe
legō, legere, lēgī, lēctus, choose, read
pellō, pellere, pepulī, pulsus, drive
premō, premere, pressī, pressus, press
quaerō, quaerere, quaesīvī, quaesītus, seek
resistō, resistere, restitī, ———, resist
trahō, trahere, trāxī, trāctus, draw
vertō, vertere, vertī, versus, turn
vīvō, vīvere, vīxī, vīctus, live

-IŌ Third Conjugation

capiō, capere, cēpī, captus, take
faciō, make, do
iaciō, throw

afficiō, afficere, affēcī, affectus, affect
dēficiō, fail
percipiō, perceive
suscipiō, undertake

rapiō, rapere, rapuī, raptus, seize
ēripiō, ēripere, ēripuī, ēreptus, rescue

Fourth Conjugation

cūstōdiō, cūstōdīre, cūstōdīvī, cūstōdītus, guard
ērudiō, teach
serviō, serve

sentiō, sentīre, sēnsī, sēnsus, feel
cōnsentiō, agree
dissentiō, disagree

EXERCISES

A. In each sentence, make the verb agree with the change of subject.

1. *Praetōrēs* laudantur.   Praetor _____.
2. *Ego* putābam eum exitūrum.   Tū _____.
3. *Litterae* trāduntur.   Gladius _____.
4. *Tū* eum ex urbe pellēbās.   Nōs _____.
5. *Rēs* ignōrābātur ā cēterīs.   Cōnsilia _____.
6. *Catilīna* hominēs dēlēctōs habēbat.   Vōs _____.
7. *Cicerō* sciēbat eōs Rōmae esse.   Ego _____.
8. *Vōs* eōs exspectātis.   Nōs _____.
9. *Ipsī* dēdūcuntur.   Vōs _____.
10. *Nōs* omnia memoriā tenēmus.   Tū _____.

B. In each sentence, substitute the equivalent forms of the verbs in parentheses for the italicized verb.

1. Servī tē *metuēbant*. (amāre, rapere, trahere)
2. *Dīcō* apertē. (dissentīre, resistere, coniūrāre)
3. Italia ad exitium *vocābātur*. (parāre, iubēre, pellere)
4. Catilīnae tēla *vītāmus*. (capere, cūstōdīre, dēlēre)
5. Ea in librīs *leguntur*. (vidēre, dēmōnstrāre, quaerere)
6. Nōnne exitum *sentīs*? (probāre, percipere, timēre)
7. Nihil tē *movet*. (premere, afficere, ērudīre)
8. Cūrae eius *mandābāris*. (committere, dare, exercēre)
9. Hanc pestem *effugiēbāmus*. (prōvidēre, vigilāre, expōnere)
10. Rem pūblicam *petēbātis*. (vāstāre, terrēre, ēripere)

C. In each sentence, give the correct form of both the present and the imperfect indicative of the italicized verb.

1. *venīre:*   Servus lentē _____; _____.
2. *vulnerāre:*   Tū mentīs _____; _____.
3. *timēre:*   Parentēs tē _____; _____.
4. *continēre:*   Nōs moenibus _____; _____.
5. *addūcere:*   Ego tē facile _____; _____.
6. *premere:*   Paucī aere aliēnō _____; _____.
7. *sentīre:*   Tū eum exspectārī in castrīs _____; _____.
8. *dīcere:*   Nōs nihil _____; _____.
9. *probāre:*   Omnēs labōrem _____; _____.
10. *rapere:*   Vōs ad mortem ā cōnsule _____; _____.

Lesson 2. FUTURE TENSE

FIRST CONJUGATION

PRINCIPAL PARTS: **iūdicō, iūdicāre, iūdicāvī, iūdicātus**
STEMS: *present,* **iūdicā-**; *perfect,* **iūdicāv-**; *participial,* **iūdicāt-**

ACTIVE		PASSIVE	
I shall judge		*I shall be judged*	
iūdicā**bō**	iūdicā**bimus**	iūdicā**bor**	iūdicā**bimur**
iūdicā**bis**	iūdicā**bitis**	iūdicā**beris** (*-re*)	iūdicā**biminī**
iūdicā**bit**	iūdicā**bunt**	iūdicā**bitur**	iūdicā**buntur**

SECOND CONJUGATION

PRINCIPAL PARTS: **dēbeō, dēbēre, dēbuī, dēbitus**
STEMS: *present,* **dēbē-**; *perfect,* **dēbu-**; *participial,* **dēbit-**

ACTIVE		PASSIVE	
dēbē**bō**	dēbē**bimus**	dēbē**bor**	dēbē**bimur**
dēbē**bis**	dēbē**bitis**	dēbē**beris** (*-re*)	dēbē**biminī**
dēbē**bit**	dēbē**bunt**	dēbē**bitur**	dēbē**buntur**

THIRD CONJUGATION

PRINCIPAL PARTS: **pellō, pellere, pepulī, pulsus**
STEMS: *present,* **pelle-**; *perfect,* **pepul-**; *participial,* **puls-**

ACTIVE		PASSIVE	
pell**am**	pell**ēmus**	pell**ar**	pell**ēmur**
pell**ēs**	pell**ētis**	pell**ēris** (*-re*)	pell**ēminī**
pell**et**	pell**ent**	pell**ētur**	pell**entur**

-IŌ THIRD CONJUGATION

PRINCIPAL PARTS: **capiō, capere, cēpī, captus**
STEMS: *present,* **cape-;** *perfect,* **cēp-;** *participial,* **capt-**

ACTIVE		PASSIVE	
capi*am*	capi*ēmus*	capi*ar*	capi*ēmur*
capi*ēs*	capi*ētis*	capi*ēris* (*-re*)	capi*ēminī*
capi*et*	capi*ent*	capi*ētur*	capi*entur*

FOURTH CONJUGATION

PRINCIPAL PARTS: **sentiō, sentīre, sēnsī, sēnsus**
STEMS: *present,* **sentī-;** *perfect,* **sēns-;** *participial,* **sēns-**

ACTIVE		PASSIVE	
senti*am*	senti*ēmus*	senti*ar*	senti*ēmur*
senti*ēs*	senti*ētis*	senti*ēris* (*-re*)	senti*ēminī*
senti*et*	senti*ent*	senti*ētur*	senti*entur*

Note:

1. The endings of the future indicative of first and second conjugation verbs, attached to the present stem, are:

ACTIVE		PASSIVE	
-bō	**-bimus**	**-bor**	**-bimur**
-bis	**-bitis**	**-beris** (**-re**)	**-biminī**
-bit	**-bunt**	**-bitur**	**-buntur**

2. The endings of the future indicative of third, **-iō** third, and fourth conjugation verbs are:

ACTIVE		PASSIVE	
-am	**-ēmus**	**-ar**	**-ēmur**
-ēs	**-ētis**	**-ēris** (**-re**)	**-ēminī**
-et	**-ent**	**-ētur**	**-entur**

3. In the passive second singular of third conjugation verbs, a long *e* distinguishes the future from the present.

pell*e*ris, *you are driven*   pell*ē*ris, *you will be driven*
   _{present} → present   future

4. With the exception of the first person singular, the forms of the *future* tense of *third* conjugation verbs resemble the forms of the *present* tense of *second* conjugation verbs.

SECOND CONJUGATION	THIRD CONJUGATION
dēbēs, *you owe* present active	pellēs, *you will drive* future active
dēbētur, *he is owed* present passive	pellētur, *he will be driven* future passive

EXERCISES

A. Change each italicized verb to the future tense.

1. Nōn *agō* obscūrē.
2. Vim nōn *timētis?*
3. Virum bonum nōn *audīs.*
4. Quid tē *impedit?*
5. *Vīvis* meīs praesidiīs obsessus.
6. Multōrum tē oculī *custōdiunt.*
7. Bellō *vāstābātur* Italia.
8. *Vidēmur* cūrā esse relevātī.
9. Vix invidiam *sustinēbam.*
10. Haec pestis *dēlētur.*

B. In each sentence, substitute the equivalent forms of the verbs in parentheses for the italicized verb.

1. Nūllum praemium *postulābō.* (merēre, quaerere)
2. Perīculum *manēbit.* (excēdere, venīre)
3. Eam rem *convincēmus.* (probāre, custōdīre)
4. Istae cōpiae *comparābuntur.* (dēligere, postulāre)
5. Eīs *persuādēbis.* (crēdere, servīre)
6. *Expōnam* vōbīs omnia. (dēmōnstrāre, dēbēre)
7. Furor tuus nōs *ēlūdet.* (opprimere, perterrēre)
8. Memoriā vestrā nostrae rēs *crēscent.* (vīvere, augēre)
9. Pauca *respondēbitis.* (dīcere, negāre)
10. Tum dēnique *interficiēre.* (necāre, rapere)

C. Change each verb to the plural.

1. dēfendet
2. faciēs
3. relinquar
4. coniūrābō
5. sentiam

6. monēberis
7. tenēbis
8. suscipiētur
9. prohibēbit
10. pōnēris

D. Change each verb to the passive.

1. pellet
2. docēbis
3. cūrābō
4. dūcēs
5. dēlēbunt

6. vincam
7. iungēmus
8. pācābit
9. vidēbimus
10. accipiētis

Lesson 3. THE PERFECT SYSTEM

FIRST CONJUGATION

PRINCIPAL PARTS: **iūdicō, iūdicāre, iūdicāvī, iūdicātus**
STEMS: *present,* **iūdicā-;** *perfect,* **iūdicāv-;** *participial,* **iūdicāt-**

ACTIVE	PASSIVE
PERFECT	
I have judged, judged, did judge	*I have been judged, was judged*
iūdicāvī iūdicāvimus	iūdicātus, {sum / es / est} -a, -um iūdicātī, {sumus / estis / sunt} -ae, -a
iūdicāvistī iūdicāvistis	
iūdicāvit iūdicāvērunt (-ēre)	
PLUPERFECT	
I had judged	*I had been judged*
iūdicāveram iūdicāverāmus	iūdicātus, {eram / erās / erat} -a, -um iūdicātī, {erāmus / erātis / erant} -ae, -a
iūdicāverās iūdicāverātis	
iūdicāverat iūdicāverant	
FUTURE PERFECT	
I shall have judged	*I shall have been judged*
iūdicāverō iūdicāverimus	iūdicātus, {erō / eris / erit} -a, -um iūdicātī, {erimus / eritis / erunt} -ae, -a
iūdicāveris iūdicāveritis	
iūdicāverit iūdicāverint	

SECOND CONJUGATION

Principal Parts: **dēbeō, dēbēre, dēbuī, dēbitus**
Stems: *present,* **dēbē-;** *perfect,* **dēbu-;** *participial,* **dēbit-**

PERFECT				
dēbuī	dēbuimus	dēbitus, -a, -um	sum es est	dēbitī, -ae, -a	sumus estis sunt
dēbuistī	dēbuistis				
dēbuit	dēbuērunt (-ēre)				

PLUPERFECT				
dēbueram	dēbuerāmus	dēbitus, -a, -um	eram erās erat	dēbitī, -ae, -a	erāmus erātis erant
dēbuerās	dēbuerātis				
dēbuerat	dēbuerant				

FUTURE PERFECT				
dēbuerō	dēbuerimus	dēbitus, -a, -um	erō eris erit	dēbitī. -ae, -a	erimus eritis erunt
dēbueris	dēbueritis				
dēbuerit	dēbuerint				

THIRD CONJUGATION

Principal Parts: **pellō, pellere, pepulī, pulsus**
Stems: *present,* **pelle-;** *perfect,* **pepul-;** *participial,* **puls-**

PERFECT				
pepulī	pepulimus	pulsus, -a, -um	sum es est	pulsī, -ae, -a	sumus estis sunt
pepulistī	pepulistis				
pepulit	pepulērunt (-ēre)				

PLUPERFECT				
pepuleram	pepulerāmus	pulsus, -a, -um	eram erās erat	pulsī, -ae, -a	erāmus erātis erant
pepulerās	pepulerātis				
pepulerat	pepulerant				

FUTURE PERFECT				
pepulerō	pepulerimus	pulsus, -a, -um	erō eris erit	pulsī, -ae, -a	erimus eritis erunt
pepuleris	pepuleritis				
pepulerit	pepulerint				

-IŌ THIRD CONJUGATION

PRINCIPAL PARTS: **capiō, capere, cēpī, captus**
STEMS: *present,* **cape-;** *perfect,* **cēp-;** *participial,* **capt-**

PERFECT

cēpī	cēpimus	captus, { sum / es / est	captī, { sumus / estis / sunt
cēpistī	cēpistis	-a, -um	-ae, -a
cēpit	cēpērunt (-ēre)		

PLUPERFECT

cēperam	cēperāmus	captus, { eram / erās / erat	captī, { erāmus / erātis / erant
cēperās	cēperātis	-a, -um	-ae, -a
cēperat	cēperant		

FUTURE PERFECT

cēperō	cēperimus	captus, { erō / eris / erit	captī, { erimus / eritis / erunt
cēperis	cēperitis	-a, -um	-ae, -a
cēperit	cēperint		

FOURTH CONJUGATION

PRINCIPAL PARTS: **sentiō, sentīre, sēnsī, sēnsus**
STEMS: *present,* **sentī-;** *perfect,* **sēns-;** *participial,* **sēns-**

PERFECT

sēnsī	sēnsimus	sēnsus, { sum / es / est	sēnsī, { sumus / estis / sunt
sēnsistī	sēnsistis	-a, -um	-ae, -a
sēnsit	sēnsērunt (-ēre)		

PLUPERFECT

sēnseram	sēnserāmus	sēnsus, { eram / erās / erat	sēnsī, { erāmus / erātis / erant
sēnserās	sēnserātis	-a, -um	-ae, -a
sēnserat	sēnserant		

FUTURE PERFECT

sēnserō	sēnserimus	sēnsus, { erō / eris / erit	sēnsī, { erimus / eritis / erunt
sēnseris	sēnseritis	-a, -um	-ae, -a
sēnserit	sēnserint		

Note:

1. The endings of the perfect system active, attached to the perfect stem, are as follows:

PERFECT ACTIVE		PLUPERFECT ACTIVE	
SINGULAR	PLURAL	SINGULAR	PLURAL
-ī	-imus	-eram	-erāmus
-istī	-istis	-erās	-erātis
-it	-ērunt (-ēre)	-erat	-erant

FUTURE PERFECT ACTIVE	
SINGULAR	PLURAL
-erō	-erimus
-eris	-eritis
-erit	-erint

2. The perfect system passive consists of two parts, the perfect passive participle and forms of the verb **esse.** For the perfect tense, the present of **esse** is used; for the pluperfect tense, the imperfect of **esse**; and for the future perfect tense, the future of **esse.**

3. The perfect passive participle resembles an adjective of the first and second declension, such as **bonus, -a, -um.** Like an adjective, it also agrees with the noun it modifies in gender, number, and case.

SINGULAR	PLURAL
Bellum **gestum** erat.	Bella **gesta** erant.

4. The perfect tense generally represents an action that is completed and final. The imperfect, on the other hand, generally represents an action in progress.

Catilīna **fugiēbat.**   Catiline was fleeing.
        imperfect

Catilīna **fūgit.**   Catiline fled.
        perfect

5. The pluperfect tense represents an action that occurred prior to another past action.

> Dōnum **āmīsī** quod **accēperam.**   I lost the gift that I
> ⎣perfect⎦   ⎣pluperfect⎦   had received.

6. The future perfect tense represents an action in future time that will be completed prior to another action in future time.

> Cum tū **perveniēs,** ego iam **discesserō.**   When you (will)
> ⎣future⎦   ⎣future perfect⎦   arrive, I shall
>   already have left.

7. In the perfect system, verbs of four or more syllables are often shortened by dropping the **vi** or the **ve**, as follows:

putāstī	for putāvistī	vigilārat	for vigilāverat
audīstis	for audīvistis	cōnsuērat	for cōnsuēverat
exīstimārunt	for exīstimāvērunt	superārit	for superāverit

EXERCISES

A. Give the full verb form for each of the following shortened forms:

1. cōnfīrmāstī
2. cōgitārat
3. cupīstis
4. complērit
5. rogāstis
6. dēlērat
7. coniūrārant
8. petīstī
9. vigilārit
10. dubitārunt

B. Change each verb in italics from the perfect to the pluperfect tense.

1. Poenam dignam *suscēpit.*
2. Dē genere bellī *dīxī.*
3. Iter *patefactum est.*
4. Praedōnēs *interfectī sunt.*
5. Quam prōvinciam *tenuistis?*
6. Tabellās prōferrī *iussimus.*
7. Ad praetōrem *vēnistī.*
8. Lēgēs dē suppliciō *rogātae sunt.*
9. Eōs in eandem spem *impulērunt.*
10. *Ēreptī estis* ex interitū.

C. In each sentence, make the verb agree with the change of subject.

1. *Pompeius* tantum bellum suscēpit.   Germānī _____.
2. *Tū* eōs ad mē mīserās.   Vōs _____.
3. *Nova* cōnstitūta sunt.   Hoc _____.
4. *Nōs* tabellās lēgimus.   Ego _____.
5. *Senātus* hoc dēcrēverit.   Cōnsulēs _____.

6. *Mithridātēs* pulsus erat.   Nōs _____.
7. *Ille* istam pestem vīderat.   Tū _____.
8. *Ego* hoc prōposueram.   Cicerō _____.
9. *Vōs* togātī vīcistis.   Nōs _____.
10. *Hoc* merīdiē iūdicātum erit.   Hae rēs _____.

D. In each sentence, substitute the equivalent form of the verb in parentheses for the italicized verb.

1. Multās prōvinciās *cōnfēcit*. (dēlēre)
2. Ā mē *rogātus est*. (ēripere)
3. Hoc multīs virīs *praedīxeram*. (mandāre)
4. Omnēs *absolūtī erunt*. (līberāre)
5. Iam ad mē *scrīpserās*. (venīre)
6. Quem socium *dēfendistis*. (cōgere)
7. Nihil *dēcrētum erat*. (merēre)
8. *Dictae sunt* fortissimae sententiae. (probāre)
9. Vincula *rūperit*. (rapere)
10. Gladiōs ā vōbīs *dēiēcimus*. (vertere)

E. Write a synopsis in the perfect system (three tenses) of the following verbs in the form indicated:

1. *facere:*   3rd plural active
2. *necāre:*   1st singular active
3. *prōvidēre:*   3rd singular passive neuter
4. *terrēre:*   2nd singular passive feminine
5. *percipere:*   1st plural active

F. Rewrite the sentences below by following the directions in parentheses. Make *all* changes required.

1. *Intrōdūxī* Volturcium. (change to the plural)
2. Hoc mihi *susceptum est*. (change to the pluperfect)
3. *Ego* semper vigilāvī. (substitute **Tū**)
4. Catilīna *discesserat*. (change to the future perfect)
5. Vincula ā cōnsule inventa sunt. (express the same idea in the active voice)
6. Eās *ostendimus* Cethēgō. (change to the pluperfect)
7. *Praesidium* comparātum est. (substitute **Cōpiae**)
8. Aliter *acciderit*. (change to the perfect)
9. *Omnia* illūstrāta sunt. (substitute **Cōnsilium**)
10. Ego dēfendī rem pūblicam. (express the same idea in the passive voice)

Lesson 4. SUM AND *POSSUM*

PRINCIPAL PARTS

sum, esse, fuī, futūrus, to be   **possum, posse, potuī,** to be able

PRESENT		PRESENT	
sum	sumus	possum	possumus
es	estis	potes	potestis
est	sunt	potest	possunt

IMPERFECT		IMPERFECT	
eram	erāmus	poteram	poterāmus
erās	erātis	poterās	poterātis
erat	erant	poterat	poterant

FUTURE		FUTURE	
erō	erimus	poterō	poterimus
eris	eritis	poteris	poteritis
erit	erunt	poterit	poterunt

PERFECT		PERFECT	
fuī	fuimus	potuī	potuimus
fuistī	fuistis	potuistī	potuistis
fuit	fuērunt	potuit	potuērunt

PLUPERFECT		PLUPERFECT	
fueram	fuerāmus	potueram	potuerāmus
fuerās	fuerātis	potuerās	potuerātis
fuerat	fuerant	potuerat	potuerant

FUTURE PERFECT		FUTURE PERFECT	
fuerō	fuerimus	potuerō	potuerimus
fueris	fueritis	potueris	potueritis
fuerit	fuerint	potuerit	potuerint

Note:

1. **Sum** and **possum** are conjugated in the active voice only.

2. **Possum** is a compound of **potis** (able), plus **sum**. Its base is **pot-** when followed by a vowel and **pos-** when followed by the letter **s.**

3. In translating forms of **posse,** *can* and *could* may be substituted for *be able.*

> Legere possum.   I am able to read; I can read.
> Exīre nōn potuit.   He was not able to leave; he could
>   not leave.

4. The third person of **esse** may sometimes be translated impersonally with the word *there.*

> Nāvis in marī est.   There is a ship on the sea.
> Erant lacrimae in eius oculīs.   There were tears in his eyes

5. Other compounds of **esse** are:

> **abesse,** to be away, absent, or distant
> **adesse,** to be near or present
> **deesse,** to be lacking or wanting
> **interesse,** to be between
> **praeesse,** to be in command or in charge

6. In conjugating the verb **abesse,** the letter **b** is dropped before the letter **f.**

> **absum,** but **āfuī**

EXERCISES

A. Change each italicized verb to the plural.

1. *Fuistī* apud Laecam.   _____ apud Laecam.
2. Ēmorī aequō animō nōn *potes.*   Ēmorī aequō animō
                         nōn _____.
3. Ubinam gentium *sum?*   Ubinam gentium _____?
4. Magnā dīligentiā *fuit.*   Magnā dīligentiā _____.
5. Vōcēs audīre *potuistī.*   Vōcēs audīre _____.
6. Illud nōn *est* obscūrum.   Illa nōn _____ obscūra.
7. *Adest* vir summā auctōritāte.   _____ virī summā
                         auctōritāte.
8. Nēmō invenīrī *poterit.*   Multī invenīrī _____.
9. Huic *praeerat.*   Huic _____.
10. *Potestne* haec lūx esse iūcunda?   _____ hī virī esse iūcundī?

B. Change the tense of each italicized verb as indicated in parentheses.

1.	Aliī *sunt* in nostrō numerō.	(perfect)
2.	Mūrus *interest.*	(imperfect)
3.	Illīs carēre nōn *poterunt.*	(present)
4.	Cōnsiliō manus *deerat.*	(future)
5.	Salvī esse *possumus.*	(imperfect)
6.	*Fuit* in illō ingenium.	(present)
7.	Nōs cōnsulēs *dēsumus.*	(pluperfect)
8.	Num id īnfitiārī *potes?*	(future)
9.	Tum *aderātis.*	(perfect)
10.	Superāre *potuērunt.*	(future perfect)

C. Write a synopsis (six tenses) of the following verbs in the form indicated:

1.	*esse:*	3rd singular	4.	*abesse:*	1st singular
2.	*posse:*	2nd singular	5.	*praeesse:*	3rd plural
3.	*adesse:*	1st plural			

D. Translate into English.

1.	erunt	6.	fuerāmus
2.	possumus	7.	adsum
3.	praeerat	8.	potuerās
4.	potuistī	9.	dēsunt
5.	āfuistis	10.	fuerit

Lesson 5. DEPONENT VERBS

A deponent verb is one that looks passive in form, but is translated as if it were active.

A semi-deponent verb is deponent in the perfect system only.

DEPONENT	SEMI-DEPONENT
vereor, verērī, veritus sum	**audeō, audēre, ausus sum**
I fear, to fear, I feared	I dare, to dare, I dared

PRINCIPAL PARTS

(*1st Conj.*)	**hortor, hortārī, hortātus sum**
(*2nd Conj.*)	**polliceor, pollicērī, pollicitus sum**
(*3rd Conj.*)	**loquor, loquī, locūtus sum**
(**-IŌ** *3rd Conj.*)	**patior, patī, passus sum**
(*4th Conj.*)	**potior, potīrī, potītus sum**

hortor

PRESENT		PERFECT			
hortor	hortā*mur*	hortātus,	*sum* / *es* / *est*	hortātī,	*sumus* / *estis* / *sunt*
hortā*ris* (*-re*)	hortā*minī*	*-a, -um*		*-ae, -a*	
hortā*tur*	hortan*tur*				

IMPERFECT		PLUPERFECT			
hortā*bar*	hortā*bāmur*	hortātus,	*eram* / *erās* / *erat*	hortātī,	*erāmus* / *erātis* / *erant*
hortā*bāris* (*-re*)	hortā*bāminī*	*-a, -um*		*-ae, -a*	
hortā*bātur*	hortā*bantur*				

FUTURE		FUTURE PERFECT			
hortā*bor*	hortā*bimur*	hortātus,	*erō* / *eris* / *erit*	hortātī,	*erimus* / *eritis* / *erunt*
hortā*beris* (*-re*)	hortā*biminī*	*-a, -um*		*-ae, -a*	
hortā*bitur*	hortā*buntur*				

WORKING VOCABULARY OF DEPONENT VERBS

First Conjugation

hortor, hortārī, hortātus sum, urge
   arbitror, think
   cōnor, try
   mīror, wonder

moror, delay
recordor, recall
vagor, wander

Second Conjugation

fateor, fatērī, fassus sum, confess
   cōnfiteor, cōnfitērī, cōnfessus sum, confess
polliceor, pollicērī, pollicitus sum, promise
vereor, verērī, veritus sum, fear

Third Conjugation

loquor, loquī, locūtus sum, speak
nancīsçor, nancīscī, nactus sum, find, obtain
nāscor, nāscī, nātus sum, be born
proficīscor, proficīscī, profectus sum, set out
sequor, sequī, secūtus sum, follow
ūtor, ūtī, ūsus sum, use

-IŌ Third Conjugation

gradior, gradī, gressus sum, walk
   ēgredior, ēgredī, ēgressus sum, go out, leave
morior, morī, mortuus sum, die
patior, patī, passus sum, endure

Fourth Conjugation

experior, experīrī, expertus sum, test, try
orior, orīrī, ortus sum, rise
potior, potīrī, potītus sum, get possession of

SEMI-DEPONENT VERBS

audeō, audēre, ausus sum, dare
fīdō, fīdere, fīsus sum, trust
   cōnfīdō, cōnfīdere, cōnfīsus sum, trust
soleō, solēre, solitus sum, be accustomed

EXERCISES

A. Change each italicized verb to the singular.

1. Dē ūnō hoste *loquēbāmur.*
2. Tē *morābuntur.*
3. Sine sensū *nāscimur.*
4. Patriam dēlēre *cōnātī erant.*
5. Repente *cōnfessī sunt.*

6. Hōc genere *ūsī estis.*
7. Iam multōs diēs *patimur.*
8. Sē cōnsequī posse *arbitrābantur.*
9. Auctōritātem *verēbiminī.*
10. Oppidō *potītī eritis.*

B. In each sentence, substitute the equivalent form of the verb in parentheses for the italicized verb.

1. Ad mē venīre *ausus est.*   (soleō)
2. Patria *loquitur.*   (morior)
3. Hoc vōbīs *pollicēmur.*   (cōnfiteor)
4. Quem nostrum ignōrāre *arbitrābāris?*   (mīror)
5. Perīcula vōs *hortantur.*   (moror)
6. Senātus sententiās *secūtus erit.*   (recordor)
7. Cōnsulēs *nactī estis.*   (vereor)
8. Silērī *patiēre.*   (cōnor)
9. Quā laetitiā *perfruentur.*   (ūtor)
10. Mihi *īnsidiātī erātis.*   (cōnfīdō)

C. Write a synopsis (six tenses) of the following verbs in the form indicated:

1. *vagor:*   3rd plural
2. *ēgredior:* 1st plural
3. *soleō:*   2nd singular

4. *orior:*   3rd singular
5. *proficīscor:* 2nd plural

D. Translate into English.

1. mortuus est
2. loquētur
3. sequēbantur
4. mīrantur
5. cōnātī sumus

6. gressus sum
7. expertus erās
8. nātī estis
9. pollicēberis
10. hortātī erimus

Lesson 6. IRREGULAR, DEFECTIVE, AND IMPERSONAL VERBS

EŌ, GO

PRINCIPAL PARTS: eō, īre, iī (īvī), itūrus

PRESENT		PERFECT	
eō	īmus	iī (īvī)	iimus
īs	ītis	īstī	īstis
it	eunt	iit	iērunt

IMPERFECT		PLUPERFECT	
ībam	ībāmus	ieram (īveram)	ierāmus
ībās	ībātis	ierās	ierātis
ībat	ībant	ierat	ierant

FUTURE		FUTURE PERFECT	
ībō	ībimus	ierō (īverō)	ierimus
ībis	ībitis	ieris	ieritis
ībit	ībunt	ierit	ierint

FERŌ, BRING

PRINCIPAL PARTS: ferō, ferre, tulī, lātus

	ACTIVE		PASSIVE	
PRES.	ferō	ferimus	feror	ferimur
	fers	fertis	ferris	feriminī
	fert	ferunt	fertur	feruntur
IMP.	ferēbam		ferēbar	
FUT.	feram		ferar	
	ferēs		ferēris	
PERF.	tulī		lātus, -a, -um sum	
PLUP.	tuleram		lātus, -a, -um eram	
FUT. PERF.	tulerō		lātus, -a, -um erō	

FĪŌ (*PASSIVE OF FACIŌ*), BE MADE, HAPPEN, BECOME

PRINCIPAL PARTS: **fīō, fierī, factus sum**

PRES.	*fīō*	——
	fīs	——
	fit	*fīunt*
IMP.	*fīēbam*	
FUT.	*fīam*	
	fīēs	
PERF.	*factus sum*	
PLUP.	*factus eram*	
FUT. PERF.	*factus erō*	

VOLŌ, WANT   NŌLŌ, NOT WANT   MĀLŌ, PREFER

PRINCIPAL PARTS:

	volō, velle, voluī	nōlō, nōlle, nōluī	mālō, mālle, māluī
PRES.	*volō*	*nōlō*	*mālō*
	vīs	*nōn vīs*	*māvīs*
	vult	*nōn vult*	*māvult*
	volumus	*nōlumus*	*mālumus*
	vultis	*nōn vultis*	*māvultis*
	volunt	*nōlunt*	*mālunt*
IMP.	*volēbam*	*nōlēbam*	*mālēbam*
FUT.	*volam*	*nōlam*	*mālam*
	volēs	*nōlēs*	*mālēs*
PERF.	*voluī*	*nōluī*	*māluī*
PLUP.	*volueram*	*nōlueram*	*mālueram*
FUT. PERF.	*voluerō*	*nōluerō*	*māluerō*

COEPĪ (*USED IN PERFECT SYSTEM ONLY*), BEGAN

PERF.	*coepī*
PLUP.	*coeperam*
FUT. PERF.	*coeperō*

LICET (*IMPERSONAL VERB*), IT IS ALLOWED

PRINCIPAL PARTS: **licet, licēre, licuit** or **licitum est**

PRES.	*licet*
IMP.	*licēbat*
FUT.	*licēbit*
PERF.	*licuit*
	licitum est
PLUP.	*licuerat*
FUT. PERF.	*licuerit*

Note: Some verbs, such as **licet** (it is allowed) and **oportet** (it is necessary), are used only impersonally. Therefore, these verbs have no forms in the first or second persons.

EXERCISES

A. In each sentence, change the italicized verb in accordance with the directions in parentheses.

1. *Ībis* tandem aliquandō. (change to the plural)
2. *Vīs* cōnflāre invidiam. (substitute the equivalent form of **nōlō**)
3. Perge quō *coepistī*. (change to the pluperfect)
4. Eī excēdere *licuit*. (change to the present)
5. Mē cōnsulem interficere *voluistī*. (substitute the equivalent form of **mālō**)
6. Cōnsul *fit*. (change to the perfect)
7. Ad audāciam ferrum *praetulistis*. (change to the imperfect)
8. Exīre *coeperāmus*. (change to the future perfect)
9. Labōrēs tuī *feruntur*. (change to the future)
10. Ad mortem tē dūcī *oportēbat*. (change to the perfect)
11. In exsilium *īverō*. (change to the second person)
12. Mē audīre *nōlent*. (substitute the equivalent form of **volō**)
13. Pācis dignitātem retinēre *vultis*. (change to the perfect)
14. Superiōra illa *tulī*. (change to the present)
15. Manēre *mālumus*. (change to the singular)

B. Write a synopsis (six tenses) of the following verbs in the form indicated:

1. *volō:* 3rd plural
2. *eō:* 2nd singular
3. *ferō:* 1st plural active

4. *fīō:* 3rd singular
5. *nōlō:* 2nd plural

C. Translate into English.

1. feruntur
2. nōluistī
3. nōn licēbat
4. coeperam
5. mālētis

6. factus erat
7. ierō
8. lātus es
9. oportēbit
10. volumus

Lesson 7. REVIEW OF THE INDICATIVE MOOD

A. In each sentence, substitute the equivalent form of the verb in parentheses for the italicized verb.

1.	Cōnsulem interficere *cōnābāmur*.	(dubitō)
2.	Lēgātōs in forō *cōnspexistī*.	(hortor)
3.	Aliquid *putābam*.	(arbitror)
4.	Crassus ā Tarquiniō *nōminātur*.	(legō)
5.	Eōs cum gladiīs *mīseram*.	(ferō)
6.	*Cōnfessus est* Italiam līberātam esse.	(dīcō)
7.	Sīc Catilīna *praecēperat*.	(cēnseō)
8.	Ā nūllō *audiēmur*.	(videō)
9.	Sēsē *ēiēcerint*.	(mandō)
10.	In senātum *vēnistis*.	(eō)
11.	C. Gracchus *interfectus erat*.	(occīdō)
12.	Nihil mē *solet* dēlectāre.	(possum)
13.	Vōs salvōs esse *volunt*.	(mālō)
14.	*Incēpistis* pollicērī omnia.	(coepī)
15.	Eum exīre *patiēre*.	(cōgō)

B. Rewrite the sentences below by following the directions in parentheses. Make *all* changes required.

1. Domum *mūnīvī*. (change to the plural)
2. Eōs *vīdistis*. (change to the imperfect)
3. Rem *exposuī*. (substitute the equivalent form of **patior**)
4. Eōs trucīdārī *oportēbat*. (change to the future)
5. *Vectīgal* cōnservārī potest. (substitute **Vectīgalia**)
6. *Tabulae novae* prōferuntur. (substitute **Tabula nova**)
7. *Nactus es* manum improbōrum. (change to the plural)
8. *Senātus* lēnitāte ūsus est. (substitute **Patria**)
9. Iūdicium eius *sequēminī*. (change to the singular)
10. Auxilium nōbīs *tulistī*. (change to the present)
11. Plēnī omnēs *sunt* librī. (change to the perfect)
12. *Volumus* ascrībī. (substitute the equivalent form of **nōlō**)
13. Impetus in mē *convertit*. (change to the future perfect)
14. *Nēmō* tē salūtāvit. (substitute **Omnēs**)
15. Duo equitēs *repertī sunt*. (change to the pluperfect)

C. Write a synopsis in the indicative (six tenses) of the following verbs in the form indicated:

1. *dēleō:* 3rd plural active
2. *suscipiō:* 3rd singular passive
3. *ēgredior:* 2nd singular
4. *possum:* 1st plural
5. *eō:* 2nd plural

D. Translate into English.

1. postulābās
2. necātus est
3. pollicēmur
4. ausus sum
5. potuistī
6. mortuus erat
7. fīunt
8. oportēbat
9. ēreptus eram
10. secūtī estis
11. coniūrābant
12. coeperint
13. prōvīderātis
14. quaerēmus
15. licēbit

E. Translate into Latin.

1. you (*plur.*) deserve
2. he avoided
3. we had been
4. it happens
5. he was urging
6. I have been able
7. will you (*sing.*) watch?
8. he had gotten possession of
9. we disagree
10. you (*sing.*) will be guarded

Unit II—Imperatives, Infinitives, Participles, Gerund

Lesson 8. IMPERATIVES AND INFINITIVES

PRESENT IMPERATIVE

First Conjugation

PRINCIPAL PARTS: **iūdicō, iūdicāre, iūdicāvī, iūdicātus**
STEMS: *present,* **iūdicā-;** *perfect,* **iūdicāv-;** *participial,* **iūdicāt-**

	ACTIVE	PASSIVE
2nd sing.	iūdic**ā**, *judge*	iūdic**āre**, *be judged*
2nd plur.	iūdic**āte**, *judge*	iūdic**āminī**, *be judged*

Second Conjugation

PRINCIPAL PARTS: **dēbeō, dēbēre, dēbuī, dēbitus**
STEMS: *present,* **dēbē-;** *perfect,* **dēbu-;** *participial,* **dēbit-**

	ACTIVE	PASSIVE
2nd sing.	dēb**ē**	dēb**ēre**
2nd plur.	dēb**ēte**	dēb**ēminī**

Third Conjugation

PRINCIPAL PARTS: **pellō, pellere, pepulī, pulsus**
STEMS: *present,* **pelle-;** *perfect,* **pepul-;** *participial,* **puls-**

	ACTIVE	PASSIVE
2nd sing.	pell**e**	pell**ere**
2nd plur.	pell**ite**	pell**iminī**

-IŌ Third Conjugation

PRINCIPAL PARTS: **capiō, capere, cēpī, captus**
STEMS: *present,* **cape-;** *perfect,* **cēp-;** *participial,* **capt-**

	ACTIVE	PASSIVE
2nd sing.	cap*e*	cap*ere*
2nd plur.	cap*ite*	cap*iminī*

Fourth Conjugation

PRINCIPAL PARTS: **sentiō, sentīre, sēnsī, sēnsus**
STEMS: *present,* **sentī-;** *perfect,* **sēns-;** *participial,* **sēns-**

	ACTIVE	PASSIVE
2nd sing.	sent*ī*	sent*īre*
2nd plur.	sent*īte*	sent*īminī*

	sum	**hortor**	**eō**
2nd sing.	es	hort*āre*	*ī*
2nd plur.	es*te*	hort*āminī*	*īte*

	ferō		**fīō**	**nōlō**
	ACTIVE	PASSIVE	ACTIVE ONLY	
2nd sing.	*fer*	*ferre*	*fī*	*nōlī*
2nd plur.	*ferte*	*feriminī*	*fīte*	*nōlīte*

Note:

1. The singular active form of the imperative is the same as the present stem. The plural is formed by adding **-te** to the singular form. However, in third and **-iō** third conjugation verbs the final **e** of the singular form is changed to **i** before **-te** is added.

2. The verbs **dīcere, dūcere, facere,** and **ferre** have shortened forms for the imperative singular active, namely **dīc, dūc, fac,** and **fer.**

3. The passive imperative singular looks exactly like the present infinitive active. The passive imperative plural looks like the present indicative passive second plural.

4. Negative commands are expressed by the present imperative of **nōlō (nōlī, nōlīte)** plus the infinitive.

INFINITIVES

ACTIVE	PASSIVE
FIRST CONJUGATION	
PRES. iūdicā*re, to judge*	iūdicā*rī, to be judged*
PERF. iūdicā*visse, to have judged*	iūdicā*tus, -a, -um esse, to have been judged*
FUT. iūdicā*tūrus, -a, -um esse, to be about to judge*	
SECOND CONJUGATION	
PRES. dēbē*re,*	dēbē*rī*
PERF. dēbu*isse*	dēbi*tus, -a, -um esse*
FUT. dēbi*tūrus, -a, -um esse*	
THIRD CONJUGATION	
PRES. pelle*re*	pell*ī*
PERF. pepul*isse*	puls*us, -a, -um esse*
FUT. puls*ūrus, -a, -um esse*	
-IŌ THIRD CONJUGATION	
PRES. cape*re*	cap*ī*
PERF. cēp*isse*	capt*us, -a, -um esse*
FUT. capt*ūrus, -a, -um esse*	
FOURTH CONJUGATION	
PRES. sentī*re*	sentī*rī*
PERF. sēns*isse*	sēns*us, -a, -um esse*
FUT. sēns*ūrus, -a, -um esse*	

sum   **possum**

	ACTIVE ONLY	
PRES.	esse	posse
PERF.	fuisse	potuisse
FUT.	futūrus, -a, -um esse	

Note: **Fore** is often used as the future infinitive of **sum**.

hortor

	ACTIVE	PASSIVE
PRES.		hortārī
PERF.		hortātus, -a, -um esse
FUT.	hortātūrus, -a, -um esse	

eō   **fīō**

	ACTIVE	PASSIVE
PRES.	īre	fierī
PERF.	īsse (īvisse)	factus, -a, -um esse
FUT.	itūrus, -a, -um esse	

ferō

	ACTIVE	PASSIVE
PRES.	ferre	ferrī
PERF.	tulisse	lātus, -a, -um esse
FUT.	lātūrus, -a, -um esse	

	volō	nōlō	mālō
	ACTIVE ONLY		
PRES.	*velle*	*nōlle*	*mālle*
PERF.	*voluisse*	*nōluisse*	*māluisse*

	coepī		licet
	ACTIVE ONLY		
PRES.			*licēre*
PERF.	*coepisse*		*licuisse*
FUT.			*licitūrum esse*

Note:

1. Most verbs have six infinitives, three in the active voice and three in the passive. The future passive infinitive is omitted in the preceding list because it is a rare form.

2. The present active infinitive of all verbs is the second principal part.

3. The present passive infinitive is formed by changing the final **e** of the present active infinitive to **ī**. However, in third and **-iō** third conjugation verbs, the final **ere** is changed to **ī**.

4. The perfect active infinitive is formed by adding the ending **-isse** to the perfect stem.

5. The perfect passive infinitive consists of the fourth principal part plus **esse**.

6. The future active infinitive is formed by adding the endings **-ūrus**, **-a**, **-um** to the participial stem plus **esse**.

7. Deponent verbs have a future infinitive that is active in *form* as well as in *meaning*.

EXERCISES

A. Rewrite the sentences below by following the directions in paren-theses. Make *all* changes required.

1. Mihi *crēde*. (change to the plural)
2. Quam ob rem *discēde*. (substitute equivalent form of **resistō**)
3. *Prohibēte* ab perīculō rem pūblicam. (change to the singular)
4. *Concitā* perditōs cīvīs. (make negative)
5. *Cape* tēcum omnīs tuōs. (substitute equivalent form of **ēdūcō**)
6. *Cōnservāte* hominem. (substitute equivalent form of **sequor**)
7. Ea vigiliīs *dēfendite*. (change to the singular)
8. *Nōlī mūtāre* istam mentem. (make affirmative)
9. *Ēgredere* ex urbe. (change to the plural)
10. *Purgā* urbem. (substitute equivalent form of **custōdiō**)
11. In vestra tēcta *discēdite*. (make negative)
12. In exsilium *proficīscere*. (substitute equivalent form of **eō**)
13. Hunc mihi timōrem *ēripe*. (change to the plural)
14. *Nōlīte percipere* dīligenter. (make affirmative)
15. *Contende* ad senātum. (substitute equivalent form of **referō**)

B. In each sentence, substitute the equivalent form of the verb in parentheses for the italicized infinitive.

1. Patriam *dēlēre* cōnāti sunt.   (servō)
2. Videor multa verba *fēcisse*.   (audiō)
3. Cōnfessus est Italiam *līberātam esse*.   (ēripiō)
4. Famem *ferre* poterat.   (patior)
5. Aquilam *mīrārī* solēbās.   (amō)
6. Dīxistī tē oppidum *occupātūrum esse*.   (capiō)
7. Ea vīdī *probārī*.   (mereō)
8. Sciō virōs *praemissōs esse*.   (legō)
9. Profitētur sē testimōnium laudis *datūrum esse*.   (quaerō)
10. Hoc facile potest *dīcī*.   (faciō)

C. Change the tense, but not the voice, of each italicized infinitive as indicated in parentheses.

1. Odiō *permōtus esse* videor.   (present)
2. Scīmus tē *parāre* manum.   (perfect)
3. Manum coniūrātōrum *exīre* putābam.   (future)
4. Vīdī eōs Rōmae *remānsisse*.   (present)
5. Negat haec ā dīs immortālibus *administrārī*.   (perfect)
6. Cēnsus indicat eum sē *gessisse* prō cīve.   (present)

7. Dīcō tē *vēnisse* in M. Laecae domum.   (future)
8. Intellegō nēminem stultum *fore*.   (perfect)
9. Sciō aquilam *praemissam esse*.   (present)
10. Fateor mē hīs studiīs *dēdī*.   (perfect)

D. Change each infinitive from the active to the passive.

1. mandāre   4. premere
2. prōvīdisse   5. dēfēcisse
3. ērudīre

E. Supply the two missing infinitives in each group.

1. necāre, necātūrus esse, necāvisse
2. iacere, iacī, iēcisse
3. dēlērī, dēlētus esse, dēlētūrus esse
4. trahere, trāxisse, trāctus esse
5. ferre, ferrī, lātus esse

Lesson 9. PARTICIPLES AND GERUND

FIRST CONJUGATION

PRINCIPAL PARTS: **iūdicō, iūdicāre, iūdicāvī, iūdicātus**
STEMS: *present,* **iūdicā-**; *perfect,* **iūdicāv-**; *participial,* **iūdicāt-**

Participles

ACTIVE	PASSIVE
PRES. iūdicā**ns, -ntis**	PERF. iūdicāt**us, -a, -um**
judging	having been judged
FUT. iūdicāt**ūrus, -a, -um**	FUT. (*Gerundive*) *iūdica***ndus, -a, -um**
about to judge	must be judged

Gerund

Genitive:	iūdica**ndī,** *of judging*
Dative:	iūdica**ndō,** *to (for) judging*
Accusative:	iūdica**ndum,** *judging*
Ablative:	iūdica**ndō,** *by judging*

SECOND CONJUGATION

PRINCIPAL PARTS: **dēbeō, dēbēre, dēbuī, dēbitus**
STEMS: *present,* **dēbē-**; *perfect,* **dēbu-**; *participial,* **dēbit-**

Participles

ACTIVE	PASSIVE
PRES. dēbē**ns, -ntis**	PERF. dēbit**us, -a, -um**
FUT. dēbit**ūrus, -a, -um**	FUT. dēbe**ndus, -a, -um**

Gerund

Gen.	dēbe**ndī**
Dat.	dēbe**ndō**
Acc.	dēbe**ndum**
Abl.	dēbe**ndō**

THIRD CONJUGATION

PRINCIPAL PARTS: **pellō, pellere, pepulī, pulsus**
STEMS: *present*, **pelle-**; *perfect*, **pepul-**; *participial*, **puls-**

Participles

ACTIVE	PASSIVE
PRES. pellē*ns, -ntis*	PERF. puls*us, -a, -um*
FUT. puls*ūrus, -a, -um*	FUT. pelle*ndus, -a, -um*

Gerund

Gen.	pelle*ndī*
Dat.	pelle*ndō*
Acc.	pelle*ndum*
Abl.	pelle*ndō*

-IŌ THIRD CONJUGATION

PRINCIPAL PARTS: **capiō, capere, cēpī, captus**
STEMS: *present*, **cape-**; *perfect*, **cēp-**; *participial*, **capt-**

Participles

ACTIVE	PASSIVE
PRES. capiē*ns, -e*ntis	PERF. capt*us, -a, -um*
FUT. capt*ūrus, -a, -um*	FUT. capie*ndus, -a, -um*

Gerund

Gen.	capie*ndī*
Dat.	capie*ndō*
Acc.	capie*ndum*
Abl.	capie*ndō*

FOURTH CONJUGATION

PRINCIPAL PARTS: **sentiō, sentīre, sēnsī, sēnsus**
STEMS: *present,* senti-; *perfect,* sēns-; *participial,* sēns-

Participles

ACTIVE	PASSIVE
PRES. sentiē*ns,* -*entis*	PERF. sēns*us,* -*a,* -*um*
FUT. sēns*ūrus,* -*a,* -*um*	FUT. sentie*ndus,* -*a,* -*um*

Gerund

Gen.	sentie*ndī*
Dat.	sentie*ndō*
Acc.	sentie*ndum*
Abl.	sentie*ndō*

DEPONENT VERBS

hortor

Participles

PRES. hortā*ns*	PERF. hortāt*us,* -*a,* -*um*
FUT. hortāt*ūrus,* -*a,* -*um*	FUT. horta*ndus,* -*a,* -*um*

Gerund

Gen.	horta*ndī*
Dat.	horta*ndō*
Acc.	horta*ndum*
Abl.	horta*ndō*

IRREGULAR VERBS

sum   **possum**

Participles

FUT. fut*ūrus, -a, -um*	PRES. pot*ēns*

eō

Participles

PRES. *iēns, euntis*
FUT. *itūrus, -a, -um*

Gerund

eundī, etc.

ferō

Participles

ACTIVE	PASSIVE
PRES. *ferēns, -entis*	PERF. *lātus, -a, -um*
FUT. *lātūrus, -a, -um*	FUT. *ferendus, -a, -um*

Gerund

ferendī, etc.

volō   **nōlō**   **fīō**

Participles

PRES. *volēns, -entis*	PRES. *nōlens, -entis*	PERF. *factus, -a, -um*
		FUT. *faciendus, -a, -um*

Note:

1. The present active participle is formed by adding the ending **-ns** to the present stem. However, in **-iō** third conjugation verbs, an **i** is inserted before the final **e** of the stem; in fourth conjugation verbs, an **e** is inserted before the **-ns** ending.

2. The future active participle is the same as the future active infinitive without **esse**.

3. The perfect passive participle is the same as the perfect passive infinitive without **esse**.

4. The future passive participle is formed by adding the endings **-ndus, -a, -um** to the present stem. However, in **-iō** third conjugation verbs, an **i** is inserted before the final **e** of the stem; in fourth conjugation verbs, an **e** is inserted before the **-ndus** ending. The future passive participle is also known as the gerundive.

5. Latin verbs lack a perfect active and a present passive participle.

6. The present and future participles of deponent verbs are active in *form* as well as in *meaning.*

7. The future passive participle of deponent verbs is passive in *meaning* as well as in *form.*

8. The gerund is formed by adding the ending **-ndī**, etc., to the present stem. However, in **iō** third conjugation verbs, an **i** is inserted before the final **e** of the stem; in fourth conjugation verbs, an **e** is inserted before the **-ndī** ending.

9. The gerund of deponent verbs is active in *form* as well as in *meaning.*

EXERCISES

A. In each sentence, substitute the equivalent form of the verb in parentheses for the italicized verb.

1. Hoc *dictūrus* sum.   (faciō)
2. Ille erat ūnus *timendus.*   (vereor)
3. Ad *dēlendam* rem pūblicam pertinuit.   (vāstō)

4. Eōs *coniūnctōs* mactābis.   (cōgō)
5. *Dissimulandī* causā in senātum vēnit.   (audiō)
6. Ipsum *ēgredientem* prōsecūtī sumus.   (discēdō)
7. Spem Catilīnae nōn *crēdendō* aluērunt.   (cōnfīdō)
8. Vidēris *invītātus* ad tuōs īsse.   (trahō)
9. Parāvistī manum cōnsulum *interficiendōrum* causā.   (necō)
10. Ad caedem *proficīscēns* hoc venerārī solēbās.   (eō)
11. *Audītā* rē, fūgit.   (videō)
12. Sibi prōcūrātiōnem *incendendae* urbis poscit.   (rapiō)
13. Hoc nōn est *postulandum*.   (ferō)
14. Cicerōne *cōnsulente*, exspectābāmus.   (cōgitō)
15. Quid exspectās auctōritātem *loquentium*?   (patior)

B. Indicate whether each verb in italics is a gerund or a gerundive.

1. Exercitātiō *dīcendī* est in mē.
2. In *cōnservandā* rē pūblicā invidia suscepta est.
3. Omne ingenium contulit ad glōriam *celebrandam*.
4. Cōnsīliōrum *reprimendōrum* causā profūgērunt.
5. Erat eī industria in *agendō*.

C. Supply the missing participle in each group.

1. vītātus, vītātūrus, vītandus
2. vīvēns, vīctus, vīctūrus
3. merēns, merendus, meritūrus
4. serviendus, servītus, servītūrus
5. suscipiēns, susceptus, suscipiendus

Unit III—Subjunctive Mood

Lesson 10. PRESENT AND IMPERFECT TENSES

FIRST CONJUGATION

PRINCIPAL PARTS: iūdicō, iūdicāre, iūdicāvī, iūdicātus

STEMS: *present*, **iūdicā-**; *perfect*, **iūdicāv-**; *participial*, **iūdicāt-**

ACTIVE		PASSIVE	
PRESENT			
iūdic*em*	iūdic*ēmus*	iūdic*er*	iūdic*ēmur*
iūdic*ēs*	iūdic*ētis*	iūdic*ēris* (*-re*)	iūdic*ēminī*
iūdic*et*	iūdic*ent*	iūdic*ētur*	iūdic*entur*
IMPERFECT			
iūdicā*rem*	iūdicā*rēmus*	iūdicā*rer*	iūdicā*rēmur*
iūdicā*rēs*	iūdicā*rētis*	iūdicā*rēris* (*-re*)	iūdicā*rēminī*
iūdicā*ret*	iūdicā*rent*	iūdicā*rētur*	iūdicā*rentur*

SECOND CONJUGATION

PRINCIPAL PARTS: dēbeō, dēbēre, dēbuī, dēbitus

STEMS: *present*, **dēbē**; *perfect*, **dēbu-**; *participial*, **dēbit-**

ACTIVE		PASSIVE	
PRESENT			
dēbe*am*	dēbe*āmus*	dēbe*ar*	dēbe*āmur*
dēbe*ās*	dēbe*ātis*	dēbe*āris* (*-re*)	dēbe*āminī*
dēbe*at*	dēbe*ant*	dēbe*ātur*	dēbe*antur*
IMPERFECT			
dēbē*rem*	dēbē*rēmus*	dēbē*rer*	dēbē*rēmur*
dēbē*rēs*	dēbē*rētis*	dēbē*rēris* (*-re*)	dēbē*rēminī*
dēbē*ret*	dēbē*rent*	dēbē*rētur*	dēbē*rentur*

THIRD CONJUGATION

PRINCIPAL PARTS: **pellō, pellere, pepulī, pulsus**
STEMS: *present,* **pelle-**; *perfect,* **pepul-**; *participial,* **puls-**

ACTIVE		PASSIVE	
PRESENT			
pell*am*	pell*āmus*	pell*ar*	pell*āmur*
pell*ās*	pell*ātis*	pell*āris* (*-re*)	pell*āminī*
pell*at*	pell*ant*	pell*ātur*	pell*antur*
IMPERFECT			
peller*em*	peller*ēmus*	peller*er*	peller*ēmur*
peller*ēs*	peller*ētis*	peller*ēris* (*-re*)	peller*ēminī*
peller*et*	peller*ent*	peller*ētur*	peller*entur*

-IŌ THIRD CONJUGATION

PRINCIPAL PARTS: **capiō, capere, cēpī, captus**
STEMS: *present,* **cape-**; *perfect,* **cēp-**; *participial,* **capt-**

ACTIVE		PASSIVE	
PRESENT			
capi*am*	capi*āmus*	capi*ar*	capi*āmur*
capi*ās*	capi*ātis*	capi*āris* (*-re*)	capi*āminī*
capi*at*	capi*ant*	capi*ātur*	capi*antur*
IMPERFECT			
caper*em*	caper*ēmus*	caper*er*	caper*ēmur*
caper*ēs*	caper*ētis*	caper*ēris* (*-re*)	caper*ēminī*
caper*et*	caper*ent*	caper*ētur*	caper*entur*

FOURTH CONJUGATION

PRINCIPAL PARTS: **sentiō, sentīre, sēnsī, sēnsus**
STEMS: *present,* **sentī-;** *perfect,* **sēns-;** *participial,* **sēns-**

ACTIVE		PASSIVE	
	PRESENT		
sentiam	sentiāmus	sentiar	sentiāmur
sentiās	sentiātis	sentiāris (-re)	sentiāminī
sentiat	sentiant	sentiātur	sentiantur
	IMPERFECT		
sentīrem	sentīrēmus	sentīrer	sentīrēmur
sentīrēs	sentīrētis	sentīrēris (-re)	sentīrēminī
sentīret	sentīrent	sentīrētur	sentīrentur

DEPONENT VERBS

hortor

PRESENT	IMPERFECT
horter	hortārer
hortēris (-re)	hortārēris (-re)
hortētur	hortārētur
hortēmur	hortārēmur
hortēminī	hortārēminī
hortentur	hortārentur

IRREGULAR VERBS

sum   **possum**

ACTIVE ONLY			
PRESENT	IMPERFECT	PRESENT	IMPERFECT
sim	essem	possim	possem
sīs	essēs	possīs	possēs
sit	esset	possit	posset
sīmus	essēmus	possīmus	possēmus
sītis	essētis	possītis	possētis
sint	essent	possint	possent

eō

ACTIVE ONLY	
PRESENT	IMPERFECT
eam	*īrem*, etc.
eās	
eat	
eāmus	
eātis	
eant	

volō   nōlō   mālō

ACTIVE ONLY		
PRES.	*velim*	*nōlim*	*mālim*
	velīs	*nōlīs*	*mālīs*
	velit	*nōlit*	*mālit*
	velīmus	*nōlīmus*	*mālīmus*
	velītis	*nōlītis*	*mālītis*
	velint	*nōlint*	*mālint*
IMP.	*vellem*, etc.	*nōllem*, etc.	*māllem*, etc.

ferō

	ACTIVE	PASSIVE
PRES.	*feram*, etc.	*ferar*, etc.
IMP.	*ferrem*, etc.	*ferrer*, etc.

fīō   licet

PRES.	*fīam*, etc.
IMP.	*fierem*, etc.

PRES.	*liceat*, etc.
IMP.	*licēret*, etc.

Note:

1. The sign of the present subjunctive in the first conjugation is **e**; in all the other conjugations, **a**.

2. In the first conjugation, the tense is formed by changing the final **ā** of the present stem to **e** and then adding the personal endings.

3. In the second conjugation, the final **e** of the present stem is kept before the endings are added.

4. In the **-iō** third conjugation, the final **e** of the present stem is changed to **i** before the endings are added.

5. In the fourth conjugation, the final **i** of the present stem is kept before the endings are added.

6. In the third, **-iō** third, and fourth conjugations, the first person singular of the present subjunctive has the same spelling as the first person singular of the future indicative.

7. The imperfect subjunctive of all verbs is formed by taking the entire present active infinitive and adding the personal endings.

8. In the case of deponent verbs, which have no present active infinitive, the passive personal endings are added to a made-up form that resembles a present active infinitive.

PRESENT PASSIVE INFINITIVE	MADE-UP INFINITIVE
hortārī	**hortāre-**
pollicērī	**pollicēre-**
loquī	**loquere-**
patī	**patere-**
potīrī	**potīre-**

EXERCISES

A. In each sentence, substitute the equivalent form of the verb in parentheses for the italicized subjunctive.

1. Cūrā ut vir *sīs*. (agō)
2. Tē ut ūlla rēs *frangat*. (afficiō)
3. Rogāstī ut domī meae tē *asservārem*. (cūstōdiō)
4. Hunc nōn *dīligam*? (admīror)

5. Est nōbīs is animus ut *cēdāmus* audāciae nullīus.   (resistō)
6. *Dēcernātur* tamen, sī placet.   (scrībō)
7. Nēmō est quī tē nōn *metuat*.   (vereor)
8. Quid est quod iam *exspectēs*.   (volō)
9. Dēlēgistī quōs Rōmae *relinquerēs*.   (vigilō)
10. Utinam cōpiam virōrum fortium *habērētis*.   (mālō)
11. Nōn nūllī sunt quī ea nōn *videant*.   (sentiō)
12. Sē abdicāvit ut eā religiōne *līberārēmur*.   (prohibeō)
13. Cum coniūrātī in aedem *dūcerentur*, signum   (pellō)
    statuēbātur.
14. Parricīdae *pereant*!   (morior)
15. Requīsīvī quem exitum tantīs malīs *spērārent*.   (polliceor)

B. With each form, make the one change indicated in parentheses.

1. susciperētur (active)   9. essēmus (present)
2. dēlērēmus (singular)   10. nōlim (3rd person)
3. postulent (imperfect)   11. ērudiam (passive)
4. vītent (2nd person)   12. ferāmus (imperfect)
5. eās (plural)   13. premerēminī (active)
6. vertātis (passive)   14. fateātur (2nd person)
7. patiāris (1st person)   15. ēriperēs (present)
8. potīrer (plural)

C. Write the present and imperfect subjunctive of the following
verbs in the form indicated:

1. *possum:* 3rd plural   4. *oportet:* 3rd singular
2. *ēgredior:* 2nd singular   5. *vereor:* 2nd plural
3. *fīō:* 1st singular

Lesson 11. PERFECT AND PLUPERFECT TENSES

FIRST CONJUGATION

PRINCIPAL PARTS: **iūdicō, iūdicāre, iūdicāvī, iūdicātus**
STEMS: *present,* **iūdicā-;** *perfect,* **iūdicāv-;** *participial,* **iūdicāt-**

ACTIVE		PASSIVE			
		PERFECT			
iūdicāverim	iūdicāverīmus	iūdicātus,	sim	iūdicātī,	sīmus
iūdicāverīs	iūdicāverītis	-a, -um	sīs	-ae, -a	sītis
iūdicāverit	iūdicāverint		sit		sint
		PLUPERFECT			
iūdicāvissem	iūdicāvissēmus	iūdicātus,	essem	iūdicātī,	essēmus
iūdicāvissēs	iūdicāvissētis	-a, -um	essēs	-ae, -a	essētis
iūdicāvisset	iūdicāvissent		esset		essent

SECOND CONJUGATION

PRINCIPAL PARTS: **dēbeō, dēbēre, dēbuī, dēbitus**
STEMS: *present,* **dēbē-;** *perfect,* **dēbu-;** *participial,* **dēbit-**

ACTIVE		PASSIVE			
		PERFECT			
dēbuerim	dēbuerīmus	dēbitus,	sim	dēbitī,	sīmus
dēbuerīs	dēbuerītis	-a, -um	sīs	-ae, -a	sītis
dēbuerit	dēbuerint		sit		sint
		PLUPERFECT			
dēbuissem	dēbuissēmus	dēbitus,	essem	dēbitī,	essēmus
dēbuissēs	dēbuissētis	-a, -um	essēs	-ae, -a	essētis
dēbuisset	dēbuissent		esset		essent

THIRD CONJUGATION

PRINCIPAL PARTS: **pellō, pellere, pepulī, pulsus**
STEMS: *present,* **pelle-;** *perfect,* **pepul-;** *participial,* **puls-**

ACTIVE		PASSIVE		
		PERFECT		
pepul*erim*	pepul*erīmus*	puls*us,* $\begin{cases} sim \\ sīs \\ sit \end{cases}$ -*a, -um*	pulsī, $\begin{cases} sīmus \\ sītis \\ sint \end{cases}$ -*ae, -a*	
pepul*erīs*	pepul*erītis*			
pepul*erit*	pepul*erint*			
		PLUPERFECT		
pepul*issem*	pepul*issēmus*	puls*us,* $\begin{cases} essem \\ essēs \\ esset \end{cases}$ -*a, -um*	pulsī, $\begin{cases} essēmus \\ essētis \\ essent \end{cases}$ -*ae, -a*	
pepul*issēs*	pepul*issētis*			
pepul*isset*	pepul*issent*			

-IŌ THIRD CONJUGATION

PRINCIPAL PARTS: **capiō, capere, cēpī, captus**
STEMS: *present,* **cape-;** *perfect,* **cēp-;** *participial,* **capt-**

ACTIVE		PASSIVE		
		PERFECT		
cēp*erim*	cēp*erīmus*	capt*us,* $\begin{cases} sim \\ sīs \\ sit \end{cases}$ -*a, -um*	captī, $\begin{cases} sīmus \\ sītis \\ sint \end{cases}$ -*ae, -a*	
cēp*erīs*	cēp*erītis*			
cēp*erit*	cēp*erint*			
		PLUPERFECT		
cēp*issem*	cēp*issēmus*	capt*us,* $\begin{cases} essem \\ essēs \\ esset \end{cases}$ -*a, -um*	captī, $\begin{cases} essēmus \\ essētis \\ essent \end{cases}$ -*ae, -a*	
cēp*issēs*	cēp*issētis*			
cēp*isset*	cēp*issent*			

FOURTH CONJUGATION

PRINCIPAL PARTS: **sentiō, sentīre, sēnsī, sēnsus**
STEMS: *present,* **sentī-;** *perfect,* **sēns-;** *participial,* **sēns-**

ACTIVE		PASSIVE	
		PERFECT	
sēnserim	sēnserīmus	sēnsus, $\begin{cases} sim \\ sīs \\ sit \end{cases}$	sēnsī, $\begin{cases} sīmus \\ sītis \\ sint \end{cases}$
sēnserīs	sēnserītis	-a, -um	-ae, -a
sēnserit	sēnserint		
		PLUPERFECT	
sēnsissem	sēnsissēmus	sēnsus, $\begin{cases} essem \\ essēs \\ esset \end{cases}$	sēnsī, $\begin{cases} essēmus \\ essētis \\ essent \end{cases}$
sēnsissēs	sēnsissētis	-a, -um	-ae, -a
sēnsisset	sēnsissent		

DEPONENT VERBS

hortor

PERFECT				PLUPERFECT			
hortātus, -a, -um	$\begin{cases} sim \\ sīs \\ sit \end{cases}$	hortātī, -ae, -a	$\begin{cases} sīmus \\ sītis \\ sint \end{cases}$	hortātus, -a, -um	$\begin{cases} essem \\ essēs \\ esset \end{cases}$	hortātī, -ae, -a	$\begin{cases} essēmus \\ essētis \\ essent \end{cases}$

IRREGULAR VERBS

sum   **possum**

ACTIVE ONLY			
PERFECT	PLUPERFECT	PERFECT	PLUPERFECT
fuerim	fuissem	potuerim	potuissem
fuerīs	fuissēs	potuerīs	potuissēs
fuerit	fuisset	potuerit	potuisset
fuerīmus	fuissēmus	potuerīmus	potuissēmus
fuerītis	fuissētis	potuerītis	potuissētis
fuerint	fuissent	potuerint	potuissent

eō

ACTIVE ONLY	
PERFECT	PLUPERFECT
ierim (*īverim*), etc.	*īssem* (*īvissem*), etc.

volō nōlō mālō

ACTIVE ONLY		
PERF.	*voluerim,* etc.	*nōluerim,* etc.	*māluerim,* etc.
PLUP.	*voluissem,* etc.	*nōluissem,* etc.	*māluissem,* etc.

ferō

	ACTIVE	PASSIVE
PERF.	*tulerim,* etc.	*lātus sim,* etc.
PLUP.	*tulissem,* etc.	*lātus essem,* etc.

coepī licet

ACTIVE ONLY		
PERF.	*coeperim,* etc.	*licuerit,* etc.
PLUP.	*coepissem,* etc.	*licuisset,* etc.

fīō

PASSIVE ONLY	
PERF.	*factus sim,* etc.
PLUP.	*factus essem,* etc.

Note:

1. The perfect active subjunctive is formed by adding to the perfect stem the following endings:

-erim	**-erīmus**
-erīs	**-erītis**
-erit	**-erint**

2. The perfect active subjunctive resembles the future perfect active indicative in all forms except the first person singular. In the first person singular, the ending is **-erim** instead of **-erō**.

3. The pluperfect active subjunctive is formed by adding to the perfect active infinitive the personal endings, **-m, -s, -t, -mus, -tis, -nt.**

4. The perfect passive subjunctive consists of two parts. The first part is the perfect passive participle; the second the present subjunctive of **esse.**

5. The pluperfect passive subjunctive also consists of two parts. The first part is the perfect passive participle; the second the imperfect subjunctive of **esse.**

6. The perfect passive participle, used in the formation of the perfect and pluperfect passive subjunctive, agrees with the subject in gender, number, and case.

7. In the perfect and pluperfect subjunctive, verbs of four or more syllables are often shortened as follows:

laudārit   for **laudāverit**
laudāssem for **laudāvissem**

EXERCISES

A. In each sentence, substitute the equivalent form of the verb in parentheses for the italicized verb.

1. Dīcam quantās rēs *gesserīmus*.   (dēleō)
2. Vidētis quā celeritāte haec *gesta sini*.   (iūdicō)
3. Cum Catilīna sociōs Rōmae *reliquisset*,   (ēripiō)
   semper vigilāvī.
4. Cum ea *putāssem*, urbem servāvī.   (faciō)

5. Cōgitā quem in locum *prōgressus sīs*. (eō)
6. Vōbīs quid senātus *cēnsuerit* expōnam. (prōvideō)
7. Cum *profectī essētis* in Siciliam, vēnit (discēdō)
Hēraclēam.
8. Tantā dīligentiā fuistī ut ad praetōrem (contendō)
vēnerīs.
9. Cum *esset respōnsum*, ea ā cīvibus suscepta (dīcō)
erant.
10. Exclūsī eōs cum illī ipsī *vēnissent*. (cōnfiteor)

B. Give the full verb form for each of the following shortened forms.

1. quaesīssēs 4. retardārint
2. iūdicārit 5. repudiāssēmus
3. līberāssem

C. With each form, make the one change indicated in parentheses.

1. coeperīs (pluperfect) 6. secūtī sītis (3rd person)
2. fuissem (plural) 7. dēlēctī essēmus (perfect)
3. dubitāvisset (1st person) 8. susceptī essent (singular)
4. potuerītis (singular) 9. iēcerim (2nd person)
5. tulerit (passive) 10. trāctī essent (active)

D. Write the perfect and pluperfect subjunctive of the following verbs in the form indicated:

1. *videō:* 3rd plural passive 4. *nōlō:* 1st singular
2. *rēgnō:* 3rd singular active 5. *afficiō:* 1st plural passive
3. *patior:* 2nd singular

Unit IV—Nouns

Lesson 12. DECLENSION OF NOUNS

FIRST DECLENSION

	SINGULAR	PLURAL
Nom.	tabula	tabulae
Gen.	tabulae	tabulārum
Dat.	tabulae	tabulīs
Acc.	tabulam	tabulās
Abl.	tabulā	tabulīs

Note:

1. Nouns of the first declension end in **-a** in the nominative singular and **-ae** in the genitive singular.

2. Nouns of the first declension are feminine unless they denote males: **terra** (land) is feminine, but **nauta** (sailor) and **Catilīna** (a man's name) are masculine.

3. Some nouns of the first declension that have been borrowed from the Greek end in **-ās** in the nominative singular: **Archiās** (a man's name). The rest of the declension is regular.

4. The base of a noun is found by dropping the ending of the *genitive singular*.

SECOND DECLENSION

	(*m.*)	(*m.*)	(*m.*)	(*m.*)	(*n.*)
	SINGULAR				
Nom.	oculus	puer	ager	vir	templum
Gen.	oculī	puerī	agrī	virī	templī
Dat.	oculō	puerō	agrō	virō	templō
Acc.	oculum	puerum	agrum	virum	templum
Abl.	oculō	puerō	agrō	virō	templō

SECOND DECLENSION

		PLURAL			
Nom.	oculī	puerī	agrī	virī	templa
Gen.	oculōrum	puerōrum	agrōrum	virōrum	templōrum
Dat.	oculīs	puerīs	agrīs	virīs	templīs
Acc.	oculōs	puerōs	agrōs	virōs	templa
Abl.	oculīs	puerīs	agrīs	virīs	templīs

Note:

1. The nominative singular of second declension nouns ends in -us,
   -er, or -ir for the masculine, and -um for the neuter. All second declension nouns end in -ī in the genitive singular.

   Humus (ground, earth) is feminine by exception.

   Locus (place) is neuter in the plural, ending in -a in the nominative
   and accusative plural.

2. Nouns ending in -ius and -ium generally have one -i in the genitive
   singular: **nūntius, nūntī, nūntiō,** etc.; **beneficium, beneficī, bene-
   ficiō,** etc.

THIRD DECLENSION

	MASCULINE & FEMININE		NEUTER	
	SINGULAR	PLURAL	SINGULAR	PLURAL
Nom.	praetor	praetōrēs	scelus	scelera
Gen.	praetōris	praetōrum	sceleris	scelerum
Dat.	praetōrī	praetōribus	scelerī	sceleribus
Acc.	praetōrem	praetōrēs	scelus	scelera
Abl.	praetōre	praetōribus	scelere	sceleribus

I-Stems

MASCULINE & FEMININE			NEUTER	
	SINGULAR	PLURAL	SINGULAR	PLURAL
Nom.	mēns*is*	mēns*ēs*	mar*e*	mar*ia*
Gen.	mēns*is*	mēns*ium*	mar*is*	mar*ium*
Dat.	mēns*ī*	mēns*ibus*	mar*ī*	mar*ibus*
Acc.	mēns*em*	mēns*ēs, -īs*	mar*e*	mar*ia*
Abl.	mēns*e*	mēns*ibus*	mar*ī*	mar*ibus*

Note:

1. The nominative singular ending of nouns of the third declension varies greatly. The genitive singular, however, always ends in **-is**.

2. The third declension contains nouns of all three genders.

3. The following nouns are masculine:
   a. Those denoting males: **senex** (old man), **cēnsor** (censor).
   b. Abstract nouns ending in **-or**: **furor** (madness), **terror** (fright).

4. The following nouns are feminine:
   a. Those denoting females: **mulier** (woman), **uxor** (wife).
   b. Those ending in **-tās, -tūs, -tūdō, -iō, -tiō,** and **-x**: **facilitās, senectūs, cōnsuētūdō, opīniō, coniūrātiō,** and **vōx**.

5. Nouns ending in **-en** and **-us** are neuter: **lūmen, scelus.**

6. The accusative plural of i-stem nouns may end in **-īs** as well as **-ēs**.

7. The irregular nouns **vīs** and **nēmō** are declined as follows:

	SINGULAR	PLURAL	SINGULAR
Nom.	*vīs*	*vīrēs*	*nēmō*
Gen.	*vīs*	*vīrium*	*nūllīus*
Dat.	*vī*	*vīribus*	*nēminī*
Acc.	*vim*	*vīrēs, īs*	*nēminem*
Abl.	*vī*	*vīribus*	*nūllō*

FOURTH DECLENSION

	MASCULINE		NEUTER	
	SINGULAR	PLURAL	SINGULAR	PLURAL
Nom.	portus	portūs	cornū	cornua
Gen.	portūs	portuum	cornūs	cornuum
Dat.	portuī	portibus	cornū	cornibus
Acc.	portum	portūs	cornū	cornua
Abl.	portū	portibus	cornū	cornibus

Note:

1. The nominative singular of fourth declension nouns ends in **-us** for the masculine and **-ū** for the neuter. The following nouns are feminine by exception: **domus, manus,** and **Īdūs.**

2. **Domus** may also be declined as a noun of the second declension.

FIFTH DECLENSION

	SINGULAR	PLURAL
Nom.	rēs	rēs
Gen.	reī	rērum
Dat.	reī	rēbus
Acc.	rem	rēs
Abl.	rē	rēbus

Note:

1. Nouns of the fifth declension end in **-ēs** in the nominative singular and **-eī** in the genitive singular.

2. Nouns of the fifth declension are feminine. **Diēs,** however, is usually masculine. It is feminine in the expression **cōnstitūtā diē** (on a set day).

COMPARISON OF NOUN ENDINGS

SINGULAR									
1st Decl.	*2nd Decl.*		*3rd Decl.*			*4th Decl.*		*5th Decl.*
	(*m.*)	(*n.*)	(*m. & f.*)	(*n.*)		(*m.*)	(*n.*)	
Nom. a	us (er,ir)	um	———	———		us	ū	ēs
Gen. ae	ī	ī	is	is		ūs	ūs	ēī
Dat. ae	ō	ō	ī	ī		uī	ū	ēī
Acc. am	um	um	em	———		um	ū	em
Abl. ā	ō	ō	e (ī)	e (ī)		ū	ū	ē
PLURAL									
	(*m.*)	(*n.*)	(*m. & f.*)	(*n.*)		(*m.*)	(*n.*)	
Nom. ae	ī	a	ēs	a (ia)		ūs	ua	ēs
Gen. ārum	ōrum	ōrum	um (ium)	um (ium)		uum	uum	ērum
Dat. īs	īs	īs	ibus	ibus		ibus	ibus	ēbus
Acc. ās	ōs	a	ēs (īs)	a (ia)		ūs	ua	ēs
Abl. īs	īs	īs	ibus	ibus		ibus	ibus	ēbus

Note: In addition to the five common cases, Latin has two cases of limited use, the *vocative* and the *locative*.

1. The *vocative* case, used to address a person, has the same form as the nominative, with the following exceptions: second declension nouns ending in **-us** form the vocative singular by changing **-us** to **-e,** while nouns ending in **-ius** change **-ius** to **-ī.** Thus,

NOMINATIVE	VOCATIVE
Catilīna	**Catilīna**
Cicerō	**Cicerō**
servus	**serve**
Antōnius	**Antōnī**

2. The *locative* case, used instead of the ablative to express place where, is found chiefly in the singular of names of towns and small islands of the first and second declensions. The locative resembles the genitive in form. Thus,

NOMINATIVE	LOCATIVE
Rōma	**Rōmae**
Corinthus	**Corinthī**

Other common locatives are **domī** (at home), **humī** (on the ground), and **rūrī** (in the country).

WORKING VOCABULARY OF NOUNS

First Declension

FEMININE

adulēscentia, youth
āra, altar
clēmentia, mercy
concordia, harmony
cōnscientia,
  conscience
culpa, fault
cūria, senate house
cūstōdia, custody

doctrīna, learning
epistula, letter
flamma, flame
grātia, favor
invidia, envy
iūstitia, justice
Kalendae (*pl.*),
  calends

lacrima, tear
mora, delay
Nōnae (*pl.*), nones
ōra, shore
sententia, feeling
sīca, dagger
tabula, writing tablet
temperantia, restraint

Second Declension

MASCULINE

animus, mind
annus, year
coniūrātī (*pl.*),
  conspirators
gladius, sword

lēgātus, envoy
morbus, disease
nūntius, messenger
oculus, eye
socius, ally

somnus, sleep
tribūnus, tribune
triumphus, triumph
ventus, wind
vīcīnus, neighbor

NEUTER

argentum, silver	factum, deed	saxum, rock
aurum, gold	ingenium, talent	subsidium, help
beneficium, favor	iūdicium, judgment	supplicium,
cōnsultum, decree	nāvigium, boat	punishment
dēlūbrum, shrine	negōtium, business	tēctum, roof
dētrīmentum, loss	officium, duty	templum, temple
exemplum, example	rōstrum, beak	vinculum, chain
exsilium, exile	of a ship	vīnum, wine

Third Declension

MASCULINE

adulēscēns,	hospes, guest	ōrdō, order
young man	īgnis, fire	praetor, judge
carcer, prison	iūdex, judge	scrīptor, writer
cēnsor, censor	labor, work	senex, old man
comes, companion	mēnsis, month	sermō, talk
cōnsul, consul	mercātor, merchant	sōl, sun
dolor, grief	mōs, custom	terror, fright
furor, madness	nēmō, no one	testis, witness
honor, honor		

FEMININE

aetās, age	facilitās, ease	ōrātiō, speech
ars, art	facultās, ability	plēbs, common people
caedēs, murder	gēns, tribe	potestās, power
coniūrātiō,	laus, praise	ratiō, method
conspiracy	lībertās, freedom	senectūs, old age
cōnsuētūdō, custom	mēns, mind	uxor, wife
cupiditās, desire	mulier, woman	vīs, force
dignitās, prestige	opīniō, opinion	vōx, voice

NEUTER

facinus, crime	lūmen, light	opus, work
frīgus, cold	moenia (pl.), walls	rūs, country
genus, kind	ōmen, omen	scelus, crime
iūs, right	onus, burden	

Fourth Declension

MASCULINE

cāsus, chance
commeātus,
    supplies
interitus,
    destruction

iussus, order
metus, fear
mōtus, movement
occāsus, setting

portus, harbor
sēnsus, feeling
ūsus, use

Fifth Declension

FEMININE

aciēs, battle line
fidēs, faith

perniciēs, ruin
rēs, thing

speciēs, appearance
spēs, hope

EXERCISES

A. Identify the case and number of the following forms:

1. ōrās	6. ratiō	11. plēbī	16. sīcā
2. perniciem	7. exemplī	12. sociōrum	17. mōrēs
3. frīgore	8. scelera	13. comitibus	18. supplicium
4. senum	9. metū	14. lēgāte	19. epistulam
5. vinculīs	10. potestās	15. facinus	20. somnō

B. Select the one noun in each group that is not in the same *case* as the others.

1. spem, oculum, vōcum, moenia, ūsum
2. morā, sermōne, gladiīs, praetōrī, gentibus
3. cupiditās, onus, opīniō, tēcta, artis
4. portuum, morbum, caedium, cūriae, generis
5. speciēī, ūsuī, vīcīnīs, tabulārum, gentibus

C. Select the one noun in each group that is not in the same *number* as the others.

1. vīrium, subsidium, annōrum, flammae, mentēs
2. laus, scrīptōrī, ratiōnem, cōnsulum, factī
3. īgnis, rēs, invidiā, testīs, dolōrem
4. lacrimīs, ventōs, iūra, sēnsūs, mora
5. grātia, coniūrātī, ōmina, comitēs, aciēbus

D. Using the same case, write each of the following nouns in the *plural*:

1. commeātū	3. vī	5. spem	7. āra	9. locus
2. iūdex	4. mōris	6. praetōrī	8. nōmen	10. lēgāte

E. Using the same case or cases, write each of the following nouns in the *singular*:

1. caedium	5. nūntiī	8. vincula
2. scelera	6. rēbus	9. lacrimīs
3. epistulās	7. portuum	10. hospitum
4. adulēscentēs		

F. Write the following specified forms:

1-2. ablative singular of *ingenium, cāsus*
3-4. genitive plural of *mercātor, annus*
5-6. accusative singular of *ōrātiō, fidēs*
7-8. accusative plural of *genus, cōnsuētūdō*
9-10. locative of *domus, Rōma*
11-12. vocative of *Mānlius, Mārcus*
13-14. ablative plural of *grātia, mēnsis*
15-16. dative singular of *aciēs, sōl*
17-18. nominative plural of *cōnsultum, mēns*
19. genitive singular of *metus*
20. dative plural of *iūdex*

G. In each sentence, substitute the equivalent form of the noun in parentheses for the italicized noun.

1. Dēsignat quemque ad *caedem*.	(mors)
2. Inclūsum est in *tabulīs*.	(littera)
3. Numerus *hostium* crēscit.	(inimīcus)
4. Intrā *moenia* sunt.	(mūrus)
5. Prīncipēs *cīvitātis* fūgērunt.	(oppidum)
6. *Servī* tē metuunt.	(Cīvis)
7. Omnēs tē *domī* exspectant.	(Rōma)
8. Priōre *nocte* vēnistī.	(diēs)
9. Magna grātia *Iovī* habenda est.	(Pompeius)
10. Patria tēcum, *Catilīna*, sīc agit.	(Mārcus)

Unit V—Adjectives and Numerals

Lesson 13. DECLENSION OF ADJECTIVES AND NUMERALS

FIRST AND SECOND DECLENSIONS

	SINGULAR		
	(*m.*)	(*f.*)	(*n.*)
Nom.	dignus	digna	dignum
Gen.	dignī	dignae	dignī
Dat.	dignō	dignae	dignō
Acc.	dignum	dignam	dignum
Abl.	dignō	dignā	dignō
	PLURAL		
	(*m.*)	(*f.*)	(*n.*)
Nom.	dignī	dignae	digna
Gen.	dignōrum	dignārum	dignōrum
Dat.	dignīs	dignīs	dignīs
Acc.	dignōs	dignās	digna
Abl.	dignīs	dignīs	dignīs

Note:

1. Some adjectives end in **-er** in the masculine nominative singular.

   līber, lībera, līberum
   miser, misera, miserum

2. Some adjectives ending in **-er** in the masculine nominative singular drop the **-e** in all other forms.

   dexter, dextra, dextrum
   sacer, sacra, sacrum

63

THIRD DECLENSION

Three Endings

	SINGULAR		
	(*m.*)	(*f.*)	(*n.*)
Nom.	celer	celer*is*	celer*e*
Gen.	celer*is*	celer*is*	celer*is*
Dat.	celer**ī**	celer**ī**	celer**ī**
Acc.	celer*em*	celer*em*	celer*e*
Abl.	celer**ī**	celer**ī**	celer**ī**

	PLURAL		
	(*m.*)	(*f.*)	(*n.*)
Nom.	celer**ēs**	celer**ēs**	celer*ia*
Gen.	celer*ium*	celer*ium*	celer*ium*
Dat.	celer*ibus*	celer*ibus*	celer*ibus*
Acc.	celer**ēs**, **-īs**	celer**ēs**, **-īs**	celer*ia*
Abl.	celer*ibus*	celer*ibus*	celer*ibus*

Note: Some adjectives ending in **-er** in the masculine nominative singular drop the **-e** in all other forms: ācer, ācris, ācre.

Two Endings

	SINGULAR		PLURAL	
	(*m. & f.*)	(*n.*)	(*m. & f.*)	(*n.*)
Nom.	grav*is*	grav*e*	grav**ēs**	grav*ia*
Gen.	grav*is*	grav*is*	grav*ium*	grav*ium*
Dat.	grav**ī**	grav**ī**	grav*ibus*	grav*ibus*
Acc.	grav*em*	grav*e*	grav**ēs**, **-īs**	grav*ia*
Abl.	grav**ī**	grav**ī**	grav*ibus*	grav*ibus*

One Ending

	SINGULAR		PLURAL	
	(m. & f.)	*(n.)*	*(m. & f.)*	*(n.)*
Nom.	āmēns	āmēns	āmentēs	āmentia
Gen.	āmentis	āmentis	āmentium	āmentium
Dat.	āmentī	āmentī	āmentibus	āmentibus
Acc.	āmentem	āmens	āmentēs, -īs	āmentia
Abl.	āmentī	āmentī	āmentibus	āmentibus

Note:

1. Third declension adjectives follow the general pattern of i-stem nouns. Adjectives with three endings have **-er** in the masculine, **-ris** in the feminine, and **-re** in the neuter. Adjectives with two endings have **-is** in the masculine and feminine, and **-e** in the neuter.

2. Adjectives of the third declension end in **-ium** in the genitive plural, and **-ī** in the ablative singular.

3. Like neuter nouns, the accusative forms of neuter adjectives are always the same as the nominative. In the plural, these forms end in **-ia**.

IRREGULAR ADJECTIVES

Some adjectives of the first and second declensions are irregular in the following cases only:

	(m.)	*(f.)*	*(n.)*
Gen. Sing.	**-īus**	**-īus**	**-īus**
Dat. Sing.	**-ī**	**-ī**	**-ī**

The following adjectives are declined in this way:

alius, alia, aliud   **uter, utra, utrum**
alter, altera, alterum   **neuter, neutra, neutrum**

ūllus, ūlla, ūllum   **sōlus, sōla, sōlum**
nūllus, nūlla, nūllum   **tōtus, tōta, tōtum**

iste, ista, istud

NUMERALS

	(m.)	(f.)	(n.)
Nom.	ūnus	ūna	ūnum
Gen.	ūnīus	ūnīus	ūnīus
Dat.	ūnī	ūnī	ūnī
Acc.	ūnum	ūnam	ūnum
Abl.	ūnō	ūnā	ūnō

	(m.)	(f.)	(n.)
Nom.	duo	duae	duo
Gen.	duōrum	duārum	duōrum
Dat.	duōbus	duābus	duōbus
Acc.	duōs	duās	duo
Abl.	duōbus	duābus	duōbus

	(m. & f.)	(n.)
Nom.	trēs	tria
Gen.	trium	trium
Dat.	tribus	tribus
Acc.	trēs	tria
Abl.	tribus	tribus

	SINGULAR	PLURAL
Nom.	mīlle	mīlia
Gen.	mīlle	mīlium
Dat.	mīlle	mīlibus
Acc.	mīlle	mīlia
Abl.	mīlle	mīlibus

Note:

1. All cardinal numbers from *four* to *one hundred* are indeclinable.

2. **Mīlle** in the singular is an indeclinable adjective; in the plural, it is a neuter noun.

WORKING VOCABULARY OF ADJECTIVES

First and Second Declensions

aeternus, eternal

cārus, dear

cēterī (pl.), the others

dignus, worthy

ēgregius, outstanding

hūmānus, human

idōneus, suitable

iūcundus, pleasant

nefārius, impious

perditus, desperate

plēnus, full

prīvātus, private

proximus, next

pūblicus, public

reliquus, remaining

sacer, sacred

salvus, safe

superus, above

tūtus, safe

ultimus, last

vērus, true

Third Declension

āmēns, mad

cīvīlis, civil

complūrēs (pl.), several

crūdēlis, cruel

frequēns, crowded

gravis, heavy

immortālis, immortal

incrēdibilis, unbelievable

iuvenis, young

levis, light

mīlitāris, military

sapiēns, wise

similis, like

singulāris, remarkable

turpis, shameful

vehemēns, strong

EXERCISES

A. Identify tne case and number of the following forms:

1. proximā nocte
2. fortēs virī
3. fīrmīs praesidiīs
4. duo equitēs
5. nefāriam caedem
6. cōnsilium vehemēns
7. iūdiciōrum gravium
8. ōrātiōnis tōtīus
9. annōs complūrēs
10. vērō comitī

B. For each noun, write the proper form of iūcundus and similis.

1. genus
2. ratiōnis
3. portum
4. mōrēs
5. facta
6. sententiā
7. sermōnum
8. officiīs
9. ingenī
10. rēbus

C. Select the adjective in parentheses that agrees with the noun.

1. vōce   (grave, gravī, gravis)
2. metum   (turpem, turpium, turpe)
3. spēbus   (aeternōs, aeternus, aeternīs)
4. ventōrum   (crūdēlium, crūdēlem, crūdēle)
5. vīcīnōs   (sapientis, sapientem, sapientīs)

D. Write the following specified forms:

nominative plural of:

1. sīca crūdēlis   2. vīnum leve   3. gēns digna

genitive singular and plural of:

4. alia vīs   5. scelus nefārium   6. noster testis

dative singular and plural of:

7. nūllus adulēscēns   8. socius sapiēns   9. ōmen pūblicum

accusative singular and plural of:

10. rēs perdita   11. templum frequēns   12. hospes cārus

ablative singular and plural of:

13. mōtus similis   14. onus grave   15. tua opīniō

E. In each sentence, substitute the equivalent form of the adjective in parentheses for the italicized adjective.

1. Tabulās *pūblicās* dēsīderās.   (similis)
2. Diēs sunt *turpēs*.   (iūcundus)
3. Rem *incrēdibilem* exposuī.   (tōtus)
4. Sēdem *omnium* rērum Rōmae locāvit.   (prīvātus)
5. In *proximīs* vīllīs fuērunt.   (trēs)
6. Commemorātiōnem *sacrī* nōminis facit.   (nūllus)
7. *Novō* genere dīcendī ūtor.   (Singulāris)
8. Animōs *nostrōs* doctrīnā colimus.   (vehemēns)
9. Erunt ducēs *nefāriī* bellī.   (crūdēlis)
10. Salūtī *vestrae* prōvīdistis.   (sōlus)

Unit VI—Comparison

Lesson 14. COMPARISON OF ADJECTIVES; FORMATION AND COMPARISON OF ADVERBS

REGULAR COMPARISON OF ADJECTIVES

POSITIVE	COMPARATIVE	SUPERLATIVE
cārus, -a, -um	cārior, -ius	cārissimus, -a, -um
turpis, -e	turpior, -ius	turpissimus, -a, -um
audāx	audācior, -ius	audācissimus, -a, -um
frequēns	frequentior, -ius	frequentissimus, -a, -um
miser, -era, -erum	miserior, -ius	miserrimus, -a, -um
sacer, -cra, -crum	sacrior, -ius	sacerrimus, -a, -um
facilis, -e	facilior, -ius	facillimus, -a, -um

Note:

1. The comparative degree is formed by adding -ior to the base of the positive for the masculine and feminine, and -ius for the neuter.

2. The superlative is formed by adding -issimus, -a, -um to the base of the positive. However,

    a. Adjectives ending in -er form the superlative by adding -rimus, -a, -um to the *nominative,* and

    b. Six adjectives ending in -lis (**facilis, difficilis, similis, dissimilis, gracilis, humilis**) form the superlative by adding -limus, -a, -um to the base.

3. The three degrees are translated as follows:

    tardus, -a, -um, slow   **tardior, -ius,** slower, rather slow
        _{positive}   _{comparative}

        tardissimus, -a, -um, slowest, very slow
             _{superlative}

IRREGULAR COMPARISON OF ADJECTIVES

POSITIVE	COMPARATIVE	SUPERLATIVE
bonus, -a, -um	melior, melius	optimus, -a, -um
malus, -a, -um	peior, peius	pessimus, -a, -um
magnus, -a, -um	maior, maius	maximus, -a, -um
parvus, -a, -um	minor, minus	minimus, -a, -um
multus, -a, -um	——, plūs	plūrimus, -a, -um

DECLENSION OF COMPARATIVES

	SINGULAR		PLURAL	
	(*m. & f.*)	(*n.*)	(*m. & f.*)	(*n.*)
Nom.	cārior	cārius	cāriōrēs	cāriōra
Gen.	cāriōris	cāriōris	cāriōrum	cāriōrum
Dat.	cāriōrī	cāriōrī	cāriōribus	cāriōribus
Acc.	cāriōrem	cārius	cāriōrēs	cāriōra
Abl.	cāriōre	cāriōre	cāriōribus	cāriōribus

FORMATION OF ADVERBS FROM ADJECTIVES

ADJECTIVE	ADVERB
altus	altē
līber	līberē
fēlīx	fēlīciter
fortis	fortiter
ācer	ācriter
vehemēns	vehementer

Note:

1. Adverbs are formed from adjectives of the first and second declensions by adding -ē to the base, and from adjectives of the third declension by adding -iter. Adjectives ending in -ēns (genitive -entis) form the adverb by adding -er to the base.

2. A few irregular formations are:

ADJECTIVE	ADVERB
audāx	audācter
bonus	bene
facilis	facile
magnus	magnopere
malus	male
multus	multum
parvus	parum

COMPARISON OF ADVERBS

POSITIVE	COMPARATIVE	SUPERLATIVE
altē	altius	altissimē
breviter	brevius	brevissimē
audācter	audācius	audācissimē
līberē	līberius	līberrimē
ācriter	ācrius	ācerrimē
facile	facilius	facillimē
bene	melius	optimē
male	peius	pessimē
magnopere	magis	maximē
parum	minus	minimē
multum	plūs	plūrimum
diū	diūtius	diūtissimē
saepe	saepius	saepissimē
vehementer	vehementius	vehementissimē

Note:

1. With the exception of **magis**, the comparative form of the adverb is the same as the neuter comparative form of the adjective.

2. With the exception of **plūrimum**, the superlative of the adverb is formed from the superlative of the adjective by changing **-us** to **-ē**.

ADJECTIVE	ADVERB
brevissimus	brevissimē
ācerrimus	ācerrimē
simillimus	simillimē
pessimus	pessimē

3. The three degrees are translated as follows:

tardē, slowly
<u>positive</u>

tardius, more slowly
<u>comparative</u>

tardissimē, most or very slowly
<u>superlative</u>

EXERCISES

A. Write the comparative and superlative of each of the following words:

1. cārus	4. similis	7. diū	10. miser	13. ācriter
2. leviter	5. bonus	8. multus	11. turpis	14. malus
3. sapiēns	6. bene	9. magnopere	12. saepe	15. parvus

B. For each noun, write the correct form of the adjective indicated.

1. potestāte   (comparative of *magnus*)
2. lūmen   (superlative of *parvus*)
3. ōrās   (comparative of *tūtus*)
4. labōris   (superlative of *difficilis*)
5. rērum   (superlative of *bonus*)

C. Write the following specified forms:

1. ablative singular of *senātus fortior*
2. accusative plural of *scelus pessimum*
3. dative singular of *ōrātiō optima*
4. accusative singular of *vīs maior*
5. genitive plural of *potentior cōnsul*

D. In each sentence, substitute the equivalent form of the word in parentheses for the italicized word.

1. Urbs *pulcherrima* vōbīs servāta est.   (nōtus)
2. Iter erat *difficillimum.*   (facilis)
3. Illa erant multō *certiōra.*   (dignus)
4. Ēreptī estis ex *crūdēlissimō* interitū.   (miser)
5. Haec studia *vehementius* colēbantur.   (ācer)
6. Erat signum *clārissimī* virī.   (sapiēns)
7. *Maximum* numerum gladiōrum extulit.   (Parvus)
8. Nōn *minōre* dolōre peritūrī sunt.   (magnus)
9. *Tardissimē* Lentulus vēnit.   (Celer)
10. Habēbat spem rērum *cārissimārum.*   (bonus)

Unit VII—Pronouns

Lesson 15. **DEMONSTRATIVE, PERSONAL, REFLEXIVE, INTENSIVE, RELATIVE, INTERROGATIVE, AND INDEFINITE PRONOUNS**

DEMONSTRATIVE PRONOUNS

is

	SINGULAR			PLURAL		
	(m.)	*(f.)*	*(n.)*	*(m.)*	*(f.)*	*(n.)*
Nom.	is	ea	id	eī (iī)	eae	ea
Gen.	eius	eius	eius	eōrum	eārum	eōrum
Dat.	eī	eī	eī	eīs (iīs)	eīs (iīs)	eīs (iīs)
Acc.	eum	eam	id	eōs	eās	ea
Abl.	eō	eā	eō	eīs (iīs)	eīs (iīs)	eīs (iīs)

hic

	SINGULAR			PLURAL		
	(m.)	*(f.)*	*(n.)*	*(m.)*	*(f.)*	*(n.)*
Nom.	hic	haec	hoc	hī	hae	haec
Gen.	huius	huius	huius	hōrum	hārum	hōrum
Dat.	huic	huic	huic	hīs	hīs	hīs
Acc.	hunc	hanc	hoc	hōs	hās	haec
Abl.	hōc	hāc	hōc	hīs	hīs	hīs

ille

	SINGULAR			PLURAL		
	(m.)	*(f.)*	*(n.)*	*(m.)*	*(f.)*	*(n.)*
Nom.	ille	illa	illud	illī	illae	illa
Gen.	illīus	illīus	illīus	illōrum	illārum	illōrum
Dat.	illī	illī	illī	illīs	illīs	illīs
Acc.	illum	illam	illud	illōs	illās	illa
Abl.	illō	illā	illō	illīs	illīs	illīs

īdem

	SINGULAR		
	(m.)	(f.)	(n.)
Nom.	īdem	eadem	idem
Gen.	eiusdem	eiusdem	eiusdem
Dat.	eīdem	eīdem	eīdem
Acc.	eundem	eandem	idem
Abl.	eōdem	eādem	eōdem

	PLURAL		
	(m.)	(f.)	(n.)
Nom.	eīdem (īdem)	eaedem	eadem
Gen.	eōrundem	eārundem	eōrundem
Dat.	eīsdem (īsdem)	eīsdem (īsdem)	eīsdem (īsdem)
Acc.	eōsdem	eāsdem	eadem
Abl.	eīsdem (īsdem)	eīsdem (īsdem)	eīsdem (īsdem)

Note:

1. **Is, hic,** and **ille** may be used both as pronouns and as adjectives. As pronouns, the masculine form means *he*, the feminine *she*, and the neuter *it*. As adjectives, **is, hic,** and **ille** are translated as follows:

   is = *this, that* (plural *these, those*)
   hic = *this* (plural *these*)
   ille = *that* (plural *those*)

2. **Īdem,** meaning *the same*, is a compound of **is** plus the suffix **-dem.** It follows the declension of **is** with a few changes in spelling.

3. Demonstrative adjectives are placed before the nouns they modify.

PERSONAL PRONOUNS

	FIRST PERSON		SECOND PERSON	
	SINGULAR	PLURAL	SINGULAR	PLURAL
Nom.	ego (*I*)	nōs (*we*)	tū (*you*)	vōs (*you*)
Gen.	meī	nostrum (nostrī)	tuī	vestrum (vestrī)
Dat.	mihi	nōbīs	tibi	vōbīs
Acc.	mē	nōs	tē	vōs
Abl.	mē	nōbīs	tē	vōbīs

Note: For the third person, the demonstrative pronouns **is, hic,** and **ille** are used.

REFLEXIVE PRONOUN

	SINGULAR	PLURAL
Nom.	——	——
Gen.	suī	suī
Dat.	sibi	sibi
Acc.	sē (sēsē)	sē (sēsē)
Abl.	sē (sēsē)	sē (sēsē)

INTENSIVE PRONOUN

ipse, self

	SINGULAR			PLURAL		
	(*m.*)	(*f.*)	(*n.*)	(*m.*)	(*f.*)	(*n.*)
Nom.	ipse	ipsa	ipsum	ipsī	ipsae	ipsa
Gen.	ipsīus	ipsīus	ipsīus	ipsōrum	ipsārum	ipsōrum
Dat.	ipsī	ipsī	ipsī	ipsīs	ipsīs	ipsīs
Acc.	ipsum	ipsam	ipsum	ipsōs	ipsās	ipsa
Abl.	ipsō	ipsā	ipsō	ipsīs	ipsīs	ipsīs

RELATIVE PRONOUN

quī, who, which

	SINGULAR			PLURAL		
	(*m.*)	(*f.*)	(*n.*)	(*m.*)	(*f.*)	(*n.*)
Nom.	quī	quae	quod	quī	quae	quae
Gen.	cuius	cuius	cuius	quōrum	quārum	quōrum
Dat.	cui	cui	cui	quibus	quibus	quibus
Acc.	quem	quam	quod	quōs	quās	quae
Abl.	quō	quā	quō	quibus	quibus	quibus

INTERROGATIVE PRONOUN

quis, who?   **quid**, what?

	SINGULAR		PLURAL		
	(*m. & f.*)	(*n.*)	(*m.*)	(*f.*)	(*n.*)
Nom.	quis	quid	quī	quae	quae
Gen.	cuius	cuius	quōrum	quārum	quōrum
Dat.	cui	cui	quibus	quibus	quibus
Acc.	quem	quid	quōs	quās	quae
Abl.	quō	quō	quibus	quibus	quibus

Note: As an adjective, the interrogative is declined like the relative pronoun **quī, quae, quod.**

   quī puer? what boy?   **quod** cōnsilium? what plan?

INDEFINITE PRONOUNS

aliquis, someone   **aliquid,** something

	SINGULAR		PLURAL		
	(*m. & f.*)	(*n.*)	(*m.*)	(*f.*)	(*n.*)
Nom.	aliquis	aliquid	aliquī	aliquae	aliqua
Gen.	alicuius	alicuius	aliquōrum	aliquārum	aliquōrum
Dat.	alicui	alicui	aliquibus	aliquibus	aliquibus
Acc.	aliquem	aliquid	aliquōs	aliquās	aliqua
Abl.	aliquō	aliquō	aliquibus	aliquibus	aliquibus

Note:

1. **Aliquis** is a compound of **quis** plus the prefix **ali-**. The prefix remains unchanged throughout the declension.

2. The adjective forms are **aliquī, aliqua, aliquod.**

3. After **sī, nisi, nē,** and **num, aliquis** and **aliquid** are shortened to **quis** and **quid.**

quīdam, a certain one

	(*m.*)	(*f.*)	(*n.*)
	SINGULAR		
Nom.	quīdam	quaedam	quiddam
Gen.	cuiusdam	cuiusdam	cuiusdam
Dat.	cuidam	cuidam	cuidam
Acc.	quendam	quandam	quiddam
Abl.	quōdam	quādam	quōdam
	PLURAL		
Nom.	quīdam	quaedam	quaedam
Gen.	quōrundam	quārundam	quōrundam
Dat.	quibusdam	quibusdam	quibusdam
Acc.	quōsdam	quāsdam	quaedam
Abl.	quibusdam	quibusdam	quibusdam

Note:

1. **Quīdam** is a compound of **quī** plus the suffix **-dam.** The suffix remains unchanged throughout the declension.

2. The letter **m** is changed to **n** before **d.**

3. The adjective forms are **quīdam, quaedam, quoddam.**

quisque, each one   **quidque,** each thing

	SINGULAR	
	(*m. & f.*)	(*n.*)
Nom.	quisque	quidque
Gen.	cuiusque	cuiusque
Dat.	cuique	cuique
Acc.	quemque	quidque
Abl.	quōque	quōque

Note:

1. **Quisque** is a compound of **quis** plus the suffix **-que.** The suffix remains unchanged throughout the declension.

2. The plural of **quisque** is rarely used.

3. The adjective forms are **quisque, quaeque, quodque.**

EXERCISES

A. Identify the case and number of the following forms:

1. hunc	4. quōque	7. cuiusdam	10. quās	13. vōs
2. alicui	5. sibi	8. quod	11. eīdem	14. illīus
3. ipsōrum	6. eīsdem	9. id	12. mē	15. tibi

B. Next to each of the following nouns are four adjectives. All of them agree with the noun except one. Write that one correctly to make it agree.

1. *iūs:* ipsum, idem, alicuius, quod
2. *perniciem:* illam, hunc, quandam, ipsam
3. *tabulīs:* quibusdam, aliquibus, eīs, eiusdem

   4. *coniūrātōs:* illōs, eīsdem, ipsōs, aliquōs
   5. *vincula:* quod, illa, quaedam, haec

   C. Write the following specified forms:

   1-2. dative singular of *illa coniūrātiō*
   3-4. nominative plural of *id flūmen*
   5-6. accusative singular of *īdem homō*
   7-8. genitive plural of *haec ōrātiō*
  9-10. accusative plural of *ego, suī*
11-12. ablative singular of *tū, quisque*
13-14. ablative plural of *quīdam cīvis*
15-16. genitive singular of *aliqua rēs*
17-18. dative plural of *cōnsul ipse*
19-20. nominative plural of *quod scelus*

   D. In each sentence, substitute the equivalent form of the word in parentheses for the italicized word.

   1. Illud *mihi* laetandum esse videō.   (tū)
   2. Ab *illō* tempore annum tertium rēgnat.   (is)
   3. Asia id *nōs* docuit.   (hic)
   4. Erant participēs *eiusdem* laudis.   (ipse)
   5. *Illīs* laus est tribuenda.   (Nōs)
   6. Est dignus *aliquibus* praemiīs.   (quīdam)
   7. Quī *huic* successit nōn satis est parātus. (ille)
   8. Ā *quō* perīculō prohibēte rem pūblicam. (quisque)
   9. Manēbō *quōdam* amōre glōriae.   (īdem)
10. Imperātor ad *id* bellum dēlēctus erat.   (aliquis)

Unit VIII—*Idioms*

Lesson 16

ad multam noctem, until late at night
amāns patriae, patriotic
apud sē, at his house, in his presence
certum mihi est, I am sure
cum prīmum, as soon as
cum ... tum, not only ... but also
domī mīlitiaeque, at home and in the field
ex cōnsuētūdine meā, according to my custom
fāmae meae servīre, to have regard for my reputation
fīnem facere, to put an end to
fortūnā secundā ūtī, to enjoy good luck
iam diū, for a long time now
iam prīdem, long since
in diēs, daily
in reliquum tempus, for the future
in viam sē dare, to start out
iūs iūrandum, an oath
multum (plūrimum) posse, to be (very) powerful
multum (plūrimum) valēre, to be (very) powerful
novīs rēbus studēre, to be eager for a revolution
ōrātiōnem habēre, to deliver a speech
orbis terrae or **orbis terrārum,** the world
patrēs cōnscrīptī, senators
post hominum memoriam, in man's memory
post urbem conditam, since the founding of the city
potius quam, rather than
quā dē causā, for this reason, for what reason
quam ob rem, for this reason, therefore
referre ad senātum, to make a motion in the senate
tantī est, it is worthwhile
tum cum, at the time when
ūnā ex parte, on one side

EXERCISES

A. Translate into idiomatic English.

1. Refer, Cicerō, ad senātum.
2. Eōrum manūs ac tēla abs tē iam diū contineō.
3. Servīlius Maelium novīs rēbus studentem occīdit.
4. Ad mortem tē dūcī iam prīdem oportēbat.
5. Quaesīvit ā Gallīs quam ob rem vēnissent.
6. Gallī iūs iūrandum sibi datum esse dīxērunt.
7. Crēscit in diēs hostium numerus.
8. Sed est tantī dum modo tua calamitās sit prīvāta.
9. Vīsne fāmae meae servīre?
10. Orbem terrae caede atque incendiīs vāstāre cupis.
11. Hoc post hominum memoriam contigit nēminī.
12. Nunc, patrēs cōnscrīptī, percipite quae dīcam.
13. Hostis potius quam inimīcus nōminābātur.
14. Ōrātiō secunda Cicerōnis ad populum habita est.
15. Quam ob rem omnia reī pūblicae causā suscēpī.

B. Complete the following Latin sentences by translating the words in parentheses.

1. Mānsērunt (until late at night).
2. Fortūnā secundā (he enjoyed).
3. Hoc sciet (for the future).
4. Agam (according to my custom).
5. (I am sure) illum esse hostem.

C. Select the correct answer in parentheses.

1. They put an end to the fight.
   Pugnae fīnem (posuērunt, dedērunt, fēcērunt).
2. He was patriotic.
   (Amāns, Volēns, Potēns) patriae erat.
3. He is very powerful.
   Plūrimum (pōnit, potest, est).
4. He excels at home and in the field.
   Domī superat (mīlitiaeque, agrōque, fīnibusque).
5. They will start out at once.
   Statim in viam sē (incipient, dabunt, pōnent).

Unit IX—Grammatical Structures

Lesson 17. THE SEVEN CASES

NOMINATIVE

1. The *subject* of a verb is in the nominative case.

    Cicerō ōrātiōnem habuit.   Cicero delivered a speech.

    Exception. The subject of an infinitive, however, is in the accusative case.

    Audīvī **Cicerōnem** ōrātiōnem   I heard that Cicero had delivered
    habuisse.   a speech.

2. A *predicate noun* or *predicate adjective* (used with the verb **sum** or a passive verb) is in the nominative.

    Catilīna erat **improbus.**   Catiline was wicked.
    Antōnius factus est **cōnsul.**   Antony was made consul.

GENITIVE

1. *Possession* is expressed by the genitive case.

    Domus **Cicerōnis** incēnsa est.   Cicero's house was burned.

2. *Description* may be expressed by the genitive with an adjective modifier.

    Erat rēs **summae**   It was a matter of the greatest
    difficultātis.   difficulty.

3. The *partitive* genitive represents the whole to which a part belongs.

    Partem **hostium**   They killed part of the enemy.
    interfēcērunt.

4. Certain *adjectives,* such as **cupidus** (desirous), **perītus** (skilled), **imperītus** (unskilled), and **plēnus** (full), take the genitive.

    Omnēs cupidī **pācis** sunt.   All are desirous of peace.

DATIVE

1. The *indirect object* of a verb is in the dative case.

   Catilīnae litterās dedit.   He gave the letter to Catiline.

2. Certain *adjectives,* such as **aequus** (equal), **amīcus** (friendly), **inimīcus** (unfriendly), **grātus** (pleasing), **similis** (like), **dissimilis** (unlike), **proximus** (nearest), **fīnitimus** (neighboring), and **idōneus** (suitable), take the dative.

   Erat similis **patrī**.   He was like his father.

3. Some *compound verbs,* such as **īnferō** (carry on), **praeficiō** (put in charge), and **praesum** (be in charge), take the dative.

   Mānlius **castrīs** praeerat.   Manlius was in charge of the camp.

   Note. Some compounds take an accusative as well as a dative.

   Praetōrēs cōpiīs praefēcit.   He put the praetors in charge of the troops.

4. Certain *intransitive verbs,* such as **crēdō** (believe), **imperō** (command), **noceō** (harm), **pāreō** (obey), **persuādeō** (persuade), **resistō** (resist), and **studeō** (be eager), take the dative.

   Mīlitēs **ducī** crēdidērunt.   The soldiers believed their leader.

5. *Purpose* is expressed by the dative, often with another dative of *reference.* This construction is called the *double dative.*

   Erat **auxiliō cōnsulī**.   He was of help to the consul.
   Est **ūsuī nōbīs**.   It is of advantage to us.

6. *Possession* may be expressed by the dative of the person with the verb **sum.**

   Mihi est domus.   I have a house.
   (The house belongs to me.)

7. The dative of *agent* (instead of the ablative) is used with the gerundive to indicate the person by whom the action must be done.

Hoc negōtium **tibi** faciendum est.	This task must be done by you. (You must do this task.)

ACCUSATIVE

1. The *direct object* of a verb is in the accusative case.

Pecūniam invēnērunt.	They found the money.

2. Certain *prepositions*, such as **ad, ante, apud, circum, contrā, inter, ob, per, post, propter,** and **trāns,** take the accusative.

Post **bellum** discessērunt.	After the war they left.

3. *Place to which* is expressed by the accusative with **ad** or **in.**

Ad **castra** properāvit.	He hurried toward the camp.

Note. The preposition is omitted with *names of towns* and the words **domus** and **rūs.**

Rōmam īre vult.	He wants to go to Rome.
Domum pervēnit.	He arrived home.
Rūs contendit.	He hurried to the country.

4. *Duration of time* is expressed by the accusative.

Multōs annōs ibi mānsērunt.	They stayed there many years.

5. *Extent of space* is expressed by the accusative.

Paucōs pedēs prōcessit.	He advanced a few feet.

6. *The subject of an infinitive* is in the accusative.

Dīxit **coniūrātōs** cōnfessōs esse.	He said that the conspirators had confessed.
Iussit **Catilīnam** discēdere.	He ordered Catiline to leave.

ABLATIVE

1. Certain *prepositions,* such as **ab, cum, dē, ex, prō,** and **sine,** take the ablative case.

    Prō **patriā** pugnāvērunt.   They fought for their country.

2. *Means* is expressed by the ablative without a preposition.

    Gladiīs pugnāvērunt.   They fought with swords.

3. *Personal agent* is expressed by the ablative with **ā** or **ab.**

    Ōrātiō ā **Cicerōne**   The speech was delivered by
       habita est.   Cicero.

4. *Accompaniment* is expressed by the ablative with **cum.**

    Cum **fīliō** pervēnit.   He arrived with his son.

Note. **Cum** is attached to the pronouns **mē, tē, sē, nōbīs, vōbīs, quō, quā,** and **quibus: mēcum** (with me), **vōbīscum** (with you), **quōcum** (with whom).

5. *Place where* or *in which* is expressed by the ablative with the preposition **in.**

    In **īnsulā** habitant.   They live on an island.

6. *Place from which* is expressed by the ablative with **ab, dē,** or **ex.**

    Ex **silvā** cucurrit.   He ran out of the forest.

Note. The preposition is omitted with *names of towns* and the words **domus** and **rūs.**

    Rōmā fūgit.   He fled from Rome.
    Domō discessērunt.   They left home.
    Rūre contendit.   He hurried from the country.

7. *Time when* or *within which* is expressed by the ablative without a preposition.

Labōratne **aestāte?**   Does he work in the summer?
Opus **paucīs annīs**   He will finish the work in a few
  cōnficiet.   years.

8. *Manner,* telling *how* something is done, is expressed by the ablative with **cum. Cum** may be omitted if an adjective modifies the noun.

Cum **virtūte** pugnāvērunt.   They fought with courage.
Magnā (cum) **laude**   They were received with great
  acceptī sunt.   honor.

9. *Cause* is expressed by the ablative without a preposition.

Perīculō bellī mulierēs   Because of the danger of war
  fūgērunt.   the women fled.

Note. The following expressions of *cause* require the preposition **dē: quā dē causā** (for this reason), **certā dē causā** (for a certain reason).

10. To *describe* a person or thing, the ablative with an adjective modifier may be used. This construction is similar to the genitive of description.

Erat vir **magnā sapientiā.**   He was a man of great wisdom.

11. *In what respect* something is true is expressed by the ablative without a preposition. This construction is sometimes called the ablative of *specification.*

Nōmine sed nōn **rē** erat rēx.   He was king in name but not in
                                 fact.

12. In denoting *comparison,* the person or thing with which the comparison is made is expressed by the ablative.

Mārcus est **sorōre** altior.   Marcus is taller than his sister.

Note. When **quam** (than) is used, both words compared are in the same case.

Mārcus est altior quam **soror.**	Marcus is taller than his sister.

13. *Degree* or *measure of difference* is expressed by the ablative without a preposition. This construction is most often found with comparatives.

Multō clārius locūtus est.	He spoke much more clearly.

14. Certain *deponent verbs,* such as **ūtor** (use), **fruor** (enjoy), and **potior** (get possession of), take the ablative.

Castrīs potiuntur.	They get possession of the camp.

15. Certain *adjectives,* such as **dignus** (worthy) and **indignus** (unworthy), take the ablative.

Magnō honōre dignus erat.	He was worthy of great honor.

16. *Separation* is expressed by the ablative with or without **ab** or **ex.**

Eōs (ab) **fīnibus** prohibuit.	He kept them from the territory.

17. The *ablative absolute* construction, a method of expressing an idea concisely, is used to denote the *time* or *circumstances* of an action. It consists of a noun or pronoun in the ablative case, with a participle in agreement. Sometimes an adjective or another noun is used instead of a participle. In translating the ablative absolute into English, we generally use the words *after, when, since,* or *while.*

Cōnsiliō captō, coniūrātī discessērunt.	After forming a plan, the conspirators left.
Mē duce, vīcistis.	With me as your leader, you have won.
Omnibus clāmantibus, domum relīquit.	While all shouted, he left home.

VOCATIVE

The vocative case is used in *addressing* a person.

Mārce Tullī, quid agis?   Marcus Tullius, what are you
                                    doing?

LOCATIVE

Place where is expressed by the locative case, which resembles the genitive in form. The locative is used (instead of the ablative) with singular names of towns and small islands of the first and second declensions. Other common locatives are **domī** (at home), **humī** (on the ground), and **rūrī** (in the country).

Rōmae habitant.   They live in Rome.
Nōn **domī** est.   He is not at home.

EXERCISES

A. Translate the following expressions into English.

1. timor populī; contrā rem pūblicam
2. mihi vidētur; manū suā
3. sine summō perīculō; mē imperante
4. proximā nocte; domī meae
5. quam ob rem; Rōmā fūgērunt
6. paucīs ante diēbus; vōbīs expōnam
7. in hōc ōrdine; mihi crēde
8. ad commūnem salūtem; brevī tempore
9. illā nocte; cuius adventū ipsō
10. propter quāsdam suspīciōnēs; certā dē causā

B. Complete the following Latin sentences by translating the words in parentheses.

1. Eī virī erant (conspirators).
2. (With the greatest diligence) labōrāvit.
3. (To Rome) celeriter contendit.
4. (Marcus), quid agis?
5. (Two hours) manēbant.
6. In forō (at that time) erāmus.
7. Nōn pugnās (against your native land).

8. (By the consul) monēbantur.
9. Omnēs resistent (Catiline).
10. Hostēs (in Rome) nōn dēbent manēre.

C. Choose the word or expression in parentheses that makes the sentence grammatically correct.

1. Puer (domum, ad domum) ībit.
2. Hoc (mihi, ā mē) agendum erat.
3. Cicerō (amīcōs, amīcīs) persuāsit.
4. Coniūrātī (gladiīs, gladiōs) ūtēbantur.
5. (Omnēs cōpiās, Omnibus cōpiīs) praeerat.
6. Ōrātiōnem (eō diē, eum diem) habuit.
7. Catilīna erat fortior quam (reliquī, reliquōs).
8. Erat indignus (praemī, praemiō).
9. Ob (perīculum, perīculō) fugient.
10. (Rōmae, Rōmā) diū manēbant.

D. Rewrite the sentences below, following the directions in parentheses. Make *all* changes required.

1. Locus *ferrō* dēlētus est. (change to **Catiline**)
2. Ex *urbe* discēde. (change to **Rome**)
3. Cīvīs *servāvī*. (substitute **nocuī**)
4. Laudem *voluit*. (change to **dignus erat**)
5. Versārī *diū* nōn potes. (substitute **one day**)
6. Dēlēgistī quōs *Rōmae* relinquerēs. (substitute **town**)
7. Pompeius imperātōrem *nōmināvit*. (change to **nōminātus est**)
8. Laetitiam *sentiēs*. (substitute **fruēris**)
9. Tū ā mē *ēiectus est*. (substitute **ēiciendus est**)
10. Eum *ad* vōs mittam. (substitute **cum**)

Lesson 18. AGREEMENT

1. A *verb* agrees with its *subject* in person and number.

Lēgēs tē **impediunt.**	The laws prevent you.
Tū aliquandō **ībis.**	You will finally go.

2. An *adjective* or *participle* agrees with its *noun* or *pronoun* in gender, number, and case.

Cīvem **perniciōsum** timent.	They fear a dangerous citizen.
Catilīnam orbem terrae vastāre **cupientem** perferēmus?	Shall we put up with Catiline who desires to destroy the world?

3. A *predicate noun* or *predicate adjective* is in the same case as the *subject.*

Galba factus est **rēx.**	Galba became king.
Scīvit eōs esse **improbōs.**	He knew that they were wicked.

4. A noun in *apposition* with another noun or pronoun agrees with it in case.

Flaccum, **praetōrem,** ad mē vocāvī.	I summoned Flaccus, the praetor.

5. A *relative pronoun* agrees with its *antecedent* in gender and number; its case depends on its use in its own clause.

Dictae sunt sententiae **quās** senātus secūtus est.	Opinions were expressed that the senate followed.

EXERCISES

A. Make the adjective in parentheses agree with the noun.

1. diem (tōtus)
2. adventū (celer)
3. scelera (omnis)
4. coniūrātīs (complūrēs)
5. epistulam (quīdam)
6. mentis (iste)
7. cōnsulī (dignus)
8. artium (vērus)
9. testīs (reliquus)
10. supplicī (vehemēns)

B. Choose the word in parentheses that makes the sentence grammatically correct.

1. Adulēscentēs erant (perditī, perdicōs).
2. Virī (quī, quōs) vīdistī amīcī meī sunt.
3. Agrī (dēlētus, dēlētī) erant.
4. Cicerō (cōnsul, cōnsulem) factus est.
5. Bellum (cīvīlis, cīvīle) gerēbātur.
6. Catilīnam (dux, ducem) coniūrātiōnis secūtī sunt.
7. Nox (nūlla, nūllus) intercessit.
8. Castra in Italiā (est, sunt).
9. Praetōrī (quī, cui) mānsit crēdidērunt.
10. Comitem (interfectus, interfectum) esse sciō.

C. Rewrite the sentences below, following the directions in parentheses. Make *all* changes required.

1. *Praetōrēs* iūre laudantur. (change to **Praetor**)
2. *Nāvibus* missīs, oppidum mūnīvit. (change to **Nāve**)
3. *Tū* tē in custōdiam dedistī. (substitute **Ille**)
4. Ad hanc *āmentiam* fortūna tē servāvit. (substitute **perīculum**)
5. Praedīxeram *eōs* ventūrōs esse. (change to **eum**)
6. Vidētis *omnia* oppressa esse. (substitute **hās rēs**)
7. *Ea* per mē illūstrāta sunt. (change to **Id**)
8. *Cōnfessiō* certior vīsa est. (substitute **Oculī**)
9. *Litterās* prōferrī iubet quās sibi datās esse dīcēbat. (substitute **Epistulam**)
10. Religiō *C. Mariō* nōn fuerat. (add **cōnsul** in apposition)

Lesson 19. THE INFINITIVE

1. COMPLEMENTARY INFINITIVE. Certain verbs, such as **possum, cōnor**, and **dubitō**, require another verb in the infinitive to complete their meaning. The subject is the same for both verbs.

Dubitāvit negōtium **suscipere.**   He hesitated to undertake the task.

2. OBJECT INFINITIVE. Some verbs, such as **cōgō, iubeō,** and **prohibeō**, take as their *object* another verb in the infinitive. Each verb has its own subject, with the subject of the infinitive always in the accusative case.

Cicerō coēgit Catilīnam   Cicero compelled Catiline to
  discēdere.   leave.

3. INFINITIVE OF INDIRECT STATEMENT. Verbs of *saying, knowing, thinking,* and *perceiving,* such as **dīcō, sciō, putō,** and **sentiō,** are often followed by an infinitive in *indirect statement.* The subject of the infinitive is in the accusative.

    a. The *present* infinitive is used if the action takes place *at the same time* as that of the main verb.

Scit Cicerōnem **manēre.**   He knows that Cicero is staying.
Scīvit Cicerōnem **manēre.**   He knew that Cicero was staying.

    b. The *perfect* infinitive is used if the action takes place *before* that of the main verb.

Scit Cicerōnem **mānsisse.**   He knows that Cicero stayed.
Scīvit Cicerōnem **mānsisse.**   He knew that Cicero had stayed.

    c. The *future* infinitive is used if the action takes place *after* that of the main verb.

Scit Cicerōnem **mānsūrum**   He knows that Cicero will stay.
  esse.
Scīvit Cicerōnem **mānsūrum**   He knew that Cicero would stay.
  esse.

Note. Complementary and *object* infinitives are found principally in the *present* tense.

EXERCISES

A. For each English verb, choose the correct infinitive in parentheses.

1. Iussit virum *to leave.* (exīre, exīsse, exitūrum esse)
2. Scīmus eōs *fought.* (pugnāre, pugnāvisse, pugnātūrōs esse)
3. Incipiunt terram *to see.* (vidēre, vīdisse, vīsūram esse)
4. Putat sē *is defeated.* (vincī, victum esse, victūrum esse)
5. Dubitāvī oppidum *to seize.* (capere, cēpisse, captūrum esse)
6. Dīxērunt sē *were coming.* (venīre, vēnisse, ventūrōs esse)
7. Exīstimat eōs fīnēs *will destroy.* (dēlēre, dēlēvisse, dēlētūrōs esse)
8. Coēgit mīlitēs *to speak.* (loquī, locūtōs esse, locūtūrōs esse)
9. Sentiēbant eum *would live.* (vīvere, vīxisse, vīctūrum esse)
10. Arbitrātus est sē *had been freed.* (līberārī, līberātum esse, līberātūrum esse)

B. Translate into Latin the words in italics.

1. Cicero decided *to call together* the senate.
2. They all wanted *to be praised.*
3. He knew that the *state was* in danger.
4. I said that the *conspirators would go* to the camp.
5. They could not *defeat* the enemy.
6. He compelled the sailors *to abandon* the ship.
7. We thought that the grain *had been burned.*
8. They ought *to undertake* the task.
9. He said that his father *had died.*
10. I know that my friends *are coming.*

C. Translate into English.

1. Dīcō tē vēnisse in M. Laecae domum.
2. Competītōrēs tuōs interficere voluistī.
3. Exīre ex urbe iubet cōnsul hostem.
4. Videō enim esse hīc in senātū quōsdam quī tēcum fuērunt.
5. Sī tē interficī iusserō, residēbit manus coniūrātōrum.
6. Eōs ad mē eō tempore ventūrōs esse praedīxeram.
7. Potestne tibi haec lūx, Catilīna, esse iūcunda?
8. Omnēs sciunt tē stetisse in forō cum tēlō.
9. Dubitāsne vītam istam fugae mandāre?
10. Tē statim itūrum esse in exsilium dīcis.

D. Rewrite the sentences below, following the directions in parentheses. Make *all* changes required.

1. Tē *interficī* iussī. (substitute the equivalent form of **necō**)
2. Occāsus imperī appropinquat. (start the sentence with **Dīxērunt**)
3. Eī Rōmae remānsērunt. (start the sentence with **Vīdī**)
4. Dīxistī tibi *esse* mora. (change to action in the past)
5. Tū iam exībis. (start the sentence with **Cōnfīrmāstī**)
6. Negāvī mē id *factūrum esse*. (change to action in the present)
7. Tē *dēfendere* audet. (substitute the equivalent form of **custōdiō**)
8. Dīcō tuōs sociōs eōdem *convēnisse*. (change to action in the future)
9. Triumphī meī in animīs vestrīs collocantur. (start the sentence with **Volō**)
10. Lēgātī ad Catilīnam missī sunt. (start the sentence with **Comperī**)

Lesson 20. THE SUBJUNCTIVE

The subjunctive mood generally expresses doubt, uncertainty, or emotion, whereas the indicative mood is the mood of fact. The subjunctive, although most frequently found in subordinate clauses, has a few uses in independent clauses.

INDEPENDENT CLAUSES

1. HORTATORY (OR VOLITIVE) SUBJUNCTIVE. The *hortatory* subjunctive is used in the *present* tense to express an exhortation or command. It is generally found in the first person plural and is translated "Let us . . . . . ." The negative is introduced by **nē**.

Urbem **relinquāmus.**	Let us leave the city.
Nē id **faciāmus.**	Let us not do it.

When used in the second or third person, the hortatory subjunctive is sometimes called the *jussive* subjunctive.

Sēcēdant improbī.	Let the scoundrels leave.

2. DELIBERATIVE SUBJUNCTIVE. The *deliberative* subjunctive is used in questions or exclamations to express surprise, doubt, or anger. This subjunctive is often introduced by **ut** in the affirmative and **nōn** in the negative. The *present* or *imperfect* subjunctive is used, depending on whether the action is in the present or past.

Tē ut ūlla rēs **frangat!**	As if anything can break your spirit!
Quid **dīcerem?**	What was I to say?

3. OPTATIVE SUBJUNCTIVE. The *optative* subjunctive is used to express a wish. This subjunctive is often introduced by **utinam** (would that) in the affirmative and **utinam nē** in the negative.

   a. The *present* tense is used when the wish is *possible* of attainment.

Utinam tibi istam mentem deī **dent!**	Would that the gods give you such an intention!

b. The *imperfect* tense is used when the wish is *impossible* of attainment in the *present.*

Utinam virōrum fortium cōpiam **habērētis!**	Would that you had a number of valiant men!

c. The *pluperfect* tense is used when the wish was *impossible* of attainment in the *past.*

Utinam nē mē **vīdisset!**	Would that he had not seen me!

4. POTENTIAL SUBJUNCTIVE. The *potential* subjunctive is used to suggest an action as *possible* or *conceivable.* The negative is introduced by **nōn.** The *present* tense is generally used for immediate time, the *imperfect* for past time.

Quis mē **reprehendat?**	Who can criticize me?
Hoc aliquem cāsum **reciperet.**	This might have involved some risk.

DEPENDENT CLAUSES

There are four tenses in the subjunctive mood. The tense to be used in a particular sentence follows the sequence of tenses.

	MAIN VERB	SUBJUNCTIVE VERB	
		INCOMPLETE ACTION	COMPLETED ACTION
PRIMARY	Present Future Future Perfect	Present	Perfect
SECONDARY	Imperfect Perfect Pluperfect	Imperfect	Pluperfect

Incomplete means that the action of the subjunctive verb takes place at the *same* time as or *after* that of the main verb.

Completed means that the action of the subjunctive verb took place *before* that of the main verb.

1. PURPOSE. The *purpose* of an action is expressed in Latin by the subjunctive introduced by **ut** or **utī** for the affirmative and **nē** for the negative. English generally uses an infinitive. The *present* subjunctive is used for primary sequence, the *imperfect* for secondary.

Sē dēfendit nē **vincātur.**	He defends himself in order not to be conquered.
Vēnērunt ut templum **vidērent.**	They came to see the temple.

a. When there is an *antecedent* in the main clause, the subjunctive clause may be introduced by **quī** instead of **ut.** This construction is called a *relative clause of purpose.*

Nūntium mīsit **quī** epistulam **obtinēret.**	He sent the messenger to get the letter.

b. A clause used as the *object* of a verb of asking, commanding, persuading, wishing, and the like, is often called a *substantive clause of purpose,* or a *substantive volitive clause.*

Catilīnae persuādet ut **discēdat.**	He persuades Catiline to leave.
Voluī ut mē **audīrēs.**	I wanted you to hear me.

2. RESULT. The *result* of an action is expressed by the subjunctive introduced by **ut** for the affirmative and **ut nōn** for the negative. A result clause can usually be recognized by the presence in the main clause of one of the following words: **tam, ita, sīc, tantus, tālis, tot.** The *present* subjunctive is used for primary sequence, the *imperfect* for secondary.

Sīc loquar ut nōn odiō permōtus esse **videar.**	I shall speak in such a way as not to seem to be moved by hatred.
Tempestās erat tanta ut **perterrērēmur.**	The storm was so great that we were frightened.

A clause used as the *object* of a verb is called a *substantive clause of result.* Such a clause is common after the following verbs: **accidit ut, fit ut** (it happens that) ; **faciō ut, efficiō ut, perficiō ut** (I see to it that).

Accidit ut Cicerō **adesset.**	It happened that Cicero was present.
Efficiam ut **eās.**	I shall see to it that you go.

3. **Cum** CLAUSES

   a. Circumstantial or descriptive. The *circumstance* under which an action took place in the past is expressed by **cum** with the subjunctive. **Cum** is translated *when* or *while*. The *imperfect* subjunctive is used for incomplete action, the *pluperfect* for completed action.

Cum virī **convēnissent**, adventum nūntiāvērunt.	When the men had assembled, they announced their arrival.

   Note. When the emphasis is on the *time* of the action, *not* the *circumstance*, the indicative is used.

Multum prōfēcī tum cum tē ā cōnsulātū **reppulī**.	I accomplished a lot when I kept you from the consulship.

   b. Causal. The *cause* or *reason* for an action may be expressed by **cum** with the subjunctive. **Cum** is translated *since* or *because*.

Quae cum ita **sint**, cūr nōn exīs?	Since this is so, why don't you leave?

   Note. Cause may also be expressed by **quod, quia,** or **quoniam**. **Quod** and **quia** take the indicative when the writer states the reason as his own; they take the subjunctive when the reason is another person's. **Quoniam** takes the indicative.

Mārcus aberat quod **erat** aeger.	Marcus was absent because (I know as a fact) he was sick.
Mārcus aberat quod **esset** aeger.	Marcus was absent because (so he says) he was sick.

   c. Concessive. Concession may be expressed by **cum** with the subjunctive. In concessive clauses, **cum** is translated *although,* and **tamen** usually appears in the main clause.

Cum **esset** senex, tamen pugnāre potuit.	Although he was old, still he was able to fight.

   Note. Concession may also be expressed by **quamquam** with the indicative.

Quamquam **est** meus amīcus, nōn cōnfīdō.	Although he is my friend, I don't trust him.

4. INDIRECT QUESTION. An *indirect question* depending on a verb of mental action is expressed by the subjunctive introduced by an interrogative word or expression.

Scīmus ubi **habitet.**   We know where he lives.

Note. The *direct question* is in the indicative.

Ubi **habitat?**   Where does he live?

5. RELATIVE CLAUSE OF CHARACTERISTIC OR DESCRIPTION. A relative clause that *characterizes* or *describes* an *indefinite* antecedent has its verb in the subjunctive. Such a clause is common after the following expressions: **sunt quī** (there are those who), **quis est quī?** (who is there who?), **sōlus est quī** (he is the only one who).

Paucī sunt quī legere nōn **possint.**   There are few people who cannot read.

Note. If the antecedent in a relative clause is *definite,* the indicative is used.

Puerum cognōvī quī legere nōn **potest.**   I know a boy who cannot read.

6. ANTICIPATORY CLAUSE. A clause *anticipating* an act that may or may not actually take place uses the subjunctive. Such a clause is common after the conjunctions **dum,** meaning *until,* and **antequam** and **priusquam,** both meaning *before.*

Exspectāre cōnstituit dum nāvis **pervenīret.**   He decided to wait until the ship should arrive. (The ship might or might not arrive.)

Priusquam capī **posset,** fūgit.   Before he could be seized, he fled.

Note. When the clause describes an act that has actually occurred, the indicative is used. **Dum,** meaning *while,* takes the *present* indicative.

Antequam discessit, mihi grātiās ēgit.   Before he left, he thanked me. (He actually left.)

7. CLAUSE AFTER A VERB OF FEARING. A verb of *fearing* is followed by the subjunctive introduced by **nē** (that) and **ut** (that not).

Timēbat nē **fierem** aeger.   He was afraid that I would be-
                                  come ill.
Vereor ut mē **videat.**   I fear that he may not see me.

Note. This use of **nē,** meaning *that,* and **ut,** meaning *that not,* is the opposite of their use in a purpose clause.

8. CLAUSE AFTER AN EXPRESSION OF DOUBT. A *negative* or *interrogative* expression of *doubt* is followed by the subjunctive introduced by **quīn.** Some such common expressions are **nōn dubitō** (I do not doubt), **nōn est dubium** (there is no doubt), and **quis dubitat?** (who doubts?).

Nōn erat dubium quīn   There was no doubt that he would
   interficerētur.   be killed.

9. CONDITIONAL SENTENCES. A *conditional* sentence contains two clauses, one expressing a condition (dependent clause) and the other a conclusion (independent clause). The condition is intro- duced by **sī, sī nōn,** or **nisi.**

   a. Future less vivid ("should-would"). A conditional sentence ex- pressing *uncertainty of fulfillment* takes the *present* subjunctive in both clauses. The translation in English is "should . . . . . . would."

Sī me **videat,** eum **dīcam.**   If he should see me, I would tell
                              him.

   b. Contrary to fact. A sentence expressing a condition that is *contrary to fact* takes the subjunctive in both clauses. The *imperfect* subjunctive is used in *present* time, the *pluperfect* in *past* time.

Sī **vīveret,** servōs **līberāret.**   If he were alive (but he isn't),
                            he would free the slaves.
Sī **vīxisset,** servōs **līberāvisset.** If he had been alive (but he
                            wasn't), he would have freed
                            the slaves.

   Note. A *simple* condition expressing a statement that may or may not be true takes the *indicative.*

Sī **adest,** fēlīx **sum.**   If he is present, I am happy.
Sī **veniet,** eī cibum **dabō.**   If he will come, I shall give him
                            food.

EXERCISES

A. Choose the word or expression in parentheses that makes the sentence grammatically correct.

1. Nēmō est quī hoc (dubitat, dubitet).
2. Senātōribus persuāsit ut (dēcernant, dēcernerent).
3. Tam altus erat mōns (ut nōn, nē) ascendere possem.
4. Sī exeat, in perīculō (sit, esset).
5. (Nē, Nōn) ibi maneāmus.
6. Quis dubitat (nē, quīn) occīsus sit?
7. Utinam virī eum (laudant, laudent)!
8. Intellegit cūr hoc (fieret, factum sit).
9. Sī (vēnerit, vēnisset), eum vīdissēmus.
10. Catilīnae imperāvit ut (discēderet, discesserit).

B. Translate into Latin the words in italics.

1. *Let us tell* him the truth.
2. *If he had done* this, *he would have been saved.*
3. *Although he sees* us, he will not stay.
4. The danger was so great *that we were frightened.*
5. *Since they were not* in Rome, they couldn't see the games.
6. We knew *where you had gone.*
7. *If they should fight, we would not remain.*
8. There is no one *who believes* him.
9. He persuaded his men *not to attack.*
10. There is no doubt *that he is afraid.*

C. Translate into English.

1. Quae cum ita sint, dubitās abīre?
2. Faciam ut intellegās quid dē tē sentiant.
3. Quam diū quisquam erit quī tē dēfendere audeat, vīvēs.
4. Quid est quod tē iam dēlectāre possit?
5. Sīc tēcum loquar nōn ut odiō permōtus esse videar.
6. Sī tē parentēs timērent, ab eōrum oculīs discēderēs.
7. Sī tēcum patria loquātur, nōnne obtinēre dēbeat?
8. Nōn nūllī sunt in hōc ōrdine quī perīculum nōn videant.
9. Itaque congregentur improbī ūnum in locum.
10. Sī hoc huic adulēscentī dīxissem, mihi senātus vim et manūs intulisset.

D. Rewrite the sentences below, following the directions in parentheses. Make *all* changes required.

1. Nōndum *addūcor* ut hoc faciam. (change to **addūcēbar**)
2. Quanta tempestās invidiae impendet? (start the sentence with **Videō**)
3. Eum hortātus sum ut ea indicāret. (make the dependent clause negative)
4. Sī hoc huic virō *dīxissem*, senātus mihi vim intulisset. (change to present time)
5. Omnēs tē prōsequentur. (start the sentence with **Nōn dubitō**)
6. Virum *mīsī* quī tēla efferret. (change to **mittō**)
7. Poenās lēgum timēs. (start the sentence with **Utinam**)
8. Tū ūllum exsilium cōgitās. (insert **ut** after **Tū**)
9. Sī tē parentēs *timērent*, ab eōrum oculīs concēderēs. (change to past time)
10. Equitātum in Italiam mīsērunt. (start the sentence with **Veritus est**)

Lesson 21. THE IMPERATIVE

The imperative mood, used to express a *command*, is found principally in the present tense, second person singular and plural. Negative commands are expressed by the present imperative of **nōlō** (**nōlī, nōlīte**) plus the infinitive.

Mūta, Catilīna, tuam mentem.	Change your mind, Catiline.
Ēgredere ex urbe.	Get out of the city.
Nōlīte manēre, amīcī.	Do not stay, friends.

Note:

1. The singular active form of the imperative is the same as the present stem. To form the plural, add **-te.** In the third conjugation, change **e** to **i** before adding **-te.**

2. **Dīcō, dūcō, faciō,** and **ferō** drop the final **e** in the imperative singular.

3. The passive imperative singular looks exactly like the present infinitive active. The passive imperative plural is the same in form as the present indicative passive second plural.

EXAMPLES OF IMPERATIVE FORMS

	INFINITIVE	IMPERATIVE SINGULAR	IMPERATIVE PLURAL
	REGULAR VERBS		
(*1st Conj.*)	**laudāre**	**laudā**	**laudāte**
(*2nd Conj.*)	**tenēre**	**tenē**	**tenēte**
(*3rd Conj.*)	**pellere**	**pelle**	**pellite**
(**-IŌ** *3rd Conj.*)	**capere**	**cape**	**capite**
(*4th Conj.*)	**audīre**	**audī**	**audīte**
	DEPONENT VERBS		
(*1st Conj.*)	**hortārī**	**hortāre**	**hortāminī**
(*2nd Conj.*)	**verērī**	**verēre**	**verēminī**
(*3rd Conj.*)	**sequī**	**sequere**	**sequiminī**
(**-IŌ** *3rd Conj.*)	**patī**	**patere**	**patiminī**
(*4th Conj.*)	**potīrī**	**potīre**	**potīminī**

EXERCISES

A. Translate into English.

1. Mihi crēde, Catilīna.
2. Recognōsce mēcum noctem illam superiōrem.
3. Proficīscere ex urbe in exsilium.
4. Ēdūc tēcum omnīs tuōs amīcōs.
5. Pūrgāte urbem, coniūrātī.
6. Quam ob rem discēde atque timōrem eripe.
7. Nōlī convocāre senātum.
8. Līberā rem pūblicam metū.
9. Percipite dīligenter quod dīcam.
10. Recordāminī, Quirītēs, omnīs cīvīlīs dissēnsiōnēs.

B. Translate into Latin.

1. Fight bravely, soldiers.
2. Do not go, Marcus.
3. Tell us the truth, Lentulus.
4. Quintus, follow the slave.
5. Fellow citizens, listen carefully.
6. Consuls, do not fear.
7. Send him to Rome, Lucius.
8. Encourage the soldiers, citizens.
9. Catiline, leave the city.
10. Do not believe him, friends.

C. Rewrite the sentences below, following the directions in parentheses. Make *all* changes required.

1. *Respice* rem pūblicam. (change to the plural)
2. *Cōnsīderā* omnia. (substitute the equivalent form of **Ferō**)
3. *Sēcerne* tē ā bonīs. (make negative)
4. *Recordāminī* omnīs dissēnsiōnēs. (change to the singular)
5. *Cognōscite,* Quirītēs. (substitute the equivalent form of **Loquor**)

Lesson 22. PARTICIPLES; GERUND AND GERUNDIVE

PARTICIPLES

The *participle* is a verbal adjective. As an adjective, the participle agrees in gender, number, and case with the noun or pronoun it modifies. As a verb, the participle has tense and voice, and may take an object. There are four participles: a present and future participle in the active voice, and a perfect and future participle in the passive voice. There is no present passive or perfect active participle. The participle is often best translated by a clause.

1. The *present participle* denotes action occurring *at the same time* as that of the main verb.

Servīlius Maelium novīs rēbus **studentem** occīdit.

Servilius killed Maelius, who was eager for a revolution.

2. The *perfect participle* denotes action occurring *before* that of the main verb.

Ā quō **repudiātus,** etiam ad mē venīre ausus es.

Having been turned down by him, you even dared to come to me.

The perfect participle of a deponent verb is passive in form but active in meaning.

Hortātus suōs, dux discessit.

After encouraging his men, the general left.

Note. For the use of the present and perfect participles in the *ablative absolute* construction, see page 87.

3. The *future active participle* is generally used with some form of the verb **sum** to express a *future* or *intended* action. This construction is often referred to as the *active periphrastic*.

Quod **dictūrus sum** nōn novum est.

What I am about to say is not new.

GERUND AND GERUNDIVE

1. The *gerundive* (future passive participle) is used principally:

    a. to express *purpose* when it modifies a noun in the accusative with **ad** (in order to), or with **causā** or **grātiā** and the genitive (for the purpose or sake of).

Vēnistī ad rem **cūrandam.**	You came in order to take care of the matter.
Vēnistī reī **cūrandae** causā (grātiā).	You came for the purpose (sake) of taking care of the matter.

    Note. The genitive always precedes **causā** or **grātiā.**

    b. to express *obligation* or *necessity* with some form of **esse.** In this use, the person by whom the action must be done is put in the dative case (*dative of agent*).

Illud quod **faciendum** fuit Cicerōnī factum est.	That which had to be done by Cicero was done.

    Note. This construction is often referred to as the *passive periphrastic.*

2. The *gerund* is a verbal noun, declined only in the singular. Lacking the nominative, the gerund is declined like a second declension noun.

gen.	**-ndī**
dat.	**-ndō**
acc.	**-ndum**
abl.	**-ndō**

In English, the gerund ends in *-ing.*

Hortātus est modum **vivendī.**	He urged a method of getting along together.
Nōn **pugnandō** sed **tacendō** superāre potuērunt.	They were able to win not by fighting, but by keeping quiet.

    Note. When the gerund has an object, Latin prefers the gerundive.

Sollicitātī sunt **bellī excitandī** causā.	They were aroused for the purpose of stirring up war.

    Instead of
Sollicitātī sunt **bellum excitandī** causā.

EXERCISES

A. Choose the word or expression in parentheses that makes the sentence grammatically correct.

1. Urbs (nōbīs, ā nōbīs) dēfendenda est.
2. Putat cīvēs (cōgendī, cōgendōs) esse.
3. Urbem (ad videndam, vidēre) vēnit.
4. Puerum (pugnāns, pugnantem) vīdimus.
5. (Vulnerātus, Vulnerātī) hominēs fūgērunt.

B. Translate into Latin the words in italics.

1. He understands the art *of speaking*.
2. I found the men *working* in the fields.
3. *He is about to write* a letter.
4. Catiline *must be removed by Cicero*.
5. Rome, *abandoned* by the people, would fall to ruin.

C. Translate the following sentences into idiomatic English.

1. Istī gladiātōrī ūnam hōram ad vīvendum nōn dabō.
2. Coniūrātiōnem nāscentem nōn crēdendō cōnfīrmāvērunt.
3. Intrōductī Gallī sibi litterās datās esse dīxērunt.
4. Condiciō nāscendī incerta est.
5. Gabīnium statim ad mē nihil suspicantem vocāvī.
6. Manum cōnsulum interficiendōrum causā parāvistī.
7. Eum dīcendī exercitātiō dēfēcit.
8. Multa invidia est in cōnservandā rē pūblicā.
9. Labōrem incendendae urbis postulāvit.
10. Mihi cum eīs coniūrātīs vīvendum est.
11. Quod sum dictūrus neque praetermittendum neque relinquendum est.
12. Invidia inertiae pertimēscenda est.
13. Illae dissēnsiōnēs nōn ad dēlendam sed ad commūtandam rem pūblicam pertinēbant.
14. Ille erat ūnus timendus ex istīs omnibus.
15. Ad certās rēs cōnficiendās certōs hominēs dēlēctōs habēbat.
16. Ut temporibus reī pūblicae cēdās nōn est postulandum.
17. Eī quī hanc urbem dēlēre cōnātī sunt morte sunt multandī.
18. Ea rēs studia hominum accendit ad cōnsulātum mandandum M. Tulliō Cicerōnī.
19. Prīmō Archiās sē ad scrībendī studium contulit.
20. Vītam agunt ad fēstōs diēs lūdōrum celebrandōs.

Lesson 23. REVIEW OF GRAMMATICAL STRUCTURES

Choose the word or expression in parentheses that makes the sentence grammatically correct.

GROUP I

1. Antōnius (hostis, hostem) appellātus est.
2. Scit ubi Catilīna (sit, esset).
3. Lēgātus (castrōrum, castrīs) praefectus est.
4. Cicerō (honōris, honōre) dignus erat.
5. (Domō, Domī) excessit.
6. Catilīna (Cicerōnī, ā Cicerōne) ēiciendus erat.
7. Tam celer erat (nē, ut nōn) caperētur.
8. Auctōritās magna (cōnsulī, ad cōnsulem) erat.
9. (Audiāmus, Audīrēmus) ōrātiōnem.
10. Multī sunt quī hunc (laudant, laudent).
11. Sī hoc (audiat, audiet) nōs laudet.
12. (Nōlī, Nē) manēre in urbe.
13. Nōn dubitāvī (ut, quīn) venīret.
14. (Auxilium, Auxiliō) servōrum ūsus est.
15. Hōc tempore cōnsul (Rōmae, Rōmam) fuit.
16. Nēmō (cōnsulem, cōnsulī) crēdidit.
17. Rogāvit ubi coniūrātī (erant, essent).
18. Urbs (quae, quam) expugnāverant dēlēta est.
19. Dīc mihi, (Mārcus, Mārce), quid velīs.
20. Dux (oppidum, oppidō) potītus est.

GROUP II

1. (Iūstitiam, Iūstitiā) semper ūtēbantur.
2. Cīvēs (nōbīs, ā nōbīs) cōnservandī sunt.
3. Nēmō est quī hoc (dubitat, dubitet).
4. Dēmōnstrābō quid ille (ageret, ēgerit).
5. Cicerō (cōnsul, cōnsulem) factus est.
6. Nōlī id cōnsilium (cape, capere).
7. Victōriam (litterīs, litterās) nūntiāvit.
8. Tria mīlia (mīlitēs, mīlitum) in urbe erant.
9. Virī veniunt ut rēgem (vident, videant).
10. Lēgātus (castra, castrīs) praeerat.
11. (Eōs īre, Eīs ut īrent) persuāsit.
12. Cicerō eō tempore (domī, domum) erat.

13. Sī ad Etrūriam ībunt (capiantur, capientur).
14. (Paucīs diēbus, Paucōs diēs) in castrīs morātī sunt.
15. (Cōpiās mittī, Ut cōpiae mittantur) dīcit.
16. Hunc poētam dēligunt, cum (est, sit) magnus.
17. (Nē, Nōn) ibi maneāmus.
18. Prīncipem (vīsus esse, vīsum esse) sciō.
19. Tantus erat timor ut (fugiant, fugerent).
20. Magna virtūs (Cicerōnī, ad Cicerōnem) erat.

GROUP III

1. Nēmō erat quī pācem nōn (amāvit, amāret).
2. (Īnsidiīs, Īnsidiās) hostium resistēmus.
3. Rogat quō modō Cicerō haec (ageret, ēgerit).
4. Ōrātiōnēs (quae, quās) Cicerō habuit optimae erant.
5. (Catilīna, Catilīnam) interficī iussit.
6. Allobrogibus (redīre, ut redīrent) imperāvit.
7. Posterō diē Catilīna (Rōmā, Rōmae) discessit.
8. Rēs pūblica (nōbīs, ā nōbīs) laudanda est.
9. Hostēs (hīs tēlīs, haec tēla) ūtentur.
10. Nōlīte (dēpōnite, dēpōnere) vestra arma.
11. (Omnem diem, Omnī diē) manēbat.
12. Sī eōs (convocat, convocet) statim conveniant.
13. Tantum perīculum est ut hostēs (fugiunt, fugiant).
14. Mānlium (castra, castrīs) praeesse dīxit.
15. Rogāvit (quis, quī) id fēcisset.
16. Puerī (domī, domum) ībunt.
17. Patientia magna (ad cōnsulem, cōnsulī) erat.
18. (Nē, Nōnne) id facere dubitent.
19. Dum haec (gerēbantur, geruntur), cōnsul advēnit.
20. Sunt quī id (dīcant, dīcerent).

Unit X—Passages for Translation and Comprehension

Lesson 24

GROUP I

Translate the following passages into English:

A

[Cicero tells the senate that Antony's followers have deserted his (Antony's) cause for that of Brutus.]

Legiō quam L. Pīsō lēgātus Antōnī dūcēbat fīliō meō sē trādidit. Altera pars equitātūs quaestōrem in Thessaliā relīquit sēsēque ad Brūtum contulit; alteram partem in Macedoniā Cn. Domitius adulēscēns summā virtūte et ingeniō ā lēgātō Syriacō abdūxit.
(5) P. Vatīnius autem, quī anteā ā vōbīs laudātus est et hōc tempore laudandus est, aperuit Dyrrachī portās Brūtō et exercitum dēdidit. Tenet igitur rēs pūblica Macedoniam et Graeciam tuētur.
—Cicero, *In Antōnium*, X, 6 (adapted)

Thessaliā (line 2) = Thessaly (northern part of Greece)
Macedoniā (line 3) = Macedonia (a country north of Greece)
Syriacō (line 4) = Syrian
Dyrrachī (line 6) = Dyrrachium (a seaport of Greece)

B

[Cicero argues that Caesar should pardon King Deiotarus for having supported Pompey in the Civil War.]

Ignōsce, ignōsce, Caesar, sī Pompeī auctōritātī rēx Dēiotarus cessit, quem nōs omnēs secūtī sumus; ad quem cum dī atque hominēs plūrima et maxima ōrnāmenta congessissent, tum tū ipse. Quamquam tuae rēs gestae cēterōrum laudibus obscūritātem
(5) attulērunt, idcircō memoria Cn. Pompeī nōn āmissa est. Quis ignōrat quantum nōmen illīus fuerit, quantae opēs, quanta in omnī genere bellōrum glōria, quanti honōrēs populī Rōmānī?
—Cicero, *Prō Rēge Dēiotarō*, IV, 12 (adapted)

ignōsce (line 1) — from *ignōscō*, pardon
congessissent (line 3) — from *congerō*, lavish
obscūritātem (line 4) = dimness
idcircō (line 5) = for that reason

C

[Cicero rallies the Romans against Antony.]

Optimō cōnsiliō et maximō studiō, Quirītēs, vigilābō prō vōbīs. Etenim quis est cīvis tam oblītus beneficī vestrī, tam neglegēns patriae, ut vestrā opīniōne nōn permoveātur? Vōs omnēs cupitis mala cōnsilia M. Antōnī ā rē pūblicā āvertere,
(5)   fūrōrem eius exstinguere, audāciam eius opprimere. Idem volunt omnēs colōniae, cūncta Italia. Vēnit tempus; hōra postpōnī nōn potest. Cīvēs Rōmānī esse servī nōn possunt; deī immortālēs eōs omnibus gentibus imperāre volunt. Nōs Rōmānōs dē lībertāte vehementer dīcere necesse est. Aliae natiōnēs
(10) servitūtem ferre possunt sed lībertās ā deīs immortālibus populō Rōmānō data est.

—Cicero, *In Antōnium*, VI, 18–19 (adapted)

oblītus (line 2) = unmindful

GROUP II

Do *not* write a translation of the following passages; read them through carefully several times and then answer in English the questions below. Use *everything* in the text that will make your answers clear and complete.

D

[Sallust describes the end of the conspiracy.]

Sed ubi, omnibus rēbus cognitīs, Petrēius tubā signum dat et cohortēs prōgredī iubet, idem facit hostium exercitus. Postquam ad eum locum vēnērunt quō proelium committī posset, pīla dēpōnunt et gladiīs rem gerunt. Intereā Catilīna cum suīs in
(5)   prīmā aciē erat, omnia providēbat, ad suōs labōrantēs auxilium mittēbat, hostēs ācriter oppugnābat. Petrēius ubi videt Catilīnam magnā vī contendere, cohortem in mediōs hostēs indūcit et eōs resistentēs interficit. Catilīna cum copiās suās oppressās esse et sē cum paucīs relictum esse vidēret, in hostēs incurrit
(10) ibique pugnāns occīditur.

—Sallust, *Bellum Catilīnae*, LX (adapted)

1. What order did Petreius give? What effect did that have on the enemy?
2. What did the combatants do when they reached the battleground?
3. What was the reaction of Petreius to what Catiline was doing in the front line?
4. What did Catiline finally see?
5. What was the outcome of this?

E

[Pompey defeats Mithridates and Tigranes, Asiatic kings, of whom one surrenders unconditionally.]

Cn. Pompeius, cum in Asiā esset, memorābile bellum contrā rēgem Mithridātem, quī post profectiōnem Lūcullī novum exercitum comparāverat, gessit. Sed ille rēx in Armeniam fūgit et petīvit Tigrānem, potentissimum rēgem eius temporis. Itaque
(5) simul Pompeius duōs rēgēs in Armeniam secūtus est. Prīmō fīlius Tigrānis ad Pompeium pervēnit. Deinde rēx ipse sē rēgnumque victōrī permīsit. Tigrānēs autem dīxit esse nēminem nisi Cn. Pompeium cui sē committeret. Sēnsit etiam nōn esse turpe vincī ab eō quem Fortūna suprā omnēs extulisset.

—C. Velleius Paterculus, *Historia Rōmāna* II, 37 (adapted)

memorābile (line 1) = memorable
Lūcullī (line 2) = of Lucullus (a Roman general, Pompey's predecessor)

1. What action did Pompey take when he was in Asia?
2. What preparation had his opponent made after the departure of Lucullus?
3. What were the next *two* acts performed by that king?
4. How does the author describe Tigranes?
5. What was Pompey's next move?
6. Who first came over to Pompey?
7. What did Tigranes say when he surrendered?
8. How did the king feel about being defeated by this particular conqueror? Why?

F

[Cicero reveals some of the secrets of the Catilinarian conspiracy.]

Vōs enim tum, iūdicēs, nihil labōrābātis neque suspicābāminī;
ego ipse tum Catilīnae et Autrōnī cōpiās et cōnātum repressī.
Quid tandem Cornēlius ipse dīcit dē illā nocte cum convēnit
ad M. Laecam eā nocte quae omnium temporum coniūrātiōnis
(5)   ācerrima fuit atque acerbissima? Tum cōnstitūta est Catilīnae
diēs exeundī, tum cēterīs manendī condiciō, tum dīscrīptiō tōtam
per urbem caedis atque incendiōrum; tum pater Cornēlī illud
sibi officium dēpoposcit ut, cum venīret prīmā lūce cōnsulem
salūtātum, mē in meō lectulō interficeret.

—Cicero, *Prō P. Sullā*, 18 (adapted)

suspicābāminī (line 1) — from *suspicārī*, to mistrust
cōnātum (line 2) = attempt
acerbissima (line 5) — from *acerbus*, bitter, violent
dīscrīptiō (line 6) = arrangement
salūtātum (line 9) = to pay his respects to
lectulō (line 9) = couch

1. Of what *two* things does Cicero accuse the jury?
2. What did Cicero himself do?
3. Where did the conspirators meet?
4. What kind of night was it?
5. What *three* decisions were made at the meeting?
6. What assignment did the elder Cornelius demand?
7. Under what circumstances was this assignment to be carried out?

GROUP III

Read the following passages carefully, but do *not* write a transla-lation. Below each passage you will find a series of incomplete statements. Write the number of the answer that best completes *each* statement *on the basis of the information given in the passage.*

G

[Cicero, writing of himself in the first person, complains about the action of Quintus Metellus, the tribune.]

Atque ille Metellus, id quod tē audīvisse sciō, mē abeuntem officiō magistrātūs, cōntiōnem habēre prohibuit. Hāc iniūriā tantā acceptā, tamen illō ipsō diē mīsī ad Metellum commūnēs amīcōs quī ōrārent ut dē illā mente dēsisteret. Hīs ille respondit
(5) sē potestātem nōn habēre quae mē pūblicē loquī paterētur; etenim paulō ante in cōntiōne dīxerat potestātem dīcendī virō darī nōn dēbēre quī sine iūdiciō aliōs animadvertisset. Senātus gravissimā poenā eōs affēcit quī urbem incendere et magistrātūs ac senātum interficere, bellum maximum incitāre voluissent.
(10) Nunc hic Metellus iūdicābit mē quī urbem incendiīs, Italiam bellō līberāvissem, eādem poenā dignum esse quā improbissimī cīvēs affectī sunt. Sī huic nōn respondissem, nēmō mē in cōnsulātū fortem fuisse exīstimāret.

—Cicero, *Ad Familiārēs*, V, 2 (adapted)

cōntiōnem (line 2) = public meeting
dēsisteret (line 4) — from *dēsistere*, to cease
paterētur (line 5) — from *patior*, permit
animadvertisset (line 7) — from *animadvertere*, to punish

1. Metellus Cicerōnem vetuit
   (1) officiō abīre   (3) omnia audīre
   (2) concilium convocāre   (4) magistrātum tenēre
2. Ut Metellus mentem mūtāret, Cicerō ūsus est
   (1) amīcīs   (3) mente suā
   (2) iniūriīs   (4) diē
3. Cicerō dīcere pūblicē nōn potuit quod
   (1) in cōntiōne dīxisset   (4) virōs sine iūdiciō poenā
   (2) potestātem aliīs dedisset   affēcisset
   (3) paulō ante respondisset
4. Metellus Cicerōnem exīstimābat
   (1) nūllā poenā dignum esse
   (2) urbem incendere passum esse

    (3) eādem condiciōne ac virī nefāriī
    (4) magistrātum improbissimum fuisse
5. Cicerō Metellō respondit quod nōn voluit in cōnsulātū
    (1) fortis vidērī   (3) timidus vidērī
    (2) improbus vidērī   (4) aliōs sē iūdicāre

H

[How Mithridates carried on war with the Roman generals.]

      Cōgitāte, iūdicēs, quid Mithridātēs effēcerit et quī vir fuerit. Tum vōs pōnētis hunc rēgem ante omnēs rēgēs quibuscum populus Rōmānus bellum gessit. Eum, cum bellum in tōtam Asiam intulisset, L. Sulla, noster imperātor, pācātum dīmīsit.

(5) Eum magnā ex parte repressum sed nōn oppressum L. Mūrēna relīquit; is rēx, aliquot annīs cōnsūmptīs ad cōnfīrmandās cōpiās bellī, tantum valuit ut putāret sē Ōceanum cum Pontō, et cōpiās Sertōrī cum suīs coniūnctūrum esse. Ad quod bellum duo cōnsulēs ita missī sunt ut alter Mithridātem persequerētur,

(10) alter Bīthȳniam tuerētur.

                          —Cicero, *Prō L. Mūrēnā*, XV, 32–33

repressum (line 5) = checked
aliquot (line 6) = several
Ōceanum (line 7) = the ocean
Pontō (line 7) — Translate as "the Black Sea."
Sertōrī (line 8) = of Sertorius (a Roman general in Spain)

1. Mithridātēs exīstimābātur
    (1) hostis potentissimus   (3) vir optimus
    (2) rēx īnfīrmus   (4) bellum longum gessisse
2. L. Sulla, dux Rōmānus,
    (1) ā Mithridāte pācātus erat
    (2) ā Mithridāte dīmissus erat
    (3) bellum in tōtam Asiam intulerat
    (4) Mithridātem superāverat
3. L. Mūrēna Mithridātem
    (1) oppressit   (3) repressit
    (2) dēfendit   (4) victum relīquit
4. Mithridātēs putāvit sē posse
    (1) cōnsūmere cōpiās bellī   (3) vincere Sertōrium
    (2) iungere Ōceanum cum Pontō   (4) cōnfīrmāre cōpiās Sertōrī
5. Alter cōnsul missus est ut Bīthȳniam
    (1) vinceret   (3) dēlēret
    (2) caperet   (4) dēfenderet

I

[Cicero states the case against Verres.]

Nunc Verrēs intellegit mē in iūdicium venīre ut vōbīs dē suīs sceleribus nārrem. Iste senātor videt etiam multōs senātōrēs esse testēs audāciae suae; videt multōs equitēs Rōmānōs, multōs cīvēs atque sociōs contrā quōs maximās iniūriās fēcerit; videt etiam

(5)   multōs lēgātōs ab amīcissimīs cīvitātibus cum pūblicā auctōritāte convēnisse. Quae cum ita sint, omnēs bonōs virōs esse malōs exīstimat et iūdicia senātōrum esse pessima arbitrātur. Semper sine timōre dīcit nōn sine causā sē cupidum pecūniae fuisse quod in pecūniā tantum auxilium esse sentiat.

—Cicero, *In C. Verrem*, I, 7–8 (adapted)

1. Cicerō in iūdicium vēnit ut
   (1) dē sceleribus suīs nārrāret
   (2) omnēs scelera sua intellegerent
   (3) Verrēs facinora intellegeret
   (4) facinora Verris nūntiāret

2. Verrēs multīs cīvibus sociīsque
   (1) nocuerat   (3) persuāserat
   (2) crēdiderat   (4) restiterat

3. Ad iūdicium convēnērunt
   (1) amīcae cīvitātēs   (3) multī lēgātī
   (2) auctōrēs pūblicī   (4) multī equitēs hostium

4. Verrēs putat
   (1) omnēs virōs esse bonōs
   (2) iūdicia senātūs esse inīquissima
   (3) senātōrēs esse pessimī
   (4) iūdicia esse bona

5. Verrēs nōn sine causā semper
   (1) auxilium petēbat   (3) pecūniam cupiēbat
   (2) timōrem sentiēbat   (4) tantum auxilium habēbat

Unit XI—Word Study and Derivation

Lesson 25. SYNONYMS

VERBS

adorior, oppugnō, attack
afferō, addūcō, bring to
afficiō, indūcō, influence
afflīgō, caedō, strike
aiō, inquam, say
aperiō, patefaciō, open
cēnseō, dēcernō, decree
cernō, percipiō, perceive
cōgitō, cōnsīderō, consider
commemorō, meminī,
     recordor, remember
comperiō, nōscō, learn, find out
concitō, permoveō, arouse
cūstōdiō, vigilō, guard, watch
dēferō, dēdūcō, bring down or
     away
dēficiō, dēsum, fail, be lacking
dēlectō, placeō, delight, please
dēleō, exstinguō, vāstō, destroy
dēserō, relinquō, desert,
     abandon
dēsīderō, cupiō, optō, volō,
     desire, want
ērudiō, doceō, teach

excellō, superō, surpass
ignōrō, nesciō, not know
impellō, hortor, urge
inclūdō, contineō, confine
indicō, dēmōnstrō, point out
metuō, timeō, vereor, fear
necō, caedō, interficiō, kill
neglegō, omittō, praetereō,
     praetermittō, pass over
nōminō, appellō, name, call
opīnor, crēdō, believe
perdō, āmittō, lose
pereō, morior, die
perferō, patior, sustineō,
     endure
permittō, mandō, entrust
prehendō, capiō, occupō, seize
quiēscō, taceō, be quiet or silent
requīrō, postulō, demand
retardō, moror, delay
suēscō, soleō, be accustomed
vādō, eō, go
vehō, ferō, portō, carry
violō, noceō, injure, harm

NOUNS

aedēs, dēlūbrum, templum,
  temple, shrine
aequitās, iūstitia, fairness
comes, socius, amīcus,
  companion
commeātūs, cōpiae, supplies
coniūnx, uxor, wife
cōnsuētūdō, īnstitūtum, mōs,
  custom
cōntiō, concilium, meeting,
  assembly
cupiditās, studium, desire
cūstōdia, praesidium, vigilia,
  watch, guard
dignitās, auctōritās, authority,
  prestige
doctrīna, disciplīna, learning,
  training
exitium, interitus, perniciēs,
  pestis, destruction

facinus, scelus, crime
fēlīcitās, fortūna, luck
flamma, īgnis, incendium, fire
humus, terra, earth
ingenium, virtūs, ability
invidia, odium, hatred
lapis, saxum, stone
lūmen, lūx, light
maleficium, iniūria, harm
metus, timor, fear
moenia, mūrī, walls
mulier, fēmina, woman
opīniō, sententia, opinion
ops, auxilium, aid
ōra, lītus, rīpa, shore
spīritus, animus, spirit
supplicium, poena, punishment
tēctum, domus, home

ADJECTIVES

adversārius, inimīcus, hostile
aeternus, perpetuus, lasting
āmēns, stultus, foolish
beātus, fēlīx, happy
cūnctus, omnis, tōtus,
  ūniversus, all, whole
domesticus, prīvātus, private
ēgregius, īnsignis, praeclārus,
  singulāris, outstanding
familiāris, amīcus, friendly
improbus, malus, nefārius,
  wicked

ingēns, maximus, huge
iūcundus, grātus, pleasing
iūstus, aequus, just
manifestus, clārus, clear
plērīque, plūrimī, most
prūdēns, sapiēns, wise
sānctus, sacer, sacred
tūtus, salvus, safe
ultimus, extrēmus, last
vehemēns, fortis, strong
vīcīnus, fīnitimus,
  propinquus, neighboring

ADVERBS

aliquandō, dēnique, tandem,
    at last
anteā, quondam, formerly
ferē, paene, almost
iterum, rūrsus, again

profectō, quidem, vērō,
    certainly, indeed
quoque, etiam, item, also
vix, aegrē, with difficulty

CONJUNCTIONS

an, num, whether
etenim, enim, nam, for
quamquam, cum, although

quoniam, cum, since
sīve (seu), aut, vel, or

EXERCISES

A. Match each word in column *A* with its nearest equivalent in column *B*.

Column A	*Column B*
1. soleō	*a.* scelus
2. coniūnx	*b.* sapiēns
3. vix	*c.* moror
4. metus	*d.* cum
5. facinus	*e.* nesciō
6. dēserō	*f.* rūrsus
7. pereō	*g.* uxor
8. quamquam	*h.* lūx
9. prūdēns	*i.* stultus
10. ferē	*j.* suēscō
11. āmēns	*k.* morior
12. retardō	*l.* timor
13. maleficium	*m.* taceō
14. iterum	*n.* aegrē
15. ops	*o.* permoveō
16. quiēscō	*p.* iniūria
17. lūmen	*q.* salvus
18. concitō	*r.* auxilium
19. ignōrō	*s.* paene
20. tūtus	*t.* relinquō

B. Select the synonym of the italicized word.

1. *moenia* — fēmina, mūrī, domus
2. *ingēns* — maximus, gēns, ingenium
3. *cōgitō* — cernō, cōgō, cōnsīderō
4. *quiēscō* — rogō, taceō, requīrō
5. *improbus* — malus, bonus, clārus
6. *aequitās* — iūstitia, amīcitia, virtūs
7. *cūstōdia* — praemium, pretium, praesidium
8. *adorior* — amō, oppugnō, cupiō
9. *etenim* — nam, cum, num
10. *quoque* — quamquam, rūrsus, etiam

C. Select the word in parentheses that is *not* a synonym of the given word.

1. dēsīderō — (optō, volō, sedeō)
2. ōra — (caput, rīpa, lītus)
3. vīcīnus — (propinquus, oppidum, fīnitimus)
4. sīve — (sīc, vel, aut)
5. dēnique — (aliquandō, tandem, deinde)
6. dēleō — (vāstō, dēlectō, exstinguō)
7. necō — (caedō, interficiō, cadō)
8. exitium — (adventus, perniciēs, pestis)
9. profectō — (vērō, eō, quidem)
10. aedēs — (auxilium, templum, dēlūbrum)

D. In each sentence, replace the italicized word with a Latin synonym.

1. Vir memoriam *perdit.*
2. *Commeātūs* mīsit.
3. *Mulierēs* pugnam prohibuērunt.
4. Cicerō *iūstus* erat.
5. *Plērīque* discessērunt.
6. Nunc nārrō dē rēbus *domesticīs.*
7. Tēcum mox *vādent.*
8. Omnibus perīculum *indicat.*
9. *Supplicium* timuit.
10. Ōrātiōnem *vehementem* habuit.

Lesson 26. ANTONYMS

VERBS

accipiō, accept	repudiō, reject
amō, love	ōdī, hate
aperiō, open	claudō, close
clāmō, shout	taceō, be silent
cōnsentiō, agree	dissentiō, disagree
cōnsulō, consult	moneō, advise
discō, learn	doceō, teach
fateor, admit	negō, deny
illūstrō, bring to light	occultō, hide
incitō, urge on	retardō, delay
inveniō, find	perdō, lose
iungō, join	sēcernō, separate
iuvō, help	noceō, harm
labōrō, work	lūdō, play
maneō, remain	dēserō, desert
occurrō, meet	vītō, shun
sciō, know	ignōrō, not to know
servō, preserve	dēleō, destroy
vīvō, live	pereō, die

NOUNS

adulēscentia, youth	senectūs, old age
amor, love	odium, hatred
beneficium, kindness	maleficium, wickedness
clēmentia, clemency	sevēritās, severity
facilitās, ease	difficultās, difficulty
iūstitia, justice	iniūria, injustice
iuvenis, young man	senex, old man
negōtium, business	ōtium, leisure
opēs, wealth	inopia, poverty
optimātēs, aristocrats	populārēs, democrats
parēns, parent	puer, child
posteritās, posterity	maiōrēs, ancestors
praemium, reward	supplicium, punishment
rūs, country	urbs, city
salūs, health	morbus, sickness

temperantia, self control
victōria, victory
vir, man
virtūs, courage

temeritās, rashness
dētrīmentum, defeat
mulier, woman
metus, fear

ADJECTIVES

amīcus, friendly
apertus, exposed
beātus, happy
bonus, good
clēmēns, merciful
crēdibilis, credible
cūnctus, all
dignus, worthy
dīvīnus, divine
honestus, honorable
ingēns, huge
iuvenis, young
lēnis, mild
manifestus, clear
mīlitāris, military
mortālis, mortal
perītus, skilled
plēnus, full
plērīque, very many
prīvātus, private
proximus, nearest
sacer, sacred
sapiēns, wise
supplex, humble
tūtus, safe

adversārius, hostile
occultus, hidden
trīstis, sad
improbus, wicked
crūdēlis, cruel
incrēdibilis, incredible
nūllus, none
indignus, unworthy
hūmānus, human
turpis, disgraceful
parvus, small
vetus, old
vehemēns, violent
obscūrus, dark, obscure
togātus, civilian
immortālis, immortal
imperītus, unskilled
vacuus, empty
paucī, few
pūblicus, public
ultimus, farthest
nefārius, impious
stultus, foolish
superbus, haughty
perīculōsus, dangerous

ADVERBS

anteā, previously
hinc, from this place
hodiē, today
inde, thence
nūper, recently
umquam, ever

posteā, afterwards
hūc, to this place
crās, tomorrow
unde, whence
prīdem, long ago
numquam, never

CONJUNCTIONS

nisi, if not   sī, if

sīve, or   neque, nor

EXERCISES

A. Choose the word that is most nearly the opposite of the capitalized word.

1. PLĒNUS   fortis, vacuus, stultus, lēnis
2. ODIUM   bellum, inopia, negōtium, amor
3. PEREŌ   inveniō, vīvō, veniō, vincō
4. NŪPER   prīdem, hodiē, hinc, umquam
5. SAPIĒNS   supplex, improbus, stultus, superbus
6. SUPPLICIUM   dolor, iniūria, auxilium, praemium
7. DISCŌ   doceō, adeō, maneō, moneō
8. FATEOR   dīcō, negō, ignōrō, clāmō
9. METUS   salūs, beneficium, virtūs, amor
10. INGĒNS   vetus, bonus, stultus, parvus

B. Match each word in column *A* with its nearest opposite in column *B*.

Column A	*Column B*
1. taceō	*a.* nefārius
2. retardō	*b.* nūllus
3. sacer	*c.* iungō
4. posteritās	*d.* hodiē
5. clēmentia	*e.* clāmō
6. temeritās	*f.* maiōrēs
7. sēcernō	*g.* neque
8. crās	*h.* temperantia
9. sīve	*i.* incitō
10. cūnctus	*j.* sevēritās

C. Write the antonym of the following Latin words, and translate each answer.

1. umquam	3. mulier	5. prīvātus	7. rūs	9. lūdō
2. aperiō	4. dignus	6. morbus	8. perdō	10. anteā

Lesson 27. RELATED WORDS

The following list contains groups of words related in meaning and resembling one another in spelling:

aedēs, temple; **aedificium,** building; **aedificō,** build
aequitās, equality; **aequō,** equalize; **aequus,** equal
aeternus, eternal; **aetās,** age
aliēnus, belonging to another; **alius,** other
āmēns, out of one's mind; **dēmēns,** out of one's mind; **mēns,** mind
anteā, previously; **ante,** before; **antequam,** before
aperiō, open; **apertus,** open
auctor, author; **auctōritās,** authority
auris, ear; **audiō,** hear
cēnseō, take the census; **cēnsor,** censor
circā, around; **circum,** around
cīvīlis, civil; **cīvis,** citizen; **cīvitās,** citizenship
clēmēns, merciful; **clēmentia,** mercy
cognōmen, family name; **praenōmen,** first name; **nōmen,** name; **nōminō,** name
commemorō, call to mind; **meminī,** remember; **memoria,** memory
coniūnx, one joined in marriage; **iungō,** join; **iugum,** yoke
coniūrātī, conspirators; **coniūrātiō,** conspiracy; **iūrō,** swear; **iūs iūrandum,** oath
cōnscientia, conscience; **scientia,** knowledge; **sciō,** know
cōnsuēscō, become accustomed; **cōnsuētūdō,** custom
cōnsulāris, consular; **cōnsul,** consul; **cōnsulātus,** consulship; **cōnsulō,** consult; **cōnsultum,** decree
crēdibilis, believable; **incrēdibilis,** unbelievable; **crēdō,** believe
cupiditās, desire; **cupidus,** desirous; **cupiō,** desire
cūstōdia, guard; **cūstōdiō,** guard; **cūstōs,** guard
dignitās, worth; **dignus,** worthy; **indignus,** unworthy
discō, learn; **disciplīna,** learning, training
dīvīnus, godlike; **deus,** god
doctrīna, teaching; **doceō,** teach
domesticus, of the home; **domus,** home
etenim, for; **enim,** for
exterus, outer; **extrā,** outside; **extrēmus,** outermost
facilitās, ease; **facile,** easily; **facilis,** easy
familiāris, of the family; **familia,** family
fēlīcitās, good fortune; **fēlīx,** fortunate
fīdus, faithful; **cōnfīdō,** have faith in; **fidēs,** faith

frūctus, enjoyment; **fruor,** enjoy
honestās, honor; **honestus,** honorable
hūmānitās, humanity; **hūmānus,** human; **homō,** human being
incendium, fire; **incendō,** set on fire
indicium, evidence; **indicō,** make evident
ingenium, natural ability; **ingēns,** unnaturally large
īnsignis, distinguished by a mark; **signum,** mark, sign
īnstitūtum, old-established custom; **īnstituō,** establish
invideō, envy; **invidia,** envy
īrāscor, be angry; **īra,** anger
iūdex, judge; **iūdicium,** judgment; **iūdicō,** judge
iussus, order; **iubeō,** order
iūstitia, justice; **iūstus,** just; **iūs,** justice, right
lūdō, play; **lūdus,** game
maleficium, bad deed; **malus,** bad
metuō, fear; **metus,** fear
mīlitāris, military; **mīles,** soldier
mortālis, subject to death, mortal; **immortalis,** immortal; **mors,** death
mōtus, movement; **moveō,** move
nāvālis, naval; **nāvis,** ship; **nāvigō,** sail; **nauta,** sailor
necō, kill; **perniciēs,** death, destruction; **perniciōsus,** deadly
nocturnus, nightly; **nox,** night
occultō, hide; **occultus,** hidden
ōdī, hate; **odium,** hatred
omnīnō, altogether; **omnis,** all
opīniō, belief; **opīnor,** believe
ops, wealth; **inopia,** scarcity
ōrnāmentum, adornment; **ōrnō,** adorn
ōtium, leisure; **negōtium,** lack of leisure, business
partim, partly; **pars,** part
patefaciō, open up; **pateō,** lie open
patrius, of a father; **pater,** father; **patria,** fatherland
paulātim, little by little; **paulō,** a little; **paulum,** a little
perditus, lost, desperate; **perdō,** lose
perīculōsus, dangerous; **perīculum,** danger
perītus, skilled; **imperītus,** unskilled
posteritās, future; **post,** after; **posteā,** afterwards; **postquam,** after; **postrīdiē,** next day
praeclārus, very famous; **clārus,** famous
probō, approve; **improbus,** disapproved of, wicked
prūdēns, foreseeing, wise; **prōvideō,** foresee; **videō,** see

quasi, as if; sī, if; nisi, if not
quiēs, rest; quiēscō, rest
quot, how many; quotiēns, how often
rēgius, kingly; rēx, king; rēgīna, queen; rēgnum, kingdom; regō, rule; rēgnō, reign
sacer, sacred; sacrificium, sacrifice; sānctus, sacred
scrīptor, writer; scrībō, write
sēdēs, seat; sedeō, sit
senectūs, old age; senex, old man
sēnsus, feeling; sentiō, feel; sententia, feeling, opinion
serviō, be a slave to; servus, slave
singulāris, singular; singulī, single, one at a time
societās, alliance; socius, ally
somnium, dream; somnus, sleep
supplex, kneeling, suppliant; supplicātiō, day of prayer, thanksgiving; supplicium, kneeling for punishment
tēctum, roof, shelter; tegō, cover, protect
temere, rashly; temeritās, rashness
testāmentum, will; testis, witness
togātus, wearing the toga; toga, toga
triumphō, celebrate a triumph; triumphus, triumph
ultimus, farthest; ulterior, farther
umquam, ever; numquam, never
uter, which (of two); neuter, neither (of two); uterque, each (of two)
ūtilitās, usefulness; ūtilis, useful; ūtor, use
varietās, variety; varius, various, different
vēritās, truth; vērō, truly; vērum, truly; vērus, true
vīvō, live; vīvus, living; vīta, life

EXERCISES

A. Choose the word that is unrelated to the other words in each group.

1. coniūrātī, iūrō, coniūnx, coniūrātiō
2. necō, nec, perniciēs, perniciōsus
3. pateō, pater, patrius, patria
4. prūdēns, videō, prōvideō, vincō
5. sēnsus, senex, sententia, sentiō
6. uter, uterque, ut, neuter
7. vēritās, vereor, vērō, vērus
8. vīvō, vīta, videō, vīvus
9. ūtilitās, ūtor, uter, ūtilis
10. iūstitia, iussus, iūstus, iūs

B. Match each word in column A with its related word in column B.

Column A	Column B
1. partim	a. cōnscientia
2. mortālis	b. īnsignis
3. coniūnx	c. improbus
4. senectūs	d. paulātim
5. āmēns	e. mōtus
6. paulum	f. prūdēns
7. dīvīnus	g. pars
8. sciō	h. iungō
9. sēnsus	i. cōnfīdō
10. video	j. mors
11. moveō	k. ingēns
12. probō	l. deus
13. fīdus	m. sentiō
14. signum	n. dēmēns
15. ingenium	o. senex

C. Choose the word in parentheses that is related to the italicized word.

1. *mortālis*	(mōs, mors, mōtus)	
2. *ops*	(opus, optō, inopia)	
3. *hūmānitās*	(homō, humus, honestus)	
4. *exterus*	(excitō, extrā, exsistō)	
5. *auris*	(audiō, aurum, āra)	
6. *cōnscientia*	(cōnsentiō, cōnsuētūdō, sciō)	
7. *aedēs*	(adeō, aedificium, adsum)	
8. *discō*	(disciplīna, discēdō, dissentiō)	
9. *partim*	(parō, pār, pars)	
10. *tēctum*	(taceō, tegō, tangō)	

Lesson 28. WORDS OFTEN CONFUSED

amāns, loving
āmēns, foolish

āra, altar
īra, anger
ōra, shore

auris, ear
aurum, gold

cōgitō, think
cōgō, compel

ferē, almost
ferre, to bring

hospes, guest
hostēs, enemy

hūmānus, human
humus, ground

iaceō, lie
iaciō, throw

impediō, hinder
impendeō, overhang

inde, from there
unde, from where

indicium, testimony
iūdicium, trial

indicō, point out
iūdicō, judge

ingenium, talent
ingēns, huge

īnsignis, distinguished
signum, signal

iter, journey
iterum, again

iūrō, swear
iuvō, help

lēnis, gentle
levis, light

laudō, praise
lūdō, play

num, whether
nunc, now

odium, hatred
ōtium, leisure

partim, partly
paulātim, gradually

perditus, lost
praeditus, endowed with

patior, suffer
potior, get possession of

praustereā, besides
praetereā, besides
praetereō, pass over

proficīscor, set out
profiteor, confess

quaerō, seek
queror, complain

quisquam, anyone
quisque, each one

quondam, once
quoniam, since

quod, because
quot, how many

serviō, serve
servō, save

sīn, but if
sine, without

somnium, dream
somnus, sleep

supplicātiō, thanksgiving
supplicium, punishment

tōtus, whole
tūtus, safe

vērus, true
vetus, old

vītō, avoid
vīvō, live

vīs, force
vix, hardly

EXERCISES

A. Match each word in column *A* with its meaning in column *B*.

Column A	*Column B*
1. cōgō	*a.* again
2. iter	*b.* testimony
3. tōtus	*c.* anger
4. iaciō	*d.* complain
5. quaerō	*e.* journey
6. cōgitō	*f.* compel
7. indicium	*g.* safe
8. ōra	*h.* throw
9. āra	*i.* seek
10. iaceō	*j.* think
11. iterum	*k.* trial
12. tūtus	*l.* shore
13. iūdicium	*m.* altar
14. queror	*n.* whole
15. īra	*o.* lie

B. Select the correct translation of the Latin word.

1. auris   (gold, ear)
2. quisque   (each one, anyone)
3. iuvō   (help, swear)
4. num   (now, whether)
5. vix   (hardly, force)
6. somnus   (sleep, dream)
7. vetus   (true, old)
8. patior   (suffer, get possession of)
9. quoniam   (once, since)
10. odium   (hatred, leisure)
11. iūdicō   (judge, point out)

12. levis   (gentle, light)
13. ferē   (to bring, almost)
14. āmēns   (loving, foolish)
15. praetereō   (pass over, besides)
16. quot   (how many, because)
17. paulātim   (partly, gradually)
18. īnsignis   (signal, distinguished)
19. lūdō   (praise, play)
20. ingenium   (huge, talent)
21. vītō   (live, avoid)
22. serviō   (save, serve)
23. sīn   (without, but if)
24. perditus   (lost, endowed with)
25. profiteor   (set out, confess)

Lesson 29. PREFIXES AND VERB FAMILIES

Compound verbs in Latin, which are more common than simple verbs, are formed by attaching prefixes to simple verbs. In most cases there is no change in spelling, but, for ease of pronunciation, certain spelling changes do occur:

1. *Assimilation.* The final letter of a prefix may change to the first letter of the simple verb.

ad + ferō = afferō   **ob + currō = occurrō**

Note. The letter **n** changes to **m** when the simple verb starts with **p.**

in + pellō = impellō   **in + pōnō = impōnō**

2. *Contraction.* The verbal element in a compound verb may be shortened by changing a diphthong to a vowel.

in + claudō = inclūdō   **re + quaero = requīrō**

3. *Weakening of vowel.* The vowel **a** or **e** of the simple verb is often weakened to **i** in the compound.

dē + faciō = dēficiō   **con + teneō = contineō**

Note:

1. Some compounds undergo both assimilation and weakening of vowel.

    ad + faciō = afficiō   **ad + tangō = attingō**

2. The attached prefix usually gives added meaning to the simple verb.

    currō (run), **concurrō** (run together), **occurrō** (run toward)

3. Prefixes can also be attached to other parts of speech besides verbs.

    dignus (worthy), **indignus** (unworthy)
    mēns (mind), **āmēns** (out of one's mind)
    paucī (few), **perpaucī** (very few)
    clārus (famous), **praeclārus** (very famous)

PREFIXES

ab (ā, abs), from, away
ad, to, toward, near
ambi, both, around
ante, before
bene, well
bi, two, twice
circum, around
con (co, com), with, together,
    deeply, completely
contrā, against
dē, from, down
dis (dī), apart, away
ex (ē), out
extrā, outside, beyond
in, in, on, upon, into
in, not, without
inter, between
intrā (intrō), within, inside

male, badly
nōn, not, without
ob, against, toward
per, through, thoroughly, very
post, after, behind
prae, ahead, before, very
praeter, by, beyond
prō, forth
quadri (quadru, quadr), four
re (red), back
retrō, backwards, back
sē (sed), apart, away
sēmi, half
sub (sus), under, up from under
super, over, beyond
trāns (trā), across, over
tri, three

COMMON VERB FAMILIES

capiō, take
    accipiō, receive
    excipiō, receive
    incipiō, take on, begin
    percipiō, take hold of, perceive

praecipiō, take in advance, direct
recipiō, take back
suscipiō, undertake

cernō, observe
    dēcernō, decide

sēcernō, separate

citō, excite
    concitō, arouse
    excitō, arouse

incitō, urge on

claudō, close
    inclūdō, enclose

currō, run
    concurrō, run together
    occurrō, run toward, meet

prōcurrō, run forward

eō, go
  abeō, go away
  adeō, go toward
  exeō, go out
  ineō, go into

  pereō, pass away
  praetereō, go by, omit
  redeō, go back
  trānseō, go across

faciō, make, do
  afficiō, affect, afflict with
  cōnficiō, do completely, finish
  dēficiō, fail, revolt
  efficiō, bring about

  interficiō, kill
  patefaciō, expose
  perficiō, do thoroughly, finish
  praeficiō, put in charge

fateor, confess
  cōnfiteor, confess

  profiteor, confess

ferō, bring
  afferō, bring to
  cōnferō, bring together
  dēferō, bring down

  differō, put off, differ
  īnferō, bring in
  perferō, carry through, endure

fīdō, trust
  cōnfīdō, trust, be confident

flīgō, strike
  afflīgō, strike at

horreō, bristle
  abhorreō, shrink from

iūrō, swear
  coniūrō, swear together, plot

memorō, mention
  commemorō, call to mind

mittō, send, let go
  āmittō, send away, lose
  committō, bring together, entrust
  dīmittō, send off, dismiss
  intermittō, interrupt, stop

  omittō, let go, pass over
  permittō, let go, allow, entrust
  praemittō, send ahead,
  praetermittō, let go, pass over
  remittō, send back

orior, rise
    adorior, rise up against, attack

pellō, drive
    dēpellō, drive down or away   **impellō,** drive on
    expellō, drive out   **repellō,** drive back

pendeō, hang
    impendeō, hang over, threaten

petō, seek
    expetō, seek out

pōnō, put
    expōnō, put out, set forth   **prōpōnō,** put forth, offer
    impōnō, put upon

prehendō, seize
    comprehendō, arrest   **dēprehendō,** seize

quaerō, seek
    requīrō, seek again, search for

rapiō, seize
    ēripiō, take away, rescue

scrībō, write
    cōnscrībō, enlist, enroll   **dēscrībō,** write down, describe

sentiō, feel
    cōnsentiō, agree   **dissentiō,** disagree

suēscō, become accustomed
    cōnsuēscō, become accustomed

sum, be
    absum, be away   **intersum,** be between
    adsum, be near   **possum,** be able
    dēsum, be lacking   **praesum,** be at the head of

tangō, touch
    attingō, touch upon, reach

tardō, delay
    retardō, hold back, check

vertō, turn
    āvertō, turn away or aside

videō, see
    invideō, look askance, envy   **prōvideō,** foresee

vocō, call
    convocō, call together   **revocō,** call back, recall

EXERCISES

A. Separate the following compound verbs into their component parts (prefix and simple verb), and give the meaning of each part.

1. afferō	**3.** intersum	**5.** prōvideō	**7.** expetō	**9.** occurrō
2. impellō	**4.** revocō	**6.** āvertō	**8.** prōpōnō	**10.** cōnferō

B. Using the simple Latin verbs, form Latin compound verbs by translating the English words.

1. eō   go out, go across, go back
2. ferō   bring in, bring down, bring together
3. mittō   send ahead, send away, send back
4. sum   be between, be near, be at the head of
5. pōnō   put forth, put out, put upon

C. Give the meaning of the following compound Latin verbs.

1. adstō	**11.** prōspiciō
2. conterreō	**12.** interpōnō
3. ēvādō	**13.** praecurrō
4. perdiscō	**14.** obdūcō
5. antecēdō	**15.** exigō
6. absūmō	**16.** sēclūdō
7. respiciō	**17.** invādō
8. dēiciō	**18.** supergredior
9. dispellō	**19.** trānslegō
10. circummūniō	**20.** subeō

D. Give the meaning of the following compound English words derived from the Latin.

1. procrastinate
2. predict
3. concur
4. transition
5. interplanetary
6. impose
7. retrogress
8. secede
9. circumvent
10. ambivalent
11. perturb
12. bilingual
13. subvert
14. superhuman
15. nondescript
16. inevitable
17. distract
18. exclude
19. tricolor
20. quadruped

Lesson 30. SUFFIXES

A suffix added to a stem determines not only the meaning of a word, but also the part of speech. By learning the meaning of suffixes, we can derive the meaning of unfamiliar words, both Latin and English, based on familiar stems. Following is a list of common Latin suffixes with their English equivalents in parentheses:

FORMING NOUNS

-culum (*-cle*), **-mentum** (*-ment*) denote the means by which an action is performed or the result of an action

vehi**culum**	vehi*cle*
testā**mentum**	testa*ment*

-ia (*-y*), **-tās** (*-ty*), **-tia** (*-ence, -ency*), **-tūdō** (*-tude*), **-tūs** (*-tude*) denote quality, condition, act of

cūstō**dia**	custod*y*
digni**tās**	digni*ty*
clēmen**tia**	clem*ency*
magni**tūdō**	magni*tude*
servi**tūs**	servi*tude*

-iō (*-ion*), **-tiō** (*-tion*) denote an act or result of an act

opīni**ō**	opin*ion*
supplicā**tiō**	supplica*tion*

-ium (*-ium*), **-tūra** (*-ture*) denote an act

od**ium**	od*ium*
agricul**tūra**	agricul*ture*

-or (*-or*) denotes a physical or mental state

fur**or**	fur*or*

-sor (*-sor*), **-tor** (*-tor*) denote one who does something

cēn**sor**	cen*sor*
vic**tor**	vic*tor*

-ellus, -olus denote a diminutive

    lib**ellus** (liber + ellus) = a small book
    gladi**olus** (gladius + olus) = a small sword

FORMING ADJECTIVES

-ālis (*-al*), **-ānus** (*-an, -ane*), **-āris** (*-ar, -ary*), **-ārius** (*-ary*), **-ēlis** (*-el*), **-ēnus** (*-en*), **-icus** (*-ic, -ical*), **-idus** (*-id*), **-īlis** (*-il, -ile*), **-īnus** (*-ine*), **-ius** (*-ious*), **-ter** (*-trian*), **-ticus** (*-tic*), **-timus** (*-time*) denote belonging to or pertaining to

nāvālis	nav*al*
hūmānus	hum*an*, hum*ane*
mīlitāris	milit*ary*
aliēnus	ali*en*
cīvīlis	civ*il*
dīvīnus	div*ine*
nefārius	nefar*ious*
domesticus	domes*tic*

-bilis (*-ble*), **-ilis** (*-ile*) denote able to be, worthy to be

crēdibilis	credi*ble*
facilis	fac*ile*

-ōsus (*-ose, -ous*) denotes full of, abounding in

perniciōsus	pernici*ous*

FORMING VERBS

-scō denotes the beginning of an action

    timēscō (timeō + scō) = begin to fear

-tō
-sō } denotes repeated or intense action

    captō (capiō + tō) = keep on seizing
    cursō (currō + sō) = run constantly

EXERCISES

A. Separate the following Latin words into their component par (stem and suffix), and give the meaning of each part.

1. fēlīcitās
2. iūstitia
3. scrīptor
4. mortālis
5. coniūrātiō
6. perīculōsus
7. pertimēscō
8. patrius
9. incendium
10. incrēdibilis
11. ōrnāmentum
12. cōnscientia
13. maleficium
14. cōnsulāris
15. senectūs
16. cōnsuētūdō
17. vīcīnus
18. aequitās
19. sacrificium
20. familiāris

B. Give the meaning of the Latin words in each group.

1. actor, actiō, actitō
2. crūdēlis, crūdēlitās, crūdēscō
3. docilis, doctor, docilitās
4. dictō, dictātor, dictiō
5. rēgius, rēgālis, rēgnātor

C. Using your knowledge of suffixes, give the meaning of the following Latin words.

1. lūcēscō
2. sapientia
3. iuventūs
4. lēnitās
5. turpitūdō
6. fidēlis
7. frequentia
8. ēreptor
9. nārrābilis
10. audītō
11. sīcārius
12. triumphālis
13. cōgitātiō
14. dēmentia
15. lūcidus
16. īnstrūmentum
17. fīliolus
18. odiōsus
19. senīlis
20. onerārius

Lesson 31. LATIN ROOTS USED IN ENGLISH WORDS

Below is a list, by no means complete, of common Latin roots used in the formation of hundreds of English words. By recognizing the Latin root, we can arrive at the essential meaning of an unfamiliar English word derived from the Latin.

ROOTS	MEANINGS	EXAMPLES
aequ (*equ*)	even, just	equilibrium
ag, act	do, perform	agenda, react
ama	love	amateur
aqu	water	aquatic
aud	dare	audacious
audi	hear	auditory
beat	happy	beatitude
bene	well	benefactor
cad, cid, cas	fall, happen	cadence, accident, casual
cap, cip, cept	take, seize	capture, incipient, precept
capit	head	decapitate
carcer	prison	incarceration
cede (*ceed*), cess	move, yield	precede, proceed, recession
celer	swift	celerity
cid, cis	cut, kill	homicide, concise
clud, clus	shut, close	conclude, inclusion
cord	heart	discord
corp, corpor	body	corpse, incorporate
cred	believe, trust	credible
cup	desire, wish	cupidity
cur, curr, curs	run	incur, recurrent, cursive
de	god	deify
dec	ten	decimal
del	destroy	indelible
delect	delight	delectable
detr	damage	detriment
dict	say, speak	dictate
doc, doct	teach	docile, doctrine
duce, duct	lead	reduce, conduct
fac, fic, fact, fect	do, make	facile, proficient, fact, infect
felic	happy	felicity
fer, lat	bear, bring, carry	refer, translate
fess	admit	confession
fid	trust, belief	infidel

fin	end	final
grad, gress	step, move, go	grade, digress
grat	pleasing	grateful
hab, hib	have, hold	habitual, inhibit
habit	live, dwell	inhabit
iac (*jac*)	lie	adjacent
iect (*ject*)	throw	inject
iur (*jur*), **iust** (*just*)	right, law	juror, injustice
leg, lect	read, choose	illegible, select
lev	light	levity
liber	free	liberal
linqu	abandon	relinquish
loca	place	location
loqu, locut	speak, talk	loquacity, elocution
luc	light	translucent
magn	large, great	magnify
mal	bad	malodorous
melior	better	amelioration
mem	memory	memorandum
mit, mitt, miss	send, let go	admit, remittance, commission
monstra	show, point out	demonstration
mort	death	immortal
mov, mot	move	movement, commotion
mult	much, many	multiply
naut	sailor	nautical
nav	ship	navy
nefar	sinful	nefarious
nomin	name	nomination
nov	new	novel
omn	all	omnipotent
par	equal	parity
ped	foot	pedestal
pel, pell, puls	drive	repel, compelling, impulsive
pet	seek, ask	competition
pon, pos, posit	put, place	deponent, repose, composition
port	carry	portable
pot	power	potential
prehend, prehens	grasp	comprehend, prehensile
press	press	compression
prim	first	primary
pug, pugn	fight	pugilist, repugnant
quies, quiet	rest	acquiesce, quietude
reg, rig, rect	guide, rule	regulate, incorrigible, direct

repud	refuse	repudiation
sacr, secr	sacred	sacred, consecrate
sci	know	scientific
scrib, script	write	inscribe, description
sed, sid, sess	sit	sediment, assiduous, session
sen	old	senile
sent	feel	consent
sequ, secut	follow, pursue	sequel, consecutive
serv	save	conserve
simil	like	similar
spec, spic, spect	look	speculate, conspicuous, respect
sta, sist	stand	station, resist
stru, struct	build	construe, instruct
stult	foolish	stultify
summ	highest	summary
tac	quiet	taciturn
tempor	time	contemporary
ten (*tain*)**, tin, tent**	hold	tenant, contain, pertinent, tentacle
tim	fear	timorous
tract	pull, draw, drag	retract
un	one	union
urb	city	suburban
util	useful	utilize
vehement	strong	vehemently
ven, vent	come	convenient, invention
ver	true	veritable
vert, vers	turn	divert, version
vid, vis	see	video, vision
vigil	watch	vigilant
vinc, vict	conquer	convince, victim
viol	injure	inviolate
vit	avoid	inevitably
vit	life	vitamin
viv	live	convivial
voc (*voke*)**, vocat**	call	convoke, invocation
volupt	pleasure	voluptuous

EXERCISES

A. Find the Latin root of each English word, and give the meaning of the root.

1. verdict
2. nominal
3. inadmissible
4. rectitude
5. reversion
6. intimidate
7. impulsive
8. omniscient
9. structural
10. multilingual
11. procedural
12. grandiloquent
13. subsequent
14. contemporary
15. infidel
16. digress
17. recurring
18. incorporate
19. illegible
20. commotion

B. For each of the following sentences, (1) write a Latin word with which the italicized word is associated by derivation, and (2) choose the word or expression in the accompanying list that best expresses the meaning of the italicized word.

1. The government may not *legislate* in this matter.
   (*a*) use force   (*b*) give advice   (*c*) make laws
   (*d*) express approval
2. She was known to be a *vivacious* person.
   (*a*) lively   (*b*) beautiful   (*c*) intelligent   (*d*) polite
3. They decided not to *protract* the meeting.
   (*a*) end   (*b*) postpone   (*c*) cut short   (*d*) drag out
4. He drove the machine with great *facility*.
   (*a*) difficulty   (*b*) ease   (*c*) danger   (*d*) display
5. The big nations agreed on a *summit* conference.
   (*a*) top-level   (*b*) planned   (*c*) full   (*d*) delayed
6. The *disparity* of tastes was very evident.
   (*a*) lowness   (*b*) equality   (*c*) inequality   (*d*) improvement
7. The man showed few signs of *senility*.
   (*a*) weakness   (*b*) intelligence   (*c*) greed   (*d*) old age
8. They were unwilling to *desecrate* the temple.
   (*a*) dedicate   (*b*) harm   (*c*) decorate   (*d*) repair
9. She had symptoms of *incipient* consumption.
   (*a*) severe   (*b*) spreading   (*c*) beginning   (*d*) advanced
10. Who would say that war is *inevitable?*
    (*a*) helpful   (*b*) destructive   (*c*) unthinkable   (*d*) unavoidable

11. This matter is of *prime* importance.
    (*a*) great   (*b*) no   (*c*) little   (*d*) secondary
12. Slum clearance lasted a *decade*.
    (*a*) lifetime   (*b*) ten years   (*c*) generation   (*d*) 100 years
13. "Eternal *vigilance* is the price of liberty."
    (*a*) defense   (*b*) watchfulness   (*c*) truth   (*d*) distrust
14. They left with a *tacit* understanding.
    (*a*) silent   (*b*) tactful   (*c*) deliberate   (*d*) questionable
15. He was *felicitated* for his work.
    (*a*) denounced   (*b*) rewarded   (*c*) congratulated   (*d*) promoted
16. She had a feeling of *concord* with the world.
    (*a*) despair   (*b*) enmity   (*c*) frustration   (*d*) agreement
17. He was *motivated* by self-interest.
    (*a*) moved   (*b*) deceived   (*c*) despondent   (*d*) assured
18. The government decided to *ameliorate* conditions in industry.
    (*a*) change   (*b*) improve   (*c*) discuss   (*d*) investigate
19. They discussed the elections *vehemently*.
    (*a*) calmly   (*b*) slowly   (*c*) excitedly   (*d*) quickly
20. He will never *relinquish* his rights.
    (*a*) insist upon   (*b*) reduce   (*c*) assert   (*d*) give up

Lesson 32. REVIEW OF WORD STUDY AND DERIVATION

A. Show your knowledge of the influence of Latin on English by completing each of the following statements with one word. Your answers should explain the italicized words.

1. *Tangible* objects are those that can be _____.
2. A person who *cogitates* is said to be deep in _____.
3. The *tempestuous* sea showed signs of a _____.
4. His mental *retardation* makes him a _____ learner.
5. His badge of *merit* was well _____.
6. The *immortals* are those who never _____.
7. He composed a *nocturne*, a song dedicated to _____.
8. The view from the plane was *obscured* by the _____ clouds.
9. Doomed to *perdition*, the tramp was _____ to society.
10. The senator, having _____ his worth, was known for his *probity*.
11. The *aperture* was too small to see through, so he tried a larger _____.
12. The *king's* servants arranged the banquet in true _____ splendor.
13. To show their *derision*, the people _____ at the beggar.
14. The *old man* showed signs of _____.
15. The *slaves* were held in constant _____.
16. In company, the *taciturn* scholar was always _____.
17. The *ultimate* is the _____ syllable of a word.
18. The *uxorious* husband rarely left the house because he was so dominated by his _____.
19. He looked so much like a Roman *god* that people referred to him as _____.
20. His *adversary* in the political contest was a strong _____.

B. For each of the following words or expressions, give an English *synonym* derived from the Latin.

1. occurring at the same time
2. truthful
3. carry across
4. unable to be seen
5. angry
6. threatening
7. pertaining to a king
8. countrified
9. a person living at the same time as another
10. leisurely
11. nightly
12. deserve
13. usefulness
14. headlong
15. accustomed to constant sitting
16. drive on
17. pertaining to youth
18. great learning
19. pleasurable
20. turn aside

C. Next to each Latin word are four English words. Three of these words are correct derivatives. Select the one that does *not* belong.

1. MITTŌ   commit, mitten, mission, missile
2. SCRĪBŌ   describe, script, scroll, scribble
3. VĒRUS   revere, verity, veracious, verify
4. FERŌ   transfer, conference, referee, ferocious
5. CRĒDŌ   credible, crescent, creed, incredulous
6. FĪDUS   fidelity, infidel, defraud, confident
7. PETŌ   compete, petal, repeat, petition
8. LĪBER   library, liberal, liberty, liberate
9. TANGŌ   intangible, tact, tactile, tacit
10. CURRŌ   recur, current, cure, curriculum

D. The words in column *A* are all derived from Latin. Write a Latin word with which each is associated by derivation. Then find the *synonym* in column *B*.

Column A	Column B
1. pernicious	a. tearful
2. incredible	b. guardian
3. alienate	c. blameworthy
4. lacrimose	d. wise
5. contiguous	e. estrange
6. exhume	f. deadly
7. custodian	g. ancient
8. culpable	h. descendants
9. prudence	i. angry
10. posterity	j. unearth
11. odious	k. unbelievable
12. occult	l. mercy
13. sapient	m. restraint
14. temerity	n. crazed
15. inveterate	o. touching
16. morbid	p. rashness
17. temperance	q. hidden
18. irascible	r. diseased
19. demented	s. foresight
20. clemency	t. hateful

E. Give the meaning of each of the italicized words, and write a Latin word with which each is associated by derivation.

1. a *ferrous* metal
2. *civic* pride
3. *lapidary* work
4. moral *turpitude*
5. *perpetual* motion
6. a *plenary* session
7. *testify* falsely
8. *universal* suffrage
9. a *somnolent* speech
10. a *vehement* reply
11. a *querulous* person
12. eternal *verities*
13. a *rural* post office
14. a *mortal* wound
15. a *sanctified* object
16. *internecine* strife
17. *extinguish* a fire
18. an *invidious* comparison
19. high *fidelity*
20. *incendiary* bombs
21. deep *cogitation*
22. *deciduous* trees
23. *frigid* atmosphere
24. constant *iteration*
25. keen *aversion*
26. an *erudite* person
27. a mild *excitant*
28. *exemplary* conduct
29. a serious *affliction*
30. an *egregious* mistake

F. For each of the following sentences, (1) write a Latin word with which the italicized word is associated by derivation, and (2) choose the word or expression in the accompanying list that best expresses the meaning of the italicized word.

1. The *utility* of his action was challenged.
   (*a*) result   (*b*) usefulness   (*c*) purpose   (*d*) cause
2. They *deleted* the entire passage.
   (*a*) removed   (*b*) revised   (*c*) rewrote   (*d*) condemned
3. The hotel had a few *transient* guests.
   (*a*) troublesome   (*b*) wealthy   (*c*) temporary   (*d*) complaining
4. *Comprehension* is very important in language training.
   (*a*) speaking   (*b*) application   (*c*) drill   (*d*) understanding
5. He was a *potent* force for good.
   (*a*) possible   (*b*) probable   (*c*) powerful   (*d*) positive
6. The treatment *alleviated* the pain.
   (*a*) lessened   (*b*) prolonged   (*c*) increased   (*d*) stopped
7. The *aggression* was planned.
   (*a*) defense   (*b*) attack   (*c*) retreat   (*d*) surrender
8. They asked for *elucidation*.
   (*a*) help   (*b*) treatment   (*c*) clarification   (*d*) praise
9. Only a few members *dissented*.
   (*a*) withdrew   (*b*) applauded   (*c*) objected   (*d*) returned

10. The college started an *accelerated* program.
    (*a*) shortened   (*b*) extended   (*c*) cultural   (*d*) speeded up

11. His *profession* of loyalty was convincing.
    (*a*) declaration   (*b*) denunciation   (*c*) admission   (*d*) analysis

12. He was *incarcerated* upstate.
    (*a*) shipped   (*b*) detained   (*c*) imprisoned   (*d*) referred

13. That was a *delectable* dish.
    (*a*) expensive   (*b*) delightful   (*c*) unbreakable   (*d*) distasteful

14. His presence was *detrimental* to the cause.
    (*a*) helpful   (*b*) devoted   (*c*) sympathetic   (*d*) harmful

15. The newspaper *commemorated* the event.
    (*a*) published   (*b*) remembered   (*c*) disregarded   (*d*) attacked

16. His *cupidity* knew no bounds.
    (*a*) desire   (*b*) enjoyment   (*c*) depression   (*d*) antagonism

17. They remarked at his *beatific* state of mind.
    (*a*) sluggish   (*b*) relaxed   (*c*) blissful   (*d*) energetic

18. The ball park was *adjacent* to the school.
    (*a*) opposite   (*b*) annoying   (*c*) helpful   (*d*) next

19. He lived a *voluptuous* life.
    (*a*) restrained   (*b*) sensual   (*c*) serious   (*d*) lonely

20. The poor man *repudiated* offerings of help.
    (*a*) requested   (*b*) accepted   (*c*) refused   (*d*) welcomed

21. She was in a *quiescent* mood.
    (*a*) still   (*b*) lively   (*c*) determined   (*d*) complaining

22. They *violated* their agreement.
    (*a*) printed   (*b*) dishonored   (*c*) notarized   (*d*) delivered

23. He witnessed *stultifying* behavior.
    (*a*) abnormal   (*b*) intelligent   (*c*) quiet   (*d*) foolish

24. His activity from a social point of view was *pestiferous*.
    (*a*) harmful   (*b*) exciting   (*c*) rewarding   (*d*) ridiculous

25. They were on a *nefarious* expedition.
    (*a*) dangerous   (*b*) secret   (*c*) salvaging   (*d*) evil

Unit XII—*Culture*

Lesson 33. THE LIFE OF MARCUS TULLIUS CICERO

SIGNIFICANT EVENTS

BIRTH

Marcus Tullius Cicero was born on January 3, 106 B.C., near Arpium, about sixty miles southeast of Rome. His father belonged to the equestrian order, the wealthy class of Rome.

EDUCATION

For his formal education, young Cicero was sent to Rome, where he studied rhetoric, poetry, and philosophy. The Greek poet Archias was one of his teachers. Upon assuming the **toga virīlis** (toga of the adult male) at the age of 16, Cicero began to specialize in the study of oratory and law. In 79 B.C., after a brief period of military service and law practice, Cicero resumed his formal education—first at Athens, and subsequently at Rhodes under the rhetorician Molo. After two years of intensive study abroad, Cicero returned to Rome, an accomplished orator.

PRIVATE LIFE

Cicero, twice married and twice divorced, had an unhappy domestic life. His first wife, Terentia, bore him two children—a daughter, Tullia, and a son, Marcus. In 46 B.C., Cicero divorced Terentia and married Publilia, but that marriage lasted only one year. Cicero's domestic troubles were further aggravated by a crushing blow from which he never recovered—the untimely death of Tullia, his favorite child.

POLITICAL CAREER

Cicero began his **cursus honōrum** as **quaestor** in Sicily in 75 B.C. He was so just and honest in his dealings with the Sicilians that in 70 B.C. they called upon him to undertake the prosecution of Verres, a corrupt ex-governor of Sicily, on charges of extortion. For his defense, Verres engaged Hortensius, the most eminent lawyer and orator of the time. However, Cicero presented his evidence so eloquently that Hortensius withdrew from the case and Verres went into voluntary exile. As a result of his prosecution of Verres, Cicero superseded Hortensius as Rome's foremost orator.

Cicero became **aedile** in 69 B.C., **praetor** in 66 B.C., and **consul** i 63 B.C. The fact that Cicero, a **novus homō** (one whose ancestors ha never held a high office), attained the consulship was a rare achiev ment, for that office traditionally had been reserved for men of th senatorial order.

During his consulship, Cicero suppressed the Catilinarian conspirac —a plot to destroy Rome. The leader of the conspiracy, Lucius Sergiu Catilina, a noble and a member of the Senate, had been disappointe in his candidacy for the consulship. By making demagogic promise to cancel all debts, Catiline successfully obtained mass support. How ever, Cicero's prompt action and persuasive oratory thwarted Catilir and ended the danger to the Republic. For his role in crushing th Catilinarian conspiracy, the grateful Romans acclaimed Cicero **pat patriae,** a title given to national heroes.

In 58 B.C., five years after the suppression of the Catilinarian co spiracy, Clodius, an unscrupulous politician, demanded Cicero's ban ishment for having put to death five of the conspirators without a tria Depressed by this turn of events, Cicero went into voluntary exile i Greece. His exile, the darkest period in Cicero's life, lasted a year an a half. Recalled to Rome in 57 B.C., he resumed his activities as lawyer and a writer on philosophy.

In 51 B.C., Cicero held his last public office as **proconsul** of Cilici. in Asia Minor. As in Sicily, he displayed an honesty and uprightnes unequalled in Roman provincial history.

In the civil war that broke out between Caesar and Pompey i 49 B.C., Cicero tried to reconcile the adversaries, but failed. After muc hesitation about choosing sides, he finally joined the forces of Pompe in Greece. Following Caesar's triumph over Pompey, Cicero returne to Rome, where he was pardoned by Caesar.

After Caesar's assassination in 44 B.C., Cicero incurred the enmit of Antony by attacking him in a series of fourteen bitter speeche known as *Philippics*. Antony, as a member of the Second Triumvirat retaliated by placing Cicero's name on the proscription list. Rome greatest orator was beheaded on December 7, 43 B.C., near his vill at Formiae.

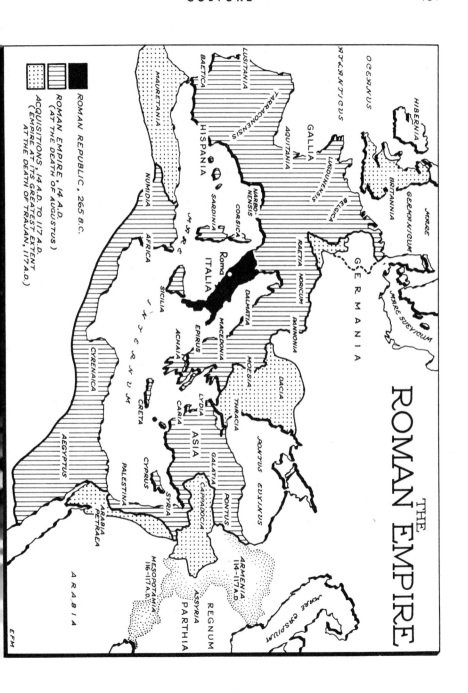

THE ROMAN EMPIRE

ROMAN REPUBLIC , 265 B.C.

ROMAN EMPIRE , 14 A.D.
(AT THE DEATH OF AUGUSTUS)

ACQUISITIONS , 14 A.D. TO 117 A.D.
(EMPIRE AT ITS GREATEST EXTENT
AT THE DEATH OF TRAJAN, 117A.D.)

HIBERNIA
BRITANNIA
GERMANICUM
OCEANUS
MARE
MARE SUEVICUM
GERMANIA
OCEANUS ATLANTICUS
LUSITANIA
BAETICA
TARRACONENSIS
GALLIA
AQUITANIA
LUGDUNENSIS
BELGICA
MAURETANIA
HISPANIA
NARBO-
NENSIS
CORSICA
SARDINIA
RAETIA
NORICUM
PANNONIA
NUMIDIA
AFRICA
Roma
ITALIA
DALMATIA
MOESIA
DACIA
SICILIA
EPIRUS
MACEDONIA
ACHAIA
THRACIA
PONTUS EUXINUS
CYRENAICA
CRETA
LYDIA
CARIA
ASIA
GALATIA
CAPPADOCIA
PONTUS
AEGYPTUS
CYPRUS
PALESTINA
SYRIA
ARMENIA
114-117A.D.
MESOPOTAMIA
116-117 A.D.
ASSYRIA
REGNUM
PARTHIA
ARABIA
PETRAEA
ARABIA
MARE CASPIUM
MARE INTERNUM

EFM

PERSONAL CHARACTERISTICS

In an age of corruption and bribery, Cicero stood out as an exceptionally upright and honest administrator. He was devoted to his family and friends, considerate and sympathetic toward his slaves.

On the other hand, Cicero was too conservative, vacillating, weak, and egotistical. Too often he lacked courage and consistency.

ACCOMPLISHMENTS AND INFLUENCE

1. **Orations.** Next to Demosthenes, Cicero is considered the world's greatest orator. Over fifty speeches of Cicero have come down to us, some delivered in defense of clients, others of a political nature. Among the best known are **In Catilīnam** (four speeches), **Prō Archiā,** and **Dē Imperiō Cn. Pompeī** (the speech on the Manilian Law).

Cicero is also regarded as the greatest Latin prose writer. His writings may be classified under two categories: essays and letters.

2. **Essays.** Cicero's essays include several treatises on oratory and a number of works on philosophy based mainly on Greek writings. His most famous essays are **Dē Orātōre, Dē Fīnibus, Dē Nātūrā Deōrum, Dē Officiīs, Dē Amīcitiā,** and **Dē Senectūte.**

3. **Letters.** Over eight hundred of Cicero's letters have been preserved. These include a group written to his best friend Atticus, a second group to various other friends, a third group addressed to his brother Quintus, and a fourth group to Brutus, one of Caesar's assassins. These letters give us a vivid picture of Roman life in Cicero's time.

Cicero has profoundly influenced succeeding generations down to the present time. His speeches, essays, and letters served as models for men such as Burke, Locke, and Montaigne. Above all, Cicero took a crude and labored language and gave it a polish and refinement unsurpassed in all Latin prose.

CHRONOLOGY OF IMPORTANT EVENTS
IN CICERO'S LIFE

B.C.

106 Born near Arpinum, Italy.

90   Began his legal studies.

88   Beginning of the war with Mithridates, king of Pontus.

81   Cicero's first appearance as a lawyer.

79   Went to Athens to continue his studies.

78   Studied under Molo at Rhodes.

77   Returned to Rome; married Terentia.

76   Birth of Tullia, Cicero's daughter.

75   Quaestor in Sicily.

70   Prosecution of Verres.

69   Aedile.

66   Elected praetor; delivered his first political speech, **Dē Imperiō Cn. Pompeī**, or the Manilian Law.

65   Birth of Marcus, Cicero's son.

63   Elected consul; suppressed the conspiracy of Catiline; delivered four Catilinarian orations.

62   Delivered the speech **Prō Archiā.**

60   Formation of the First Triumvirate by Caesar, Pompey, and Crassus.

58   Forced into exile by Clodius.

57   Recalled to Rome.

51   Appointed proconsul of Cilicia.

49   Returned to Rome; civil war between Caesar and Pompey; Cicero joined Pompey in Greece.

48   Pompey defeated by Caesar; Cicero returned to Italy; pardoned by Caesar.

46   Divorced Terentia; married Publilia.

45   Divorced Publilia; death of Tullia.

44   Assassination of Caesar; Cicero began his **Philippics** against Antony.

43   Formation of the Second Triumvirate by Octavian, Antony, and Lepidus; Cicero put to death by order of Antony.

EXERCISES

A. Find in column *B* the description that matches each name in column *A*.

<table>
<tr><td colspan="2">*Column A*</td><td colspan="2">*Column B*</td></tr>
<tr><td>**1.**</td><td>Molo</td><td>*a.*</td><td>daughter of Cicero</td></tr>
<tr><td>**2.**</td><td>Verres</td><td>*b.*</td><td>Cicero beheaded</td></tr>
<tr><td>**3.**</td><td>Cilicia</td><td>*c.*</td><td>speeches against Antony</td></tr>
<tr><td>**4.**</td><td>Tullia</td><td>*d.*</td><td>Cicero quaestor</td></tr>
<tr><td>**5.**</td><td>Terentia</td><td>*e.*</td><td>famous rhetorician</td></tr>
<tr><td>**6.**</td><td>Philippics</td><td>*f.*</td><td>caused Cicero's exile</td></tr>
<tr><td>**7.**</td><td>Archias</td><td>*g.*</td><td>Cicero proconsul</td></tr>
<tr><td>**8.**</td><td>Sicily</td><td>*h.*</td><td>Cicero's teacher</td></tr>
<tr><td>**9.**</td><td>Clodius</td><td>*i.*</td><td>wife of Cicero</td></tr>
<tr><td>**10.**</td><td>Formiae</td><td>*j.*</td><td>corrupt governor</td></tr>
</table>

B. Place the following events in correct chronological order:

1. exile of Cicero
2. divorce of Cicero and Terentia
3. impeachment of Verres
4. praetorship of Cicero
5. conspiracy of Catiline
6. Cicero's education at Athens and Rhodes
7. Cicero's proconsulship in Cilicia
8. formation of the Second Triumvirate
9. Cicero's quaestorship in Sicily
10. assassination of Caesar

C. Select the word or expression that best completes each of the following statements:

1. Cicero's first wife was (1) Publilia (2) Tullia (3) Terentia (4) Calpurnia.
2. The letters of Cicero furnish us with historical information about the (1) last years of the Republic (2) Punic Wars (3) early years of the Empire (4) overthrow of the Monarchy.
3. Cicero was called upon by the Sicilians to help prosecute (1) Sulla (2) Marius (3) Clodius (4) Verres.
4. Cicero's best friend, to whom he wrote many of his letters, was (1) Atticus (2) Brutus (3) Antonius (4) Caesar.
5. The law discussed in the speech *Dē Imperiō Cn. Pompeī* was the (1) Silvan (2) Carbonian (3) Manilian (4) Gabinian.

6. Cicero was born in (1) 100 B.C. (2) 106 B.C. (3) 90 B.C. (4) 110 B.C.
7. The direct cause of Cicero's death was the (1) assassination of Caesar (2) *Philippics* (3) trial of Clodius (4) formation of the Second Triumvirate.
8. Cicero studied oratory and philosophy under the rhetorician (1) Molo (2) Hortensius (3) Archias (4) Atticus.
9. Cicero's claim to fame rests principally upon his ability as (1) a philosopher (2) a statesman (3) a writer (4) an administrator.
10. In politics, Cicero would be classified as (1) conservative (2) progressive (3) radical (4) reactionary.
11. In 66 B.C., Cicero was elected (1) aedile (2) quaestor (3) consul (4) praetor.
12. *Dē Amīcitiā* is one of Cicero's famous (1) essays (2) speeches (3) letters (4) poems.
13. Cicero began his cursus honōrum as quaestor in (1) Cilicia (2) Sicily (3) Rhodes (4) Athens.
14. Cicero was forced into exile by (1) Manilius (2) Hortensius (3) Clodius (4) Maelius.
15. After suppressing the Catilinarian conspiracy, Cicero was called (1) novus homō (2) pater patriae (3) pater cōnscrīptus (4) homō equester.
16. In 58 B.C., Cicero was (1) beheaded (2) elected consul (3) married to Publilia (4) exiled.
17. Cicero's birthplace was near (1) Arpinum (2) Rome (3) Formiae (4) Faesulae.
18. Cicero's favorite child was (1) Marcus (2) Quintus (3) Tullia (4) Terentia.
19. In 88 B.C., Rome was engaged in a war with Mithridates, king of (1) Armenia (2) Pontus (3) Cilicia (4) Syria.
20. Cicero's chief rival as a lawyer was (1) Atticus (2) Antonius (3) Pompey (4) Hortensius.

D. Indicate whether each of the following statements is *true* or *false*. If a statement is false, correct it.

1. About one hundred letters of Cicero have come down to us.
2. Cicero's father belonged to the equestrian order.
3. The death of Cicero's favorite child, Marcus, dealt him a crushing blow.
4. In 58 B.C., Cicero went into exile in Asia Minor.
5. Cicero suppressed the Catilinarian conspiracy in 53 B.C.
6. Cicero was second only to Demosthenes in the field of oratory.

7. Cicero received his education in Rome, Athens, and Rhodes.
8. Cicero was put to death in 43 B.C. by order of Clodius.
9. *Dē Senectūte* is considered one of Cicero's greatest speeches.
10. Cicero's two marriages ended in divorce.

Lesson 34. ORATORY IN CICERO'S DAY

Oratory, the only mass medium of communication in antiquity, exercised a very important role in Roman public life. By playing upon the emotions of his audience, a skillful orator could sway people to his point of view. For example, Cicero won over to his side a mob sympathetic to Catiline.

Speeches were mainly of the following types:

1. **Ad Iūdicēs.** These were speeches addressed to a jury in cases of prosecution or defense. An example of a speech of prosecution is **In Verrem** (against Verres); one of defense is **Prō Archiā** (in behalf of Archias).

2. **Ad Patrēs Cōnscrīptōs.** Two types of speeches were delivered to the senators—one type either praised or censured someone; the other either advocated or opposed some measure. An example of the first type is the First Oration against Catiline; of the second type, the speech on the Consular Provinces.

3. **Ad Quirītēs.** These speeches, delivered to the Roman people from the Rostra in the Forum, dealt with matters of public interest. The speech on Pompey's Commission is an example of this type.

DIVISIONS OF AN ORATION

There are six parts to a typical Roman oration:

exōrdium—introductory remarks designed to arouse interest.

nārrātiō—the statement of the case.

prōpositiō—a statement setting forth the points to be proved.

cōnfīrmātiō—the affirmative argument, or proof of the case.

refūtātiō—the rebuttal, refuting the arguments of the opposing side.

perōrātiō—the conclusion, summing up the main points and often appealing to the sympathy of the audience.

CICERO'S MOST FAMOUS ORATIONS

First Oration Against Catiline—delivered November 8, 63 B.C., in the temple of Jupiter Stator at a special meeting of the Senate.

Finding Catiline present, Cicero attacks him bitterly and exposes the conspiracy. He urges Catiline to leave Rome and delivers a prayer to Jupiter.

Second Oration Against Catiline—delivered November 9, 63 B.C., to the people from the Rostra in the Forum.

Cicero explains to the people the events of the preceding day, congratulates them on the departure of Catiline, and tries to frighten the rest of the conspirators into leaving Rome.

Third Oration Against Catiline—delivered December 3, 63 B.C., to the people from the Rostra in the Forum.

Cicero tells in detail the events of that morning—the attempt by the conspirators to win the support of the Allobroges, the arrest of several leading conspirators, and finally their confession at a meeting of the Senate.

Fourth Oration Against Catiline—delivered December 5, 63 B.C., to the Senate in the Temple of Concord.

In discussing the fate of the prisoners, Cicero states his preference for the death penalty proposed by Silanus, rather than life imprisonment suggested by Caesar.

The Speech on Pompey's Commission, or the Manilian Law—delivered in 66 B.C. to the people from the Rostra in the Forum; this represents Cicero's first political speech.

Cicero speaks in support of a bill proposed by C. Manilius, a tribune, giving Pompey full command of the war against Mithridates, king of Pontus. Pompey, claims Cicero, has the four qualifications necessary for an ideal general: knowledge of military science, character, prestige, and good luck.

The Speech in Behalf of Archias—delivered in 62 B.C. in a court presided over by Cicero's brother Quintus, who was then praetor.

Cicero defends the poet Archias, who was accused of illegally enjoying Roman citizenship. The charge was made by Grattius, a lawyer who wanted to embarrass Archias' patron, Lucullus. Cicero's defense of Archias is famous for its eulogy of literature.

EXERCISES

A. Match each item in column *A* with its proper description in column *B*.

Column A	*Column B*
1. refūtātiō	*a.* patron of Archias
2. Mithridates	*b.* introduction of a speech
3. Lucullus	*c.* proposed a bill involving Pompey
4. Manilius	*d.* Cicero's brother
5. perōrātiō	*e.* rebuttal in a speech
6. Grattius	*f.* Roman senators
7. exōrdium	*g.* king of Pontus
8. patrēs cōnscrīptī	*h.* Roman people
9. Quirītēs	*i.* questioned Archias' citizenship
10. Quintus	*j.* conclusion of a speech

B. Indicate whether each of the following statements is *true* or *false*. If a statement is false, correct it.

1. Cicero's *First Oration Against Catiline* was delivered ad Quirītēs.
2. The nārrātiō in an oration is the statement of the case.
3. There are six parts to a typical oration.
4. According to Cicero, the four qualifications necessary for an ideal general are: birth, knowledge of military science, character, and good fortune.
5. Cicero's speech in behalf of Archias is famous for the method of delivery.
6. Cicero's speech on Pompey's Commission was his first political oration.
7. All of Cicero's speeches against Catiline were delivered in 63 B.C.
8. Speeches addressed ad iūdicēs were generally delivered from the Rostra in the Forum.
9. Cicero's speech in behalf of Archias was delivered in a court presided over by his brother Quintus, who was then aedile.
10. In his *Third Oration Against Catiline,* addressed to the Senate, Cicero tells of the conspirators' attempt to win the support of the Allobroges.

Lesson 35. ROMAN GOVERNMENT

SOCIAL CLASSES

There were three orders of society to which freeborn Roman citizens belonged:

Ōrdō Senātōrius (Optimātēs), the senatorial order, consisted of the nobles who actually governed Rome. Its members either were descended from a magistrate or had held office themselves. The Optimātēs were prevented by law from engaging in business.

Ōrdō Equester (Equitēs), the equestrian order, or knights, consisted of those who possessed at least $20,000. The Equitēs included the wealthy businessmen, bankers, and pūblicānī (tax collectors in the provinces).

Ōrdō Plēbēius (Plēbs, or Populārēs), the plebeian order, consisted of the rest of the freeborn citizens. The Plēbs were small tradesmen, manual workers, and peasants.

In addition to the three orders of society described above, the following groups also enjoyed varying degrees of Roman citizenship:

Lībertīnī (freedmen, or ex-slaves), whose rights were limited to voting and owning property. The freedmen could not hold office.

Colōniae (colonies), whose members enjoyed full citizenship.

Mūnicipia (self-governing towns), subject to taxation and military service.

Cīvitātēs Foederātae (federated communities), which enjoyed special treaty privileges with Rome.

POPULAR ASSEMBLIES

Two important assemblies (comitia) in ancient Rome exercised administrative and legislative powers.

Comitia Centūriāta was an assembly organized into centuries, or hundreds, each century possessing one vote. Its main function was the election of the higher magistrates: consuls, praetors, and censors. The Comitia Centūriāta also had the right to declare war. It met regularly in the Campus Martius.

Comitia Tribūta was an assembly organized into tribes, each tribe possessing one vote. Besides being the chief legislative body, the Comitia Tribūta elected tribunes, quaestors, aediles, and minor officials. It met either in the Forum or in the Campus Martius.

In addition to the two assemblies mentioned above, there was a **cōntiō** (mass meeting), called by a magistrate to discuss an issue before it was voted upon in the comitia.

THE SENATE

The Senate (**senātus**), whose members held office for life, was originally an advisory body. By Cicero's time, the Senate had become the dominant power in Rome, performing some of the duties previously exercised by the assemblies. The Senate had the power to:

1. enter into diplomatic negotiations, including peace treaties, with other nations.
2. appoint governors to provinces.
3. declare war, with the approval of the Comitia Centūriāta.
4. levy troops.
5. control all financial matters.
6. grant a **supplicātiō** (triumphal celebration) to a general.
7. declare special religious festivals.

An ordinary decree of the Senate was called a **senātūs cōnsultum.**

During a crisis, the Senate could grant the consuls dictatorial powers (**senātūs cōnsultum ultimum**) corresponding to martial law in modern times.

The meeting place of the Senate was either in the **Cūria** (senate house) or in some temple.

ROMAN OFFICIALS

Magistrates were elected for a term of one year, with the exception of the censors, who served for a year and a half. The important offices, comprising the **cursus honōrum,** had to be held in the following sequence: quaestor, praetor, consul. A candidate was required to wait at least two years between one office and the next, and at least ten years before running for re-election to the same office. The powers and duties of the various officials were as follows:

Consuls. The minimum age requirement for consul was 43. Two consuls were elected, one serving as a check upon the other. They were the chief executives of the Roman state, and presided over the Senate and assemblies. The consuls also had the power to appoint a dictator in times of crisis. A consul, after his election but before taking office, was called **cōnsul dēsīgnātus** (consul-elect). After his term of office, a **cōnsulāris** (ex-consul) was often sent to a province as **prōcōnsul** (governor).

Praetors. The minimum age requirement for praetor was 40. There were eight praetors, whose chief duty was to serve as judges in civil and criminal cases. After his term of office, a praetor was often sent to a province as **prōpraetor** (governor).

Quaestors. The minimum age requirement for quaestor was 31. There were twenty quaestors, who served as public treasurers—two in Rome, four in other parts of Italy, and the rest in the provinces.

Aediles. Although not in the cursus honōrum, the aedileship, coming after the quaestorship, was used to gain popularity for election to higher office. There were four aediles, who sponsored public games and festivals, and supervised the care of streets and public buildings.

Censors. There were two censors, usually ex-consuls, elected every five years for a period of a year and a half. Their chief duties were to take the census, assess property, supervise public morals, and arrange for the collection of taxes in the provinces.

Tribunes of the People. There were ten tribunes (**tribūnī plēbis**), elected from the plebeian class to defend its interests. The tribunes had the right to veto any decree or law passed by the Senate or assemblies, and had the power to convene and preside over the Senate.

Dictator. In times of emergency, a **dictātor,** appointed by the consuls at the request of the Senate, was given absolute power for a period of six months.

EXERCISES

A. Select the word or expression that best completes each of the following statements:

1. One of the chief powers of the Roman Senate was to (1) veto bills (2) make treaties (3) take the census (4) elect officials.
2. The Comitia Centūriāta met regularly in the (1) Campus Martius (2) Cūria (3) Forum (4) Comitium.

3. After completing a term of office, a magistrate could not run for a higher office until after a period of (1) 1 (2) 2 (3) 5 (4) 10 years had elapsed.

4. In times of emergency, a dictator was appointed by the (1) Senate (2) tribunes of the people (3) consuls (4) censors.

5. After his election but before he took office, a consul was called (1) cōnsulāris (2) prōcōnsul (3) cōnsul (4) cōnsul dēsīgnātus.

6. The first step in the cursus honōrum was the (1) aedileship (2) quaestorship (3) consulship (4) praetorship.

7. The minimum age requirement for the consulship was (1) 31 (2) 35 (3) 40 (4) 43.

8. A magistrate could be appointed governor after serving as (1) praetor (2) aedile (3) quaestor (4) tribune.

9. The tax collectors of ancient Rome were called (1) equitēs (2) populārēs (3) pūblicānī (4) optimātēs.

10. The common people of Rome had as special defenders of their interests the (1) aediles (2) tribunes (3) quaestors (4) censors.

11. The class at Rome that corresponded to our present-day financiers was called the (1) equitēs (2) plēbs (3) optimātēs (4) cōnsulārēs.

12. The communities outside Rome that were subject to taxation and military service were called (1) colōniae (2) cīvitātēs foederātae (3) oppida (4) mūnicipia.

13. The number of praetors elected annually was (1) 2 (2) 4 (3) 6 (4) 8.

14. The supervision of public games and festivals was entrusted to (1) quaestors (2) praetors (3) aediles (4) propraetors.

B. Match each item in column *A* with its proper description in column *B*.

Column A	*Column B*
1. cōntiō	*a.* treasurer
2. supplicātiō	*b.* legislative assemblies
3. praetor	*c.* ex-consul
4. comitia	*d.* senate house
5. prōpraetor	*e.* mass meeting
6. cōnsulāris	*f.* judge
7. senātūs cōnsultum	*g.* triumphal celebration
8. Cūria	*h.* senatorial class
9. quaestor	*i.* governor
10. Optimātēs	*j.* senatorial decree

Lesson 36. ROMAN RELIGION

Religion in Rome was a function of the government; church and state were not separated. In fact, many men outstanding in public life also held religious offices. Believers in polytheism (the worship of many gods), the Romans courted the favor and blessing of the deities by establishing sacred colleges (**collēgia**). These consisted of:

Pontificēs (pontiffs, or priests). Fifteen pontiffs, including the **pontifex maximus** (chief priest), supervised all religious matters and regulated the calendar. In addition to his other duties, the pontifex maximus appointed fifteen **flāminēs** (priests), who devoted themselves to the service of particular gods.

Augurēs (augurs). Fifteen augurs prophesied the future by taking the auspices (**auspicia**)—observing the actions of birds in flight. Before any important step was undertaken by the government, the augurs were consulted to determine if the omens were favorable.

Fētiālēs (heralds). A college of twenty Roman priests whose chief duties were to perform various religious rites in connection with the declaration of war and to preside at the formal ratification of peace.

In addition to the three sacred colleges, there were other groups connected with the state religion. These were:

Vestālēs (Vestal Virgins). Six Vestal Virgins kept the sacred fire forever burning in the Temple of Vesta.

Haruspicēs (soothsayers). These soothsayers, originally from Etruria, claimed the ability to prophesy by examining the entrails of animals and interpreting natural phenomena, such as lightning, eclipses, and earthquakes.

Keepers of the Sibylline Books. Fifteen men guarded the Sibylline Books, which were supposed to contain oracular sayings dealing with the destiny of Rome. The Sibylline Books were consulted in times of great danger.

EXERCISES

A. Match each item in column *A* with its proper description in column *B*.

Column A	Column B
1. pontifex maximus	a. soothsayers
2. augurēs	b. kept the sacred fire burning
3. haruspicēs	c. heralds who conducted foreign affairs
4. Sibylline Books	d. belief in many gods
5. Vestal Virgins	e. chief priest
6. fētiālēs	f. regulated the calendar
7. flāminēs	g. in charge of the auspices
8. polytheism	h. omens
9. pontificēs	i. priests devoted to particular gods
10. auspicia	j. contained oracular sayings

B. Indicate whether each of the following statements is *true* or *false*. If a statement is false, correct it.

1. The haruspicēs prophesied by examining the entrails of animals.
2. The three most important collēgia were those of the pontificēs, the augurēs, and the vestālēs.
3. One of the duties of the augurēs was to regulate the calendar.
4. There were twenty fētiālēs whose chief duty was to conduct affairs with foreign powers.
5. The Sibylline Books were guarded by fifteen men who consulted them regularly.
6. The flāminēs were appointed by the college of pontificēs.
7. The augurs took the auspices to determine if the omens were favorable.
8. There were fifteen members in the college of pontificēs.
9. Men active in Roman political life never held religious offices.
10. Phenomena such as lightning and earthquakes were often interpreted by the haruspicēs.

Lesson 37. PROMINENT CONTEMPORARIES OF CICERO

Antonius, Gaius. Colleague of Cicero in the praetorship and consulship.

Antonius, Marcus (Mark Antony). Member of the Second Triumvirate along with Octavian and Lepidus. Antony ordered Cicero, his bitter enemy, put to death for attacking him in the speeches called *Philippics*.

Archias. Greek poet, born at Antioch, in whose defense Cicero delivered one of his most famous orations, *Prō Archiā*.

Ariobarzanes. King of Cappadocia, in Asia Minor.

Atticus. Most intimate friend of Cicero and recipient of many of Cicero's letters.

Brutus, Marcus Iunius. Friend of Cicero. The two men carried on an extensive correspondence with each other.

Caesar, Gaius Iulius. Outstanding general, statesman, and writer. Caesar was a member of the First Triumvirate along with Pompey and Crassus. Caesar's lust for power was feared by Cicero, a firm believer in constitutional government.

Cassius, Lucius. One of the Catilinarian conspirators assigned the task of setting fire to Rome. Cassius also had a part in the negotiations with the Allobroges. His fate is unknown.

Catilina, Lucius Sergius. Originator and leader of the conspiracy against the Roman government during Cicero's consulship. Catiline died fighting at the head of his troops in Etruria.

Cato, Marcus Porcius. Debated the fate of the Catilinarian conspirators. By his persuasive oratory, Cato convinced the Senate to enact the death penalty.

Ceparius, Marcus. One of the Catilinarian conspirators whose task was to stir up an insurrection among the shepherds of Apulia. Ceparius was arrested, placed in custody, and later executed.

Cethegus, Gaius Cornelius. One of the most desperate of the Catilinarian conspirators. A cache of weapons found in his house and his letter to the Allobroges were the evidence on which Cethegus was convicted and executed.

Cicero, Quintus. Younger brother of Marcus Tullius Cicero; served as one of Caesar's leading generals in the Gallic War.

Clodius. Powerful politician responsible for Cicero's exile to Greece.

Crassus, Marcus Licinius. Famed for his wealth and for his victory over Spartacus in the Servile War. Crassus' death on an expedition against the Parthians resulted in the breakup of the First Triumvirate.

Glabrio. Unsuccessful general in the war against Mithridates.

Grattius. Roman lawyer who brought charges against Archias.

Hortensius. Roman orator, Cicero's principal rival, and unsuccessful defender of Verres.

Laeca. Roman Senator at whose home members of the Catilinarian conspiracy met and plotted.

Lentulus, Publius Cornelius. Consul and descendant of an illustrious family. Lentulus was one of the leading figures in the Catilinarian conspiracy. He was executed for his part in the conspiracy.

Lepidus, Marcus Aemilius. Consul with Julius Caesar in 46 B.C., Lepidus was a member of the Second Triumvirate along with Octavian and Antony.

Lucullus (brothers **Lucius** and **Marcus**). Roman generals; patrons of the poet Archias.

Manilius. Roman tribune and author of the Manilian Law, which placed Pompey in command of the war against Mithridates.

Manlius. Member of the Catilinarian conspiracy in charge of the camp at Faesulae.

Marius. Leader of the Populārēs. Marius' opposition to the aristocrat Sulla resulted in a bloody civil war.

Mithridates. King of Pontus who waged war with Rome for many years.

Murena. Roman general who received a triumphal celebration for his indecisive victory over Mithridates.

Nicomedes. King of Bithynia in Asia Minor. Nicomedes bequeathed his kingdom to Rome in 75 B.C.

Octavianus. Adopted son of Julius Caesar. Assuming the name Augustus, Octavian became the first Roman emperor, reigning from 27 B.C. until his death in 14 A.D.

Pompeius, Gnaeus Magnus. Known as Pompey the Great. He was a member of the First Triumvirate along with Caesar and Crassus. Pompey gained fame by clearing the seas of pirates and defeating Mithridates. Vanquished by Caesar in the Civil War, Pompey was killed in Egypt.

Roscius. Friend of Cicero and famous actor. Cicero, as an aid to his oratory, studied Roscius' technique.

Sallust. Roman historian who wrote an account of the Catilinarian conspiracy.

Sertorius. Roman general in Spain; loyal to Marius in the war with Sulla. Sertorius helped Mithridates in return for the promise of a fleet.

Silanus. Consul-elect who advocated the death penalty for the Catilinarian conspirators, rather than life imprisonment suggested by Caesar.

Sulla. Dictator of Rome and leader of the Optimātēs in the struggle against Marius. Sulla was given a triumphal celebration for his limited victory over Mithridates.

Tigranes. King of Armenia and son-in-law of Mithridates, whom he helped in the war against Rome.

Tiro. Cicero's slave who was freed and given the name Marcus Tullius Tiro. As Cicero's confidential secretary and literary consultant, Tiro was instrumental in having Cicero's letters published.

Verres. Corrupt politician. He was prosecuted for criminal acts committed while serving as governor of Sicily.

Volturcius, Titus. Member of the Catilinarian conspiracy. After his arrest at the Mulvian Bridge, Volturcius turned state's evidence and was pardoned.

EXERCISES

A. Find in column *B* the description that matches each name in column *A*.

Column A   *Column B*

1. Hortensius   *a.* cause of Cicero's banishment
2. Manlius   *b.* famous actor-friend of Cicero
3. Clodius   *c.* colleague of Cicero
4. Sertorius   *d.* member of the Second Triumvirate
5. Roscius   *e.* lawyer in Verres' defense
6. Manilius   *f.* Catilinarian conspirator
7. Antonius   *g.* patron of Archias
8. Lepidus   *h.* Roman general in Spain
9. Lentulus   *i.* author of bill on Pompey's commission
10. Lucullus   *j.* Catiline's general at Faesulae

B. Select the word or expression that best completes each of the following statements:

1. The members of the First Triumvirate were Caesar, Pompey, and (1) Lepidus (2) Crassus (3) Antony (4) Octavian.
2. The Roman lawyer who brought charges against Archias was (1) Grattius (2) Clodius (3) Hortensius (4) Roscius.
3. The relationship of Atticus to Cicero was (1) colleague (2) personal enemy (3) brother (4) intimate friend.
4. Three important members of the Catilinarian conspiracy were Lentulus, Cassius, and (1) Verres (2) Silanus (3) Murena (4) Volturcius.
5. Marius and Sulla were (1) colleagues in the consulship (2) bitter foes (3) Catilinarian conspirators (4) friends of Cicero.
6. Sallust, a Roman historian, wrote an account of the (1) Catilinarian conspiracy (2) Civil War (3) wars with Mithridates (4) Second Triumvirate.
7. Verres was prosecuted for criminal acts while serving as governor of (1) Cilicia (2) Sicily (3) Pontus (4) Spain.
8. An unsuccessful general in the war against Mithridates was (1) Cethegus (2) Tiro (3) Glabrio (4) Sertorius.
9. Silanus, as consul-elect, proposed for the Catilinarian conspirators (1) life imprisonment (2) limited freedom (3) exile (4) death.
10. Mithridates received help in his wars with Rome from Tigranes, king of (1) Pontus (2) Asia Minor (3) Armenia (4) Syria.

C. Indicate whether each of the following statements is *true* or *false*. If a statement is false, correct it.

1. Cicero defended Atticus in an oration called *Prō Archiā*.
2. Tiro was Cicero's confidential secretary and literary adviser.
3. Nicomedes bequeathed his kingdom, Bithynia, to Rome.
4. Catiline was executed for his part in the conspiracy.
5. Cato recommended life imprisonment for the Catilinarian conspirators.
6. Octavian, using the name Augustus, became the first Roman emperor.
7. Quintus Cicero, brother of the orator, was a general in Caesar's army.
8. Murena was one of the Roman generals who fought against Mithridates.
9. Laeca was responsible for Cicero's banishment to Greece.
10. Cassius and Cethegus were members of the Second Triumvirate.

Lesson 38. PLACES OF INTEREST IN CONNECTION WITH CICERO

Arpinum. Small town southeast of Rome; the birthplace of Cicero.

Basilicae. Halls and arcades used as law courts and business exchanges. The basilicas were located in or near the Forum.

Brundisium. Important seaport in the southeastern part of Italy; the chief port of departure for Greece.

Capitoline Hill. Formed the northwestern boundary of the Forum; contained the **arx** (citadel) and the Temple of Jupiter.

Carcer. Prison in the Forum; used for the detention of prisoners awaiting trial.

Comitium. Small open square north of the Forum; formerly served as the meeting place of the popular assemblies (**comitia**).

Curia Hostilia. Regular meeting place of the Senate, located near the Comitium.

Faesulae. City in Etruria, north of Rome. The camp for training Catiline's troops was located in Faesulae.

Forum Romanum. Located between the Capitoline and Palatine hills, the Forum, originally the marketplace of Rome, became the center of business and social activity. The Forum contained **tabernae** (shops), statues, temples, and public buildings.

Heraclea. Federated city in southern Italy, which granted citizenship to Archias.

Mulvian Bridge. One of the bridges over the Tiber where the Catilinarian conspirators were arrested on Cicero's orders.

Ostia. Seaport of Rome; located at the mouth of the Tiber River, sixteen miles from Rome.

Palatine Hill. Most famous of the seven hills of Rome; the residential section of the wealthy.

Pompeii. City in southern Italy near Naples; buried by the eruption of Vesuvius in 79 A.D.

Praeneste. City southeast of Rome that Catiline was prevented from seizing. Catiline had planned to use Praeneste as a military base for his attack on Rome.

Reate. Sabine town northeast of Rome that furnished the troops that arrested the Catilinarian conspirators.

Rostra. Platform in the Forum decorated with the beaks (**rōstra**) of captured ships. Orators addressed the people from the Rostra.

Syracuse. City in Sicily; famous for its works of art.

Tabularium. Building on the Capitoline Hill where state records were kept.

Templa. The most famous temples of Rome were:

1. **Temple of Castor and Pollux.** Located in the Forum; the repository of weights and measures; the meeting place of the Senate.

2. **Temple of Concord.** Built in the fourth century B.C. in the Forum to commemorate the end of the struggle between the patricians and the plebeians. Cicero's *Fourth Oration Against Catiline* was delivered in the Temple of Concord.

3. **Temple of Jupiter Capitolinus.** Located on the Capitoline Hill; the most famous of all the Roman temples; dedicated to Jupiter, Juno, and Minerva.

4. **Temple of Jupiter Stator.** Located on the Palatine Hill; the scene of the delivery of Cicero's *First Oration Against Catiline*.

5. **Temple of Saturn.** Located in the Forum; used as the state treasury (**aerārium**) and the repository of senatorial decrees and the bronze tablets on which the laws were inscribed.

6. **Temple of Vesta.** Located in the Forum; the most sacred place in Rome; contained the sacred fire kept ever-burning by the Vestal Virgins.

Tiber River. Famous river in western Italy on which Rome is situated. The Tiber was crossed by eight bridges.

Tullianum. Lower dungeon of the **Carcer** (prison) where five of the Catilinarian conspirators were executed by strangulation.

Viae. The Romans built a vast network of roads connecting Rome with other parts of Italy. The principal roads were:

1. **Via Appia.** The Appian Way, often called the **Rēgīna Viārum,** was the most famous of the Roman roads. It connected Rome with Brundisium, a port on the southeastern coast of Italy.

2. **Via Aurelia.** Military road leading north from Rome to Etruria. In his flight from Rome, Catiline took this route.

3. **Via Flaminia.** Crossed the Mulvian Bridge and led north toward Umbria on the east coast of Italy.

4. **Via Latina.** Led south toward Campania, where it joined the Via Appia.

5. **Via Sacra.** Principal street in Rome along which triumphal processions marched to the Forum.

EXERCISES

A. Find in column *B* the description that matches each place name in column *A*.

Column A	Column B
1. Curia	a. dungeon of Rome's prison
2. Temple of Jupiter Stator	b. queen of roads
3. Tullianum	c. location of Catiline's camp
4. Via Sacra	d. scene of Cicero's First Catilinarian Oration
5. Arpinum	e. senate house
6. Faesulae	f. port of departure for Greece
7. Temple of Jupiter Capitolinus	g. seaport of Rome
8. Brundisium	h. principal street in Rome
9. Via Appia	i. most famous Roman temple
10. Ostia	j. Cicero's birthplace

B. Indicate whether each of the following statements is *true* or *false*. If a statement is false, correct it.

1. The citadel and the Temple of Jupiter stood on the Capitoline Hill.
2. The city that granted citizenship to Archias was Praeneste.
3. The Tabularium was the regular meeting place of the Roman Senate.
4. The Tiber River was crossed by eight bridges.

5. The route taken by Catiline in his flight from Rome was along the Via Appia.
6. The city of Pompeii was buried by the eruption of Vesuvius in 79 B.C.
7. The Rostra was a speaker's platform in the Forum decorated with the beaks of captured ships.
8. The Palatine Hill contained residences of wealthy men.
9. The Carcer was a small open square in the Roman Forum.
10. Catiline's camp was located in Faesulae.

Lesson 39. ADDITIONAL BACKGROUND INFORMATION

RHETORICAL FIGURES

Many writers employ *rhetorical figures,* or figures of speech, in order to produce a more powerful or more pleasing effect. Some rhetorical devices tend to give imagery and picturesqueness to language, thus imparting a poetic feeling. The more important rhetorical figures used by Cicero are:

Alliteration. The repetition of the same initial letter in two or more words.

> Urbem ē flammā atque ferrō ac paene ex faucibus fātī ēreptam vidētis.
>
> The city, you see, has been snatched from fire and sword and almost from the jaws of fate.

Anaphora. The repetition of a word at the beginning of a series of phrases or clauses.

> **Nihil** agis, **nihil** mōlīris, **nihil** cōgitās quod nōn ego audiam.
>
> There is nothing that you do, nothing that you undertake, nothing that you plan, that I do not hear of.

Antithesis. The contrasting of two ideas, with the contrasting words in the same corresponding position.

> Adulēscentia ad scientiam reī mīlitāris **non aliēnīs praeceptīs, sed suīs imperiīs** est ērudīta.
>
> His youth was trained to a mastery of military science, not by other people's instructions, but by his own experiences as a commander.

Chiasmus. The contrasting of two ideas, with the contrasting words in opposite or crisscross order.

> Et **pācis ōrnāmenta** et **subsidia bellī** requīrētis.
>   gen.   acc.   acc.   gen.
>
> You will miss both the treasures of peace and the sinews of war.

Climax. The arrangement of a series of ideas with increasing interest or force.

Hanc **tam taetram, tam horribilem, tamque īnfēstam** pestem totiēns effūgimus.

This scourge, so vile, so dreadful, so deadly, we have so often escaped.

Hyperbole. An overstatement or exaggeration.

Persaepe etiam prīvātī in hāc rē pūblicā perniciōsōs cīvīs morte multārunt.

Very often even private citizens in this republic have punished dangerous citizens by death. (*Very often* is a gross exaggeration, for Cicero could give only one example of such an occurrence.)

Irony. The use of sarcasm, implying the opposite of what is said.

Ad sodālem tuum, **virum optimum,** dēmigrāstī, quem tū **vidēlicet ad cūstōdiendum tē dīligentissimum** fore putāstī.

You went over to your crony, an honorable man, who, I suppose, you thought would make every effort to keep an eye on you.

Metaphor. An implied comparison of a person or thing with another.

Mithridātēs ita rēgnat ut sē nōn Pontī **latebrīs occultāre** velit.

Mithridates reigns in such a way as to show no desire to confine himself to the lair of Pontus. (Mithridates is here compared to a beast of the jungle.)

Metonymy. The use of a word that is related to, or suggestive of, a more commonly used word.

Cerēs in nāvēs ferēbātur.

Grain was carried onto the ships. (The name of the goddess of grain is here used instead of the usual word for grain, **frūmentum.**)

Personification. The act of attributing human characteristics to something not human.

Sī mēcum **patria loquātur,** bene attendam.

If my country should speak with me, I would listen carefully.

Preterition. Mentioning a fact by pretending to pass over it.

Praetermittō ruīnās fortūnārum tuārum.
I pass over the loss of your possessions.

Simile. A comparison whereby a person or thing is likened to another. In Latin, the simile is introduced by some word meaning *as* or *like:* **quālis, similis, ut, velut.**

Ut saepe **hominēs aegrī** morbō gravī, sī aquam gelidam bibērunt, prīmō relevārī videntur, deinde multō gravius afflīctantur, **sīc hic morbus in rē pūblicā** ingravēscet.
As often happens when men sick with a serious disease drink cold water and seem relieved at first, but later become much worse, so this disease in the republic will become more serious.

Symmetry. A balanced arrangement of ideas.

Iam intellegēs multō mē vigilāre ācrius **ad salūtem** quam tē **ad perniciem** reī publicae.
You will soon realize that my concern for the country's welfare is keener than yours for its destruction.

Synecdoche. The use of a part for the whole, or the reverse.

In vestra **tēcta** discēdite.
Leave for your homes (literally *roofs*).

Triad. The use of three elements in a group.

Nōn **feram,** nōn **patiar,** nōn **sinam.**
I won't bear it, I won't endure it, I won't allow it.

Wordplay. A play on words, humorously or seriously, where two words of similar sound but different meanings are employed.

Tantum prōfēcī ut **exsul** potius temptāre quam **cōnsul** vexāre rem pūblicam possēs.
I accomplished this much—that you should attack the republic as exile, rather than harm it as consul.

THE ROMAN CALENDAR

The Roman calendar, revised by Julius Caesar in 45 B.C. and further modified by Pope Gregory XIII in 1582, is the calendar in use today. The Roman year (**annus**) had 365 days (**diēs**), divided into twelve months (**mēnsēs**). The names of the months and their abbreviations are:

Iānuārius	(Iān.)	Iūlius	(Iūl.)
Februārius	(Feb.)	Augustus	(Aug.)
Mārtius	(Mārt.)	September	(Sept.)
Aprīlis	(Apr.)	Octōber	(Oct.)
Māius	(Māi.)	November	(Nov.)
Iūnius	(Iūn.)	December	(Dec.)

Note:

1. Each name of a month is really an adjective modifying the noun **mēnsis**, understood.

2. **Mārtius** was originally the first month of the year, thus accounting for the names *September*, *Octōber*, *November*, and *December*.

3. **Iūlius** was named after Julius Caesar, **Augustus** after Caesar Augustus.

RECKONING TIME

The Year. The Romans indicated a particular year by:

1. Naming the two consuls in office for that year. The names were put in the ablative absolute construction with the word **cōnsulibus**.

   Mariō et Catulō cōnsulibus
   in the consulship of Marius and Catulus, or 102 B.C.

2. Counting from the date of the founding of Rome (753 B.C.), using the initials A.U.C. (**ab urbe conditā** or **annō urbis conditae**). However, since the Romans included both ends in their reckoning, we must add one to the result. Thus, A.U.C. 652 = 753 − 652 + 1, or 102 B.C.

The Month and Day. The Roman calendar did not divide the month into weeks and therefore had no names for the days of the week. Unlike the modern method of indicating a date by reference to a particular day of the week, the Romans reckoned time *backwards* from three fixed points in a month:

1. **Kalendae (Kal.)**, the Calends, the first day of each month.

2. **Nōnae (Nōn.)**, the Nones, the fifth day of each month, except in March, May, July, and October, when the Nones fell on the seventh day.

3. **Īdūs (Īd.)**, the Ides, the thirteenth day of each month, except in March, May, July, and October, when the Ides fell on the fifteenth day.

Dates occurring precisely on the Calends, the Nones, or the Ides of a particular month were expressed by the ablative of time.

> **Kalendīs Novembribus (Kal. Nov.)**
> the Calends of November, or November 1
>
> **Nōnīs Novembribus (Nōn. Nov.)**
> the Nones of November, or November 5
>
> **Īdibus Novembribus (Īd. Nov.)**
> the Ides of November, or November 13

The day before any of the three fixed points in a month was expressed by the word **prīdiē (pr.)**, used as a preposition with the accusative case.

> **pr. Īd. Mart.**
> the day before the Ides of March, or March 14

To calculate other days of the month, the Romans counted *back* from the next fixed point. In counting back, the Romans included the fixed point as a full day. This construction was expressed by the words **ante diem (a.d.)**, followed by the ordinal number indicating the particular day before the fixed point, the fixed point itself, and the month —all in the accusative case.

a.d. IV Kal. Māi. (ante diem quārtum Kalendās Māiās)
the fourth day before the Calends of May, or April 28

a.d. V Nōn. Oct. (ante diem quīntum Nōnās Octōbrēs)
the fifth day before the Nones of October, or October 3

a.d. VI Īd. Apr. (ante diem sextum Īdūs Aprīlēs)
the sixth day before the Ides of April, or April 8

EXERCISES

A. Indicate the rhetorical figure or figures in each of the following quotations:

1. Abiit, excessit, ēvāsit, ērūpit.
2. Ille, ille Iuppiter restitit; ille Capitōlium, ille haec templa, ille cūnctam urbem, ille vōs omnīs salvōs esse voluit.
3. Hoc bellum quis arbitrārētur aut ab omnibus imperātōribus ūnō annō aut omnibus annīs ab ūnō imperātōre cōnficī posse?
4. Ut in perpetuā pāce esse possītis prōvidēbō.
5. Tūne eum exīre patiēre, ut abs tē nōn ēmissus ex urbe, sed immissus in urbem esse videātur?
6. Mercātōribus mare tūtum nōn fuisse dīcam cum duodecim secūrēs in praedōnum potestātem pervēnerint.
7. Nōnne hunc in vincula dūcī, nōn ad mortem rapī, nōn summō suppliciō mactārī imperābis?
8. Calamitās tanta fuit ut eam ad aurīs imperātōris nōn ex proeliō nūntius, sed ex sermōne rūmor afferret.
9. Ēreptī estis sine caede, sine sanguine, sine exercitū, sine dīmicātiōne.
10. Intellegō hanc reī pūblicae pestem paulisper reprimī, nōn in perpetuum comprimī posse.
11. Sī interficī iusserō, crēdō, erit verendum mihi nē quisquam crūdēlius factum esse dīcat.
12. Illa nimis antīqua praetereō, quod C. Servīlius Ahāla Sp. Maelium manū suā occīdit.
13. Cum bellō vāstābitur Italia, vexābuntur urbēs, tēcta ārdēbunt, tum tē nōn exīstimās invidiae incendiō cōnflagrātūrum?
14. Castrōrum imperātōrem ducemque hostium in senātū vidētis.
15. Num mē fefellit rēs tanta, tam atrōx tamque incrēdibilis.
16. Nōs autem, fortēs virī, satis facere reī pūblicae vidēmur, sī istīus furōrem ac tēla vītāmus.

17. Dēlenda vōbis est illa macula Mithridāticō bellō superiōre concepta.

18. Illa omittō, vīsās nocturnō tempore ab occidente facēs.

19. Est ūnus Pompeius quī nōn modo eōrum hominum quī nunc sunt glōriam sed etiam antīquitātis memoriam virtūte superārit.

20. Tempus nōn ad oblīviōnem veteris bellī sed ad comparātiōnem novī contulit.

B. Give the English equivalent of the following Latin dates:

1. Kal. Sept.

2. Nōn. Iūl.

3. Īd. Feb.

4. pr. Kal. Aug.

5. pr. Īd. Apr.

6. a.d. V Kal. Dec.

7. pr. Nōn. Nov.

8. a.d. XI Kal. Iūn.

9. a.d. III Nōn. Oct.

Lesson 40. REVIEW OF CULTURE

CULTURE REVIEW A

Select the word or expression that best completes each of the following statements:

1. The date *pr. Kal. Iān.* refers to (1) Jan. 1st (2) Jan. 13th (3) Dec. 31st (4) Jan. 5th.
2. The Asiatic ruler whose military triumphs led to the appointment of Pompey as commander-in-chief was (1) Mithridates (2) Ariobarzanes (3) Tigranes (4) Nicomedes.
3. Archias spent part of his adult life in the home of his patrons, the (1) Octavii (2) Hortensii (3) Drusi (4) Luculli.
4. The city of Syracuse was famed in Cicero's day for its (1) military exploits (2) works of art (3) ships of war (4) gold coins.
5. The main route from Rome to Brundisium was the Via (1) Aurelia (2) Latina (3) Appia (4) Flaminia.
6. Cicero mourned greatly the death of his daughter (1) Terentia (2) Publilia (3) Tullia (4) Quinta.
7. The Tullianum was a (1) theater (2) temple (3) law court (4) dungeon.
8. The quotation "pūblicam prīstinus perennis" is an example of the rhetorical figure called (1) anaphora (2) simile (3) alliteration (4) chiasmus.
9. Roman orators delivered speeches from a platform called the (1) Basilica (2) Rostra (3) Curia (4) Comitia.
10. Cicero was proconsul in (1) Spain (2) Gaul (3) Cilicia (4) Sicily.

CULTURE REVIEW B

Select the word or expression that best completes each of the following statements:

1. The training camp for Catiline's troops was located at (1) Formiae (2) Faesulae (3) Ostia (4) Praeneste.
2. Pompeii was buried by the eruption of (1) Vesuvius (2) Aetna (3) Heraclea (4) Reate.
3. Cicero was exiled on the charge that he had (1) accepted bribes (2) held office illegally (3) attacked Antony (4) executed citizens without proper trial.

4. The Gallic tribe that the Catilinarian conspirators tried to win over was the (1) Nervii (2) Sequani (3) Allobroges (4) Bituriges.
5. After Cicero's return from exile, he devoted himself to writings that were mainly (1) historical (2) philosophical (3) scientific (4) grammatical.
6. The part of a Roman oration that stated the case was called the (1) nārrātiō (2) perōrātiō (3) exōrdium (4) cōnfīrmātiō.
7. An oration of Cicero that brought about the conviction of a former provincial governor was (1) *In Catilīnam* (2) *In Antōnium* (3) *In Verrem* (4) *In Caecilium*.
8. The group in Roman society that controlled banking and commerce was the (1) Optimātēs (2) Plēbs (3) Populārēs (4) Equitēs.
9. The chief duty of the pūblicānī was to (1) take the census (2) collect taxes in the provinces (3) administer justice (4) supervise the care of buildings.
10. Much of our knowledge of the Roman way of life toward the end of the Republic has been gained from Cicero's (1) letters (2) speeches (3) essays (4) poems.

CULTURE REVIEW C

Select the word or expression that best completes each of the following statements:

1. Cicero lost his life because of the hatred of (1) Caesar (2) Clodius (3) Antony (4) Pompey.
2. The Forum lay between the Palatine Hill and the (1) Capitoline (2) Aventine (3) Esquiline (4) Quirinal.
3. The most notable event in Cicero's consulship was the (1) trial of Verres (2) conspiracy of Catiline (3) assassination of Caesar (4) defeat of Mithridates.
4. Cicero's chief rival as a lawyer was (1) Antonius (2) Pompey (3) Cassius (4) Hortensius.
5. Cicero was known as a novus homō, a man (1) whose ancestors never held public office (2) who was a foreigner (3) whose family were aristocrats (4) who had been a dictator.
6. Five of the Catilinarian conspirators were executed in the (1) Rostra (2) Tullianum (3) Curia (4) Tabularium.
7. In times of crisis, the Roman Republic was ruled by a (1) censor (2) consul (3) dictator (4) proconsul.
8. The people who esteemed Cicero as much as they hated Verres were the (1) Sicilians (2) Cilicians (3) Greeks (4) Allobroges.

9. An office in the cursus honōrum was that of (1) tribune (2) censor (3) pontifex maximus (4) praetor.
10. The oration *Prō Archiā* is famous for its discussion of (1) government (2) literature (3) citizenship (4) religion.

CULTURE REVIEW D

Select the word or expression that best completes each of the following statements:

1. Cicero was consul in the year (1) 66 (2) 63 (3) 59 (4) 48 B.C.
2. A conspirator denounced by Cicero was (1) Lentulus (2) Atticus (3) Hortensius (4) Caesar.
3. The date *a.d. IV Īd. Feb.* refers to (1) Feb. 10th (2) Feb. 9th (3) Feb. 2nd (4) Jan. 29th.
4. The introductory remarks of a Latin oration constituted the (1) nārrātiō (2) perōrātiō (3) cōnfīrmātiō (4) exōrdium.
5. In Cicero's time, the provinces were governed by (1) praetors (2) proconsuls (3) aediles (4) censors.
6. The decree that gave the consuls dictatorial power was known as a (1) supplicātiō (2) senātūs cōnsultum (3) senātūs cōnsultum ultimum (4) sententia.
7. When Cicero delivered the speech *Prō Archiā,* his brother Quintus presided as (1) censor (2) quaestor (3) tribune (4) praetor.
8. Haruspicēs (1) took the census (2) foretold the future (3) guarded the sacred fire (4) kept the Sibylline Books.
9. The quotation "amoenitās locōrum, urbium pulchritūdō" is an example of the rhetorical figure called (1) antithesis (2) preterition (3) symmetry (4) chiasmus.
10. The city that granted citizenship to Archias was (1) Heraclea (2) Arpinum (3) Brundisium (4) Praeneste.

Unit XIII—*Vocabularies*

Lesson 41. LATIN MASTERY LIST

NOUNS

adulēscēns, -entis (*m.*), young man

adulēscentia, -ae (*f.*), youth

aetās, -ātis (*f.*), age

ars, artis (*f.*), art, skill

beneficium, -ī (*n.*), benefit, favor, kindness

caedēs, -is (*f.*), murder, slaughter

cāsus, -ūs (*m.*), chance, accident

comes, -itis (*m.*), companion

coniūrātī, -ōrum (*m. pl.*), conspirators

coniūrātiō, -ōnis (*f.*), conspiracy

cōnsul, -ulis (*m.*), consul

cūria, -ae (*f.*), senate house

dētrīmentum, -ī (*n.*), loss, harm, defeat

dignitās, -ātis (*f.*), prestige, dignity, honor

dolor, -ōris (*m.*), pain, grief, suffering, sorrow

epistula, -ae (*f.*), letter

exemplum, -ī (*n.*), example, precedent

exsilium, -ī (*n.*), exile, banishment

facilitās, -ātis (*f.*), ease, courtesy

factum, -ī (*n.*), deed, act

facultās, -ātis (*f.*), ability, opportunity

gēns, gentis (*f.*), family, nation, tribe

genus, -eris (*n.*), race, birth, kind

grātia, -ae (*f.*), gratitude, favor, influence

honor, -ōris (*m.*), honor, office

īgnis, -is (*m.*), fire

ingenium, -ī (*n.*), ability, talent, nature

iūdex, -icis (*m.*), judge, juror

iūdicium, -ī (*n.*), judgment, verdict, trial, court

iūs, iūris (*n.*), right, law

labor, -ōris (*m.*), work, task

laus, laudis (*f.*), praise, merit

lībertās, -ātis (*f.*), liberty, freedom

mēns, mentis (*f.*), mind

mēnsis, -is (*m.*), month

mercātor, -ōris (*m.*), trader, merchant

metus, -ūs (*m.*), fear

mora, -ae (*f.*), delay

mōs, mōris (*m.*), custom

negōtium, -ī (*n.*), business, task

nēmō, nūllīus (*m.*), no one

nihil (*n.*), nothing

occāsus, -ūs (*m.*), setting, downfall

oculus, -ī (*m.*), eye

officium, -ī (*n.*), duty, service

opīniō, -ōnis (*f.*), opinion, belief, expectation

opus, operis (*n.*), work

ōrātiō, -ōnis (*f.*), speech

ōrdō, -inis (*m*.), order, rank

plēbs, plēbis (*f*.), common people

portus, -ūs (*m*.), harbor, port

potestās, -ātis (*f*.), power

praetor, -ōris (*m*.), praetor, judge

ratiō, -ōnis (*f*.), method, plan, reason

scelus, -eris (*n*.), crime

senex, senis (*m*.), old man

sententia, -ae (*f*.), feeling, opinion

sermō, -ōnis (*m*.), talk, conversation

sōl, sōlis (*m*.), sun

subsidium, -ī (*n*.), aid, support

supplicium, -ī (*n*.), punishment, torture

templum, -ī (*n*.), temple

testis, -is (*m*.), witness

ūsus, -ūs (*m*.), use, experience, practice

vīs, vīs (*f*.), force, violence, strength

vōx, vōcis (*f*.), voice, word

ADJECTIVES AND PRONOUNS

aliquis, -qua, -quid, someone, something

alius, -a, -ud, other, another

alter, -era, -erum, the other (of two)

cēterī, -ae, -a, the others, the rest

complūrēs, -a, several, many

dignus, -a, -um, worthy

ēgregius, -a, -um, outstanding, remarkable

gravis, -e, heavy, severe, serious

hūmānus, -a, -um, human, kind, cultured

idōneus, -a, -um, suitable, fit

immortālis, -e, immortal

incrēdibilis, -e, unbelievable, extraordinary

iste, ista, istud, that (of yours), that fellow

iūcundus, -a, -um, pleasant, agreeable

levis, -e, light, mild

nefārius, -a, -um, impious, wicked

perditus, -a, -um, lost, desperate, corrupt

plēnus, -a, -um, full, abounding in

prīvātus, -a, -um, private, personal

proximus, -a, -um, nearest, next, last

pūblicus, -a, -um, public

quīdam, quaedam, quoddam, a certain

quisquam, quicquam, anyone, anything

quisque, quidque, each one, each thing

reliquus, -a, -um, remaining, rest of

salvus, -a, -um, safe, sound

similis, -e, similar, like

singulāris, -e, unique, remarkable, unusual

sōlus, -a, -um, alone, only

superus, -a, -um, upper, above

tūtus, -a, -um, safe, secure

ūllus, -a, -um, any

uterque, utraque, utrumque, each (of two), both

vehemēns, violent, vigorous, strong

vērus, -a, -um, true, real

VERBS

coepī, coepisse, coeptus, began

cōgitō, -āre, -āvī, -ātus, think, consider, plan

cōgō, -ere, coēgī, coāctus, compel, collect

cōnor, -ārī, -ātus sum, try, attempt

cōnscrībō, -ere, -scrīpsī, -scrīptus, enlist, enroll

crēdō, -ere, -idī, -itus, believe

dēleō, -ēre, -ēvī, -ētus, blot out, destroy

dubitō, -āre, -āvī, -ātus, doubt, hesitate

ēiciō, -ere, -iēcī, -iectus, throw out, drive out

ēripiō, -ere, -uī, -reptus, take away, rescue

fīō, fierī, factus sum, become, be made, happen

hortor, -ārī, -ātus sum, urge, encourage

incendō, -ere, -cendī, -cēnsus, set fire to, burn

iūdicō, -āre, -āvī, -ātus, judge, decide

iungō, -ere, iūnxī, iūnctus, join

legō, -ere, lēgī, lēctus, choose, read

licet, licēre, licuit, it is permitted, one may

loquor, -quī, -cūtus sum, speak, say

mālō, mālle, māluī, prefer

mandō, -āre, -āvī, -ātus, entrust, order

morior, morī, mortuus sum, die

moror, -ārī, -ātus sum, delay, stay

nāscor, nāscī, nātus sum, be born

nōlō, nōlle, nōluī, not want, be unwilling

opprimō, -ere, -pressī, -pressus, crush, subdue

orior, orīrī, ortus sum, rise

ostendō, -ere, -dī, -tus, show, display

patior, patī, passus sum, suffer, allow

pellō, -ere, pepulī, pulsus, drive, rout

polliceor, -ērī, -icitus sum, promise

postulō, -āre, -āvī, -ātus, demand

premō, -ere, pressī, pressus, press, oppress

prōvideō, -ēre, -vīdī, -vīsus, foresee, provide, take care

quaerō, quaerere, -sīvī, -sītus, seek, ask

resistō, -ere, -stitī, resist, oppose

sentiō, -īre, sēnsī, sēnsus, feel, perceive

stō, -āre, stetī, stātūrus, stand

studeō, -ēre, studuī, be eager for, desire

suscipiō, -ere, -cēpī, -ceptus, undertake

trahō, -ere, trāxī, trāctus, draw, drag

valeō, -ēre, -uī, -itūrus, be well, be strong

vertō, -ere, -tī, -sus, turn

vigilō, -āre, -āvī, -ātus, keep awake, watch

vīvō, -ere, vīxī, vīctūrus, live

ADVERBS, CONJUNCTIONS, PREPOSITIONS

apud (*with acc.*), among, in the presence of, near
autem, however, but, moreover
causā (*with gen.*), for the sake of
deinde, then, next
dum, while, until
igitur, therefore
mox, soon, presently
neque (nec), and not, nor
nisi, if not, unless
numquam, never

quam, how, as, than
quasi, as if, so to speak
quoque, also, even
satis, enough
sī, if
sīc, thus, so
simul, at the same time; **simul atque (ac),** as soon as
statim, immediately, at once
tamen, however, still, yet, nevertheless
tandem, at last, finally
vel, or, even

EXERCISES

A. Match the words in column A with those in column B.

Column A

1. quoque
2. mēnsis
3. facilitās
4. nāscor
5. ingenium
6. mox
7. vigilō
8. dolor
9. scelus
10. cēterī
11. tandem
12. perditus
13. mora
14. patior
15. supplicium
16. mōs
17. superus
18. quisque
19. sentiō
20. plēnus

Column B

a. lost
b. soon
c. be born
d. the others
e. punishment
f. also
g. month
h. at last
i. ease
j. feel
k. each one
l. custom
m. upper
n. full
o. delay
p. keep awake
q. ability
r. pain
s. suffer
t. crime

B. Choose the word that is most nearly *synonymous* with the italicized word.

1.	*comes:*	adventus, socius, hostis, mēnsis
2.	*subsidium:*	auxilium, perīculum, officium, iūdicium
3.	*iūcundus:*	idōneus, plēnus, bonus, grātus
4.	*cōgitō:*	cōgō, hortor, putō, legō
5.	*cōnor:*	temptō, incendō, rapiō, sciō
6.	*igitur:*	itaque, statim, quod, quoque
7.	*apud:*	propter, praeter, inter, interim
8.	*tūtus:*	omnis, uterque, superus, salvus
9.	*opus:*	passus, labor, ōrdō, ōrātiō
10.	*ostendō:*	pateō, vertō, dēleō, dēmōnstrō

C. Find the word in column *B* that is most nearly *opposite* in meaning to the word in column *A*.

Column A	Column B
1. vīvō	*a.* aliquid
2. orior	*b.* adulēscēns
3. sī	*c.* cadō
4. nihil	*d.* sedeō
5. levis	*e.* morior
6. stō	*f.* prīvātus
7. senex	*g.* semper
8. metus	*h.* nisi
9. pūblicus	*i.* virtūs
10. numquam	*j.* gravis

D. Choose the Latin word that best translates the English word.

1.	WHILE	tamen, vel, dum, deinde
2.	MONTH	mēnsis, mēns, metus, mōns
3.	AGE	aestās, genus, gēns, aetās
4.	ANYONE	quisque, quīdam, quisquam, quidque
5.	SUITABLE	idōneus, iūcundus, salvus, tūtus
6.	THROW OUT	ēripiō, exeō, excēdō, ēiciō
7.	DEMAND	pellō, polliceor, premō, postulō
8.	ABILITY	grātia, facultās, dignitās, cāsus
9.	HARBOR	porta, portō, portus, praetor
10.	FORCE	vix, vōx, vīs, ūsus

Lesson 42. LATIN-ENGLISH VOCABULARY

ā, ab (*with abl.*), from, by

abeō, -īre, -iī, -itūrus, go away

abhorreō, -ēre, -uī, shrink from, be inconsistent with

absum, -esse, āfuī, āfutūrus, be away, be absent, be distant

accēdō, -ere, -cessī, -cessūrus, go to, approach

accidō, -ere, -cidī, befall, happen

accipiō, -ere, -cēpī, -ceptus, receive

ācer, ācris, ācre, sharp, fierce

aciēs, -ēī (*f.*), line of battle

ācriter, sharply, fiercely

ad (*with acc.*), to, toward, near

addūcō, -ere, -dūxī, -ductus, lead to, influence

adeō, -īre, -iī, -itūrus, go to, approach

adhūc, up to this time, thus far, still

aditus, -ūs (*m.*), approach

adorior, -īrī, -ortus sum, rise against, attack

adsum, -esse, -fuī, -futūrus, be near, be present

adulēscēns, -entis (*m.*), young man

adulēscentia, -ae (*f.*), youth

adventus, -ūs (*m.*), arrival, approach

adversārius, -ī (*m.*), opponent, enemy

aedēs, -is (*f.*), temple; (*pl.*), house

aedificium, -ī (*n.*), building

aedificō, -āre, -āvī, -ātus, build

aeger, -gra, -grum, sick

aequitās, -ātis (*f.*), evenness, calmness, fairness

aequō, -āre, -āvī, -ātus, make equal or even

aequus, -a, -um, equal, level, fair

aestās, -ātis (*f.*), summer

aetās, -ātis (*f.*), age

aeternus, -a, -um, eternal, everlasting

afferō, -ferre, attulī, allātus, bring to, apply, cause

afficiō, -ere, -fēcī, -fectus, affect, afflict

afflīgō, -ere, -flīxī, -flīctus, strike, afflict

ager, agrī (*m.*), field, land

aggredior, -gredī, -gressus sum, attack

agmen, -inis (*n.*), marching column

agō, -ere, ēgī, āctus, drive, do

agricola, -ae (*m.*), farmer

aiō, say, assert

aliēnus, -a, -um, belonging to another, foreign

aliquandō, at some time, at last

aliquī, -qua, -quod, some, any

aliquis, -quid, someone, something

alius, -a, -ud, other, another

alter, -era, -erum, the other (of two)

altitūdō, -inis (*f.*), height, depth

altus, -a, -um, high, deep

ambulō, -āre, -āvī, -ātus, walk

āmēns, out of one's senses, foolish, mad

amīcitia, -ae (*f.*), friendship

amīcus, -a, -um, friendly
amīcus, -ī (m.), friend
āmittō, -ere, -mīsī, -missus, send away, lose
amō, -āre, -āvī, -ātus, love, like
amor, -ōris (m.), love
amplus, -a, -um, large, spacious
an, or, whether
animadvertō, -ere, -tī, -sus, notice, punish
animus, -ī (m.), mind, spirit
annus, -ī (m.), year
ante (with acc.), before, in front of
anteā, previously, formerly
antequam, before
aperiō, -īre, aperuī, apertus, open, disclose
apertus, -a, -um, open, exposed
appellō, -āre, -āvī, -ātus, name
appropinquō, -āre, -āvī, -ātus, approach
apud (with acc.), among, in the presence of, near
aqua, -ae (f.), water
aquila, -ae (f.), eagle
āra, -ae (f.), altar
arbitror, -ārī, -ātus sum, think
arbor, -oris (f.), tree
argentum, -ī (n.), silver
arma, -ōrum (n. pl.), arms
armō, -āre, -āvī, -ātus, arm, equip
ars, artis (f.), art, skill
at, but
atque (ac), and, and especially
ātrium, -ī (n.), atrium
attingō, -ere, -tigī, -tāctus, touch, reach, attain
auctor, -ōris (m.), author, authority
auctōritās, -ātis (f.), influence, authority
audācia, -ae (f.), boldness

audācter, boldly
audāx, bold, daring
audeō, -ēre, ausus sum, dare
audiō, -īre, -īvī, -ītus, hear
augeō, -ēre, auxī, auctus, increase
auris, -is (f.), ear
aurum, -ī (n.), gold
auspicium, -ī (n.), augury; (pl.), auspices
aut, or; aut . . . aut, either . . . or
autem, however, but, moreover
auxilium, -ī (n.), aid, help
āvertō, -ere, -tī, -sus, turn away or aside

barbarus, -a, -um, foreign, uncivilized, savage
barbarus, -ī (m.), barbarian, native
beātus, -a, -um, happy, rich, fortunate
bellum, -ī (n.), war
bene, well
beneficium, -ī (n.), benefit, favor, kindness
bis, twice
bonus, -a, -um, good
brevis, -e, short

cadō, -ere, cecidī, cāsūrus, fall
caedēs, -is (f.), murder, slaughter
caedō, -ere, cecīdī, caesus, cut, kill
caelum, -ī (n.), sky
calamitās, -ātis (f.), disaster
campus, -ī (m.), plain, field
capiō, -ere, cēpī, captus, take, seize, capture
captīvus, -ī (m.), prisoner
caput, -itis (n.), head
carcer, -eris (m.), prison

cārus, -a, -um, dear, precious
casa, -ae (*f.*), hut
castra, -ōrum (*n. pl.*), camp
cāsus, -ūs (*m.*), chance, accident
causa, -ae (*f.*), cause, reason
causā (*with gen.*), for the sake of
cēdō, -ere, cessī, cessūrus, move, yield
celebrō, -āre, -āvī, -ātus, frequent, crowd, celebrate
celer, -eris, -ere, swift
celeritās, -ātis (*f.*), speed, swiftness
celeriter, quickly
cēnseō, -ēre, -suī, -sus, assess, enroll, decree
cēnsor, -ōris (*m.*), censor
centum, one hundred
centuriō, -ōnis (*m.*), centurion
cernō, -ere, crēvī, crētus, perceive, discern
certus, -a, -um, certain, sure
cēterī, -ae, -a, the others, the rest
cibus, -ī (*m.*), food
circā, around, about
circiter, about
circum (*with acc.*), around
circumdō, -dare, -dedī, -datus, place around, surround
circumveniō, -īre, -vēnī, -ventus, surround
citerior, -ius, nearer
cīvīlis, -e, civil
cīvis, -is (*m.*), citizen
cīvitās, -ātis (*f.*), state, citizenship
clāmō, -āre, -āvī, -ātus, shout
clāmor, -ōris (*m.*), shout, noise
clārus, -a, -um, clear, famous
classis, -is (*f.*), fleet
claudō, -ere, clausī, clausus, close
clēmēns, merciful, kind, gentle

clēmentia, -ae (*f.*), mercy
coepī, coepisse, coeptus, began
cōgitō, -āre, -āvī, -ātus, think, consider, plan
cognōmen, -inis (*n.*), family name
cognōscō, -ere, -nōvī, -nitus, find out, learn
cōgō, -ere, coēgī, coāctus, compel, collect
cohors, -tis (*f.*), cohort
cohortor, -ārī, -ātus sum, encourage
collis, -is (*m.*), hill
collocō, -āre, -āvī, -ātus, put together, station
colloquium, -ī (*n.*), conference
colō, -ere, -uī, cultus, cultivate, honor, worship
comes, -itis (*m.*), companion
comitia, -ōrum (*n. pl.*), assembly, election
comitium, -ī (*n.*), meeting place
commeātus, -ūs (*m.*), movement, supplies
commemorō, -āre, -āvī, -ātus, remind, mention
committō, -ere, -mīsī, -missus, join, entrust
commoveō, -ēre, -mōvī, -mōtus, move deeply, alarm
commūnis, -e, common
comparō, -āre, -āvī, -ātus, get together, prepare
comperiō, -īre, -perī, -pertus, find out, discover
compleō, -ēre, -ēvī, -ētus, fill
complūrēs, -a, several, many
comportō, -āre, -āvī, -ātus, bring together
comprehendō,   -ere,   -hendī, -hēnsus, seize, arrest
concēdō, -ere, -cessī, -cessūrus,

yield, withdraw

concilium, -ī (n.), meeting

concitō, -āre, -āvī, -ātus, arouse, stir up

concordia, -ae (f.), harmony

concurrō, -ere, -currī, -cursus, run together, rush

condiciō, -ōnis (f.), terms, agreement

condō, -ere, -didī, -ditus, put together, found, establish

cōnferō, -ferre, -tulī, collātus, bring together, collect

cōnficiō, -ere, -fēcī, -fectus, finish

cōnfīdō, -ere, -fīsus sum, trust, be confident, rely on

cōnfīrmō, -āre, -āvī, -ātus, encourage, strengthen

cōnfiteor, -ērī, -fessus sum, confess, admit, acknowledge

coniciō, -ere, -iēcī, -iectus, hurl

coniungō, -ere, -iūnxī, -iūnctus, join, unite

coniūnx, -iugis (m. and f.), husband, wife

coniūrātī, -ōrum (m. pl.), conspirators

coniūrātiō, -ōnis (f.), conspiracy

coniūrō, -āre, -āvī, -ātus, plot

cōnor, -ārī, -ātus sum, try, attempt

cōnscientia, -ae (f.), consciousness, conscience

cōnscrībō, -ere, -scrīpsī, -scrīptus, enlist, enroll

cōnsentiō, -īre, -sēnsī, -sēnsus, agree

cōnsequor, -ī, -secūtus sum, pursue, overtake

cōnservō, -āre, -āvī, -ātus, preserve, keep

cōnsīderō, -āre, -āvī, -ātus, consider

cōnsīdō, -ere, -sēdī, -sessūrus, sit down, encamp

cōnsilium, -ī (n.), plan, advice

cōnsistō, -ere, -stitī, -stitūrus, take one's stand, halt

cōnspectus, -ūs (m.), sight

cōnspiciō, -ere, -spexī, -spectus, notice

cōnstituō, -ere, -stituī, -stitūtus, decide, station

cōnsuēscō, -ere, -suēvī, -suētus, become accustomed

cōnsuētūdō, -inis (f.), custom, habit

cōnsul, -ulis (m.), consul

cōnsulāris, -e, consular

cōnsulāris, -is (m.), ex-consul

cōnsulātus, -ūs (m.), consulship

cōnsulō, -ere, -uī, -tus, consult, consider

cōnsultum, -ī (n.), decree

cōnsūmō, -ere, -sūmpsī, -sūmptus, use up, spend

contendō, -ere, -tendī, -tentus, hasten, fight

contentus, -a, -um, content, satisfied

contineō, -ēre, -tinuī, -tentus, hold together, hem in

continuus, -a, -um, continuous, successive

cōntiō, -ōnis (f.), assembly, meeting

contrā (with acc.), against, opposite

conveniō, -īre, -vēnī, -ventus, come together, assemble

convocō, -āre, -āvī, -ātus, call together, summon

cōpia, -ae (f.), supply, abundance; (pl.), troops, forces

cornū, -ūs (n.), horn, wing (of an army)

corpus, -oris (n.), body
crās, tomorrow
crēdibilis, -e, credible, believable
crēdō, -ere, -idī, -itus, believe
crūdēlis, -e, cruel
culpa, -ae (f.), fault, guilt, blame
cum (with abl.), with
cum, when, since, although
cūnctus, -a, -um, all, whole
cupiditās, -ātis (f.), desire
cupidus, -a, -um, desirous, eager
cupiō, -ere, -īvī, -ītus, wish, desire
cūr, why
cūra, -ae (f.), care, anxiety
cūria, -ae (f.), senate house
cūrō, -āre, -āvī, -ātus, care for, attend to
currō, -ere, cucurrī, cursūrus, run
currus, -ūs (m.), chariot
cursus, -ūs (m.), running, course
cūstōdia, -ae (f.), guard, custody, protection
cūstōdiō, -īre, -īvī, -ītus, guard, protect, watch
cūstōs, -ōdis (m.), guard, guardian

dē (with abl.), down from, concerning, about
dea, -ae (f.), goddess
dēbeō, -ēre, -uī, -itus, owe, ought
decem, ten
dēcernō, -ere, dēcrēvī, dēcrētus, decree, decide, vote
decimus, -a, -um, tenth
dēditiō, ōnis (f.), surrender
dēdō, -ere, dēdidī, dēditus, surrender, devote
dēdūcō, -ere, -dūxī, -ductus, bring or lead down, launch
dēfendō, -ere, -fendī, -fēnsus, defend, protect

dēfēnsor, -ōris (m.), defender
dēferō, -ferre, -tulī, -lātus, carry off, report, bestow
dēficiō, -ere, -fēcī, -fectus, fail, revolt
dēiciō, -ere, -iēcī, -iectus, throw down, dislodge
deinde, then, next
dēlectō, -āre, -āvī, -ātus, please, delight, charm
dēleō, -ēre, -ēvī, -ētus, blot out, destroy
dēligō, -ere, -lēgī, -lēctus, choose
dēlūbrum, -ī (n.), shrine, temple
dēmēns, mad, insane
dēmōnstrō, -āre, -āvī, -ātus, point out, show
dēnique, finally, at last, in short
dēns, dentis (m.), tooth
dēpellō, -ere, -pulī, -pulsus, drive away, remove
dēprehendō, -ere, -dī, -sus, seize, detect
dēscrībō, -ere, -scrīpsī, -scrīptus, describe, write down
dēserō, -ere, -uī, -tus, desert, abandon
dēsīderō, -āre, -āvī, -ātus, desire, long for, miss
dēsignātus, -a, -um, elect, chosen
dēspērō, -āre, -āvī, -ātus, despair, lose hope
dēsum, -esse, -fuī, -futūrus, fail, be lacking
dētrīmentum, -ī (n.), loss, harm, defeat
deus, -ī (m.), god
dexter, -tra, -trum, right
dīcō, -ere, dīxī, dictus, say, speak, tell
diēs, -ēī (m.), day
differō, -ferre, distulī, dīlatus, differ, postpone

difficilis, -e, hard, difficult

difficultās, -ātis (f.), difficulty

digitus, -ī (m.), finger

dignitās, -ātis (f.), prestige, dignity, honor

dignus, -a, -um, worthy

dīligēns, careful

dīligentia, -ae (f.), carefulness, diligence

dīmittō, -ere, -mīsī, -missus, send away, let go

discēdō, -ere, -cessī, -cessūrus, leave, depart

disciplīna, -ae (f.), training

discō, -ere, didicī, learn

dissentiō, -īre, -sēnsī, -sēnsus, disagree, differ

dissimilis, -e, unlike

diū, for a long time

dīvidō, -ere, -vīsī, -vīsus, divide

dīvīnus, -a, -um, divine, godlike

dō, dare, dedī, datus, give

doceō, -ēre, -uī, -tus, teach, explain

doctrīna, -ae (f.), learning, instruction

dolor, -ōris (m.), pain, grief, suffering, sorrow

domesticus, -a, -um, domestic, private

domicilium, -ī (n.), home

domina, -ae (f.), mistress

dominus, -ī (m.), master

domus, -ūs (f.), house, home

dōnō, -āre, -āvī, -ātus, give

dōnum, -ī (n.), gift

dormiō, -īre, -īvī, -ītus, sleep

dubitō, -āre, -āvī, -ātus, doubt, hesitate

dūcō, -ere, dūxī, ductus, lead

dum, while, until

duo, duae, duo, two

dux, ducis (m.), leader, general

ē, ex (with abl.), out of, from

ēdūcō, -ere, -dūxī, -ductus, lead out

efficiō, -ere, -fēcī, -fectus, bring about, accomplish

ego, meī, I; (pl.), we

ēgredior, -gredī, -gressus sum, go out, leave

ēgregius, -a, -um, outstanding, remarkable

ēiciō, -ere, -iēcī, -iectus, throw out, drive out

emō, -ere, ēmī, ēmptus, buy

enim, for

ēnūntiō, -āre, -āvī, -ātus, declare, announce

eō, īre, īvī (iī), itūrus, go

eō, there, to that place

eōdem, to the same place

epistula, -ae (f.), letter

eques, -itis (m.), horseman

equitātus, -ūs (m.), cavalry

equus, -ī (m.), horse

ēripiō, -ere, -uī, -reptus, take away, rescue

ērudiō, -īre, -īvī, -ītus, teach, train

et, and; et . . . et, both . . . and

etenim, for, and indeed

etiam, even, also

etsī, although

excēdō, -ere, -cessī, -cessūrus, go out, depart

excellō, -ere, excel, surpass

excipiō, -ere, -cēpī, -ceptus, receive

excitō, -āre, -āvī, -ātus, arouse, stir up

exemplum, -ī (n.), example, precedent

exeō, -īre, -iī, -itūrus, go out

exerceō, -ēre, -ercuī, -ercitus, train

exercitus, -ūs (*m.*), army
exīstimō, -āre, -āvī, -ātus, think
exitium, -ī (*n.*), destruction, ruin, death
exitus, -ūs (*m.*), outcome, departure
expellō, -ere, -pulī, -pulsus, drive out
experior, -īrī, expertus sum, try, test
expetō, -ere, -īvī, -ītus, seek out, demand
explōrātor, -ōris (*m.*), scout
explōrō, -āre, -āvī, -ātus, search out, reconnoiter
expōnō, -ere, -posuī, -positus, put out, set forth
expugnō, -āre, -āvī, -ātus, capture
exsilium, -ī (*n.*), exile, banishment
exsistō, -ere, -stitī, stand out, appear
exspectō, -āre, -āvī, -ātus, wait (for)
exstinguō, -ere, -stīnxī, -stīnctus, extinguish, destroy
exterus, -a, -um, outer, foreign
extrā, outside of, beyond
extrēmus, -a, -um, farthest

fābula, -ae (*f.*), story
facile, easily
facilis, -e, easy
facilitās, -ātis (*f.*), ease, courtesy
facinus, -oris (*n.*), crime
faciō, -ere, fēcī, factus, make, do
factum, -ī (*n.*), deed, act
facultās, -ātis (*f.*), ability, opportunity
fāma, -ae (*f.*), report, rumor, reputation
familia, -ae (*f.*), household
familiāris, -e, domestic, friendly
familiāris, -is (*m.*), intimate friend
fateor, -ērī, fassus sum, confess, admit
fātum, -ī (*n.*), fate
fēlīcitās, -ātis (*f.*), happiness, good luck
fēlīx, happy, fortunate
fēmina, -ae (*f.*), woman
ferē, almost, about
ferō, ferre, tulī, lātus, bear, carry, bring
ferrum, -ī (*n.*), iron, weapon
fidēs, -eī (*f.*), faith, trust
fīdō, -ere, fīsus sum, trust
fīdus, -a, -um, faithful
fīlia, -ae (*f.*), daughter
fīlius, -ī (*m.*), son
fīniō, -īre, -īvī, -ītus, limit
fīnis, -is (*m.*), end, boundary; (*pl.*), territory
fīnitimus, -a, -um, neighboring
fīō, fierī, factus sum, become, be made, happen
fīrmus, -a, -um, strong
flamma, -ae (*f.*), flame, fire
flūmen, -inis (*n.*), river
foedus, -eris (*n.*), treaty, alliance
fōrma, -ae (*f.*), shape, beauty
fortis, -e, brave, strong
fortiter, bravely
fortitūdō, -inis (*f.*), courage, strength
fortūna, -ae (*f.*), fortune, luck
forum, -ī (*n.*), forum, marketplace
fossa, -ae (*f.*), trench
frāter, -tris (*m.*), brother
frequēns, frequent, crowded
frīgus, -oris (*n.*), cold
frūctus, -ūs (*m.*), fruit, enjoyment, reward

frūmentārius, -a, -um, abounding in grain, fertile
frūmentum, -ī (n.), grain
fruor, -ī, frūctus sum, enjoy
frūstrā, in vain
fuga, -ae (f.), flight
fugiō, -ere, fūgī, fugitūrus, flee
furor, -ōris (m.), madness

gēns, gentis (f.), family, nation, tribe
genus, -eris (n.), race, birth, kind
gerō, -ere, gessī, gestus, carry on, wage
gladiātor, -ōris (m.), gladiator
gladius, -ī (m.), sword
glōria, -ae (f.), glory, fame
gradior, gradī, gressus sum, step, walk
grātia, -ae (f.), gratitude, favor, influence
grātus, -a, -um, pleasing, grateful
gravis, -e, heavy, severe, serious

habeō, -ēre, -uī, -itus, have
habitō, -āre, -āvī, -ātus, live, dwell
hīberna, -ōrum (n. pl.), winter quarters
hīc, here
hic, haec, hoc, this, he, she, it
hiemō, -āre, -āvī, -ātūrus, spend the winter
hiems, -emis (f.), winter
hinc, from here, hence
hodiē, today
homō, -inis (m.), man, person
honestās, -ātis (f.), honor
honestus, -a, -um, honorable
honor, -ōris (m.), honor, office
hōra, -ae (f.), hour
hortor, -ārī, -ātus sum, urge, encourage
hospes, -itis (m.), stranger, host, guest

hostis, -is (m.), enemy
hūc, to this place, here
hūmānitās, -ātis (f.), humanity, kindness, culture
hūmānus, -a, -um, human, kind, cultured
humus, -ī (f.), ground, earth

iaceō, -ēre, -uī, lie
iaciō, -ere, iēcī, iactus, throw
iam, already, soon, now
ibi, there
īdem, eadem, idem, the same
idōneus, -a, -um, suitable, fit
Īdūs, -uum (f. pl.), Ides
igitur, therefore
īgnis, -is (m.), fire
ignōrō, -āre, -āvī, -ātus, not know, be ignorant
ignōtus, -a, -um, unknown
ille, illa, illud, that, he, she, it
illūstrō, -āre, -āvī, -ātus, bring to light, glorify
immortālis, -e, immortal
impedīmentum, -ī (n.), hindrance; (pl.), baggage
impediō, -īre, -īvī, -ītus, hinder
impellō, -ere, -pulī, -pulsus, drive on, influence
impendeō, -ēre, overhang, threaten
imperātor, -ōris (m.), general, commander
imperītus, -a, -um, inexperienced, ignorant
imperium, -ī (n.), command, rule
imperō, -āre, -āvī, -ātus, command, order
impetus, -ūs (m.), attack
impōnō, -ere, -posuī, -positus, put upon, impose

improbus, -a, -um, wicked, base

in (*with abl.*), in, on; (*with acc.*), into

incendium, -ī (*n.*), fire

incendō, -ere, -cendī, -cēnsus, set fire to, burn

incertus, -a, -um, uncertain

incipiō, -ere, -cēpī, -ceptus, begin

incitō, -āre, -āvī, -ātus, urge on, arouse

inclūdō, -ere, -clūsī, -clūsus, enclose, confine

incola, -ae (*m.*), inhabitant

incolumis, -e, unharmed, safe

incrēdibilis, -e, unbelievable, extraordinary

inde, from there, thence

indicium, -ī (*n.*), testimony, proof, evidence

indicō, -āre, -āvī, -ātus, point out, accuse

indignus, -a, -um, unworthy

ineō, -īre, -iī, -itūrus, enter upon

īnfēlīx, unhappy, unfortunate

īnferō, -ferre, -tulī, illātus, bring in, wage, inflict

ingenium, -ī (*n.*), ability, talent, nature

ingēns, huge, vast

inimīcus, -a, -um, unfriendly

inīquus, -a, -um, unequal, uneven, unfavorable

initium, -ī (*n.*), beginning

iniūria, -ae (*f.*), injury, wrong, injustice

inopia, -ae (*f.*), lack, scarcity

inquam, say

īnsequor, -sequī, -secūtus sum, follow after, pursue

īnsidiae, -ārum (*f. pl.*), ambush, treachery

īnsignis, -e, notable, distinguished

īnstituō, -ere, -stituī, -stitūtus, establish, decide

īnstitūtum, -ī (*n.*), custom

īnstruō, -ere, -strūxī, -strūctus, draw up, arrange

īnsula, -ae (*f.*), island

integer, -gra, -grum, whole, untouched, unharmed

intellegō, -ere, -lēxī, -lēctus, realize, understand

inter (*with acc.*), between, among

intereā, meanwhile

interficiō, -ere, -fēcī, -fectus, kill

interim, meanwhile

interitus, -ūs (*m.*), destruction, death

intermittō, -ere, -mīsī, -missus, stop, discontinue

interrogō, -āre, -āvī, -ātus, ask, question

intersum, -esse, -fuī, -futūrus, be between, take part, differ

intervāllum, -ī (*n.*), space between, distance

intrā, within

inveniō, -īre, -vēnī, -ventus, find, come upon

invideō, -ēre, -vīdī, -vīsus, envy

invidia, -ae (*f.*), envy, unpopularity

ipse, ipsa, ipsum, -self, very

īra, -ae (*f.*), anger

īrāscor, -ī, īrātus sum, be angry

is, ea, id, this, that, he, she, it

iste, ista, istud, that (of yours), that fellow

ita, so, thus

itaque, and so, therefore

item, likewise

iter, itineris (*n.*), march, journey, route

iterum, again

iubeō, -ēre, iussī, iussus, order

iūcundus, -a, -um, pleasant, agreeable

iūdex, -icis (*m.*), judge, juror

iūdicium, -ī (*n.*), judgment, verdict, trial, court

iūdicō, -āre, -āvī, -ātus, judge, decide

iugum, -ī (*n.*), yoke, ridge

iungō, -ere, -iūnxī, -iūnctus, join

iūrō, -āre, -āvī, -ātus, swear

iūs, iūris (*n.*), right, law

iussus, -ūs (*m.*), order

iūstitia, -ae (*f.*), justice

iūstus, -a, -um, just, proper

iuvenis, -e, young

iuvenis, -is (*m.*), young man

iuvō, -āre, iūvī, iūtus, help, aid

Kalendae, -ārum (*f. pl.*), Calends

labor, -ōris (*m.*), work, task

labōrō, -āre, -āvī, -ātus, work

lacrima, -ae (*f.*), tear

lapis, -idis (*m.*), stone

lātitūdō, -inis (*f.*), width

latus, -eris (*n.*), side

lātus, -a, -um, wide

laudō, -āre, -āvī, -ātus, praise

laus, laudis (*f.*), praise, merit

lēgātus, -ī (*m.*), lieutenant, envoy

legiō, -ōnis (*f.*), legion

legō, -ere, lēgī, lēctus, choose, read

lēnis, -e, gentle, mild, smooth

levis, -e, light, mild

lēx, lēgis (*f.*), law

libenter, gladly, willingly

liber, -brī (*m.*), book

līber, -era, -erum, free

līberī, -ōrum (*m. pl.*), children

līberō, -āre, -āvī, -ātus, free

lībertās, -ātis (*f.*), liberty, freedom

licet, licēre, licuit, it is permitted, one may

lingua, -ae (*f.*), tongue, language

littera, -ae (*f.*), letter (of the alphabet); (*pl.*), communication

lītus, -oris (*n.*), shore

locō, -āre, -āvī, -ātus, place

locuplēs, rich

locus, -ī (*m.*); (*pl.*), loca, -ōrum (*n.*), place

longus, -a, -um, long

loquor, -quī, -cūtus sum, speak, say

lūdō, -ere, lūsī, lūsus, play

lūdus, -ī (*m.*), game, school

lūmen, -inis (*n.*), light

lūna, -ae (*f.*), moon

lūx, lūcis (*f.*), light

magis, more

magister, -trī (*m.*), teacher

magistrātus, -ūs (*m.*), magistrate, office

magnitūdō, -inis (*f.*), greatness, size

magnopere, greatly

magnus, -a, -um, great, large

maiōrēs, -um (*m. pl.*), ancestors

maleficium, -ī (*n.*), evil deed, crime

mālō, mālle, māluī, prefer

malus, -a, -um, bad, evil

mandō, -āre, -āvī, -ātus, entrust, order

maneō, -ēre, mānsī, mānsūrus, remain, stay

manifestus, -a, -um, clear, obvious

manus, -ūs (*f.*), hand, band

mare, -is (*n.*), sea

maritimus, -a, -um, maritime

māter, -tris (*f.*), mother
māteria, -ae (*f.*), timber
mātūrus, -a, -um, mature, ripe, early
maximē, most of all, especially
medius, -a, -um, middle (of)
meminī, -isse, remember
memoria, -ae (*f.*), memory
mēns, mentis (*f.*), mind
mēnsa, -ae (*f.*), table
mēnsis, -is (*m.*), month
mercātor, -ōris (*m.*), trader, merchant
mereō, -ēre, -uī, -itus, deserve, earn
merīdiēs, -ēī (*m.*), noon
metuō, -ere, -uī, fear
metus, -ūs (*m.*), fear
meus, -a, -um, my, mine
mīles, -itis (*m.*), soldier
mīlitāris, -e, military
mīlle, one thousand
mīror, -ārī, -ātus sum, wonder at, admire
miser, -era, -erum, wretched, poor
mittō, -ere, mīsī, missus, send
modo, only
modus, -ī (*m.*), manner, way
moenia, -ium (*n. pl.*), walls, fortifications
moneō, -ēre, -uī, -itus, advise, warn
mōns, montis (*m.*), mountain
mōnstrō, -āre, -āvī, -ātus, show
monumentum, -ī (*n.*), monument, record
mora, -ae (*f.*), delay
morbus, -ī (*m.*), disease
morior, morī, mortuus sum, die
moror, -ārī, -ātus sum, delay, stay
mors, mortis (*f.*), death

mortālis, -e, mortal
mōs, mōris (*m.*), custom
mōtus, -ūs (*m.*), movement, activity
moveō, -ēre, mōvī, mōtus, move
mox, soon, presently
mulier, -eris (*f.*), woman
multitūdō, -inis (*f.*), multitude, crowd
multus, -a, -um, much, many
mūnicipium, -ī (*n.*), free town
mūniō, -īre, -īvī, -ītus, fortify, build
mūnītiō, -ōnis (*f.*), fortification
mūrus, -ī (*m.*), wall
mūtō, -āre, -āvī, -ātus, change

nam, for
nancīscor, -ī, nactus sum, find, obtain
nārrō, -āre, -āvī, -ātus, tell, relate
nāscor, nāscī, nātus sum, be born
nātiō, -ōnis (*f.*), nation, tribe
nātūra, -ae (*f.*), nature
nauta, -ae (*m.*), sailor
nāvālis, -e, naval
nāvigium, -ī, boat
nāvigō, -āre, -āvī, -ātus, sail
nāvis, -is (*f.*), ship
-ne (sign of a question)
nē, in order not
nē . . . quidem, not even
necessārius, -a, -um, necessary
necesse, necessary
necō, -āre, -āvī, -ātus, kill
nefārius, -a, -um, impious, wicked
neglegō, -ere, -lēxī, -lēctus, neglect, disregard
negō, -āre, -āvī, -ātus, deny, say no
negōtium, -ī (*n.*), business, task
nēmō, nūllīus, no one

neque (nec), and not, nor; neque
... neque, neither ... nor
nesciō, -īre, -īvī, not know
neuter, -tra, -trum, neither (of
two)
nihil, nothing
nisi, if not, unless
nōbilis, -e, noble, famous
nōbilitās, -ātis (f.), nobility,
fame
noceō, -ēre, -uī, -itūrus, harm
nocturnus, -a, -um, nocturnal
nōlō, nōlle, nōluī, not want, be
unwilling
nōmen, -inis (n.), name
nōminō, -āre, -āvī, -ātus, name,
call
nōn, not
Nōnae, -ārum (f. pl.), Nones
nōndum, not yet
nōnne, not?
nōnus, -a, -um, ninth
nōscō, -ere, nōvī, nōtus, learn,
find out, know
noster, -tra, -trum, our, ours
nōtus, -a, -um, known, famous
novem, nine
novus, -a, -um, new, strange
nox, noctis (f.), night
nūllus, -a, -um, no, none
num, whether (also used in questions expecting a negative answer)
numerus, -ī (m.), number
numquam, never
nunc, now
nūntiō, -āre, -āvī, -ātus, announce
nūntius, -ī (m.), messenger, message
nūper, recently

ob (with acc.), on account of
obscūrus, -a, -um, obscure, dark

obses, obsidis (m.), hostage
obsideō, -ēre, -sēdī, -sessus, be-
siege
obtineō, -ēre, -tinuī, -tentus, hold,
possess
occāsus, -ūs (m.), setting, downfall
occīdō, -ere, -cīdī, -cīsus, kill
occultō, -āre, -āvī, -ātus, hide
occultus, -a, -um, hidden, secret
occupō, -āre, -āvī, -ātus, seize
occurrō, -ere, -currī, -cursus, run
against, meet
ōceanus, -ī (m.), ocean
octāvus, -a, -um, eighth
octō, eight
oculus, -ī (m.), eye
ōdī, ōdisse, hate
odium, -ī (n.), hatred
officium, -ī (n.), duty, service
ōlim, once, formerly
ōmen, -inis (n.), omen
omittō, -ere, -mīsī, -missus, pass
over, disregard
omnīnō, altogether, in all
omnis, -e, all, every
onus, -eris (n.), burden, load
opīniō, -ōnis (f.), opinion, belief,
expectation
opīnor, -ārī, -ātus sum, believe,
imagine, judge
oportet, -ēre, -uit, it is necessary
oppidum, -ī (n.), town
opportūnus, -a, -um, suitable, appropriate
opprimō, -ere, -pressī, -pressus,
crush, subdue
oppugnō, -āre, -āvī, -ātus, attack
ops, opis (f.), help; (pl.), wealth,
resources
optimātēs, -ium (m. pl.), aristocrats, nobility
optō, -āre, -āvī, -ātus, wish, desire

opus, operis (*n.*), work
ōra, -ae (*f.*), shore
ōrātiō, -ōnis (*f.*), speech
ōrātor, -ōris (*m.*), orator
orbis, -is (*m.*), circle; **orbis terrae** or **terrārum**, world
ōrdō, -inis (*m.*), order, rank
orior, orīrī, ortus sum, rise
ōrnāmentum, -ī (*n.*), decoration, distinction
ōrnō, -āre, -āvī, -ātus, adorn, equip, honor
ōrō, -āre, -āvī, -ātus, beg, plead
ostendō, -ere, -dī, -tus, show, display
ōtium, -ī (*n.*), leisure, quiet, peace

pācō, -āre, -āvī, -ātus, subdue
paene, almost
pār, equal, like
parātus, -a, -um, prepared, ready
parēns, -entis (*m.*), parent
pāreō, -ēre, -uī, -itūrus, obey
parō, -āre, -āvī, -ātus, prepare
pars, partis (*f.*), part
partim, partly
parvus, -a, -um, small, little
passus, -ūs (*m.*), pace, step
patefaciō, -ere, -fēcī, -factus, lay open, expose
pateō, -ēre, -uī, lie open, extend
pater, -tris (*m.*), father
patior, patī, passus sum, suffer, allow
patria, -ae (*f.*), country, native land
patrius, -a, -um, fatherly, ancestral
paucī, -ae, -a, few
paulātim, little by little, gradually
paulō, a little

paulum, a little
pāx, pācis (*f.*), peace
pecūnia, -ae (*f.*), money.
pedes, -itis (*m.*), infantryman
pellō, -ere, pepulī, pulsus, drive, rout
pendeō, -ēre, pependī, depend, hang
per (*with acc.*), through
percipiō, -ere, -cēpī, -ceptus, perceive, feel, get
perditus, -a, -um, lost, desperate, corrupt
perdō, -ere, -didī, -ditus, lose, destroy
pereō, -īre, -iī, -itūrus, perish, die
perferō, -ferre, -tulī, -lātus, bring, endure
perficiō, -ere, -fēcī, -fectus, finish
perīculōsus, -a, -um, dangerous
perīculum, -ī (*n.*), danger
perītus, -a, -um, skilled, experienced
permittō, -ere, -mīsī, -missus, allow, entrust
permoveō, -ēre, -mōvī, -mōtus, move deeply, arouse
perniciēs, -ēī (*f.*), ruin, destruction
perniciōsus, -a, -um, destructive, dangerous
perpetuus, -a, -um, continuous, lasting
persequor, -sequī, -secūtus sum, pursue
perspiciō, -ere, -spexī, -spectus, notice, perceive
persuādeō, -ēre, -suāsī, -suāsūrus, persuade
perterreō, -ēre, -uī, -itus, terrify
pertimēscō, -ere, -timuī, become frightened
pertineō, -ēre, -tinuī, reach, ex-

tend, pertain

perturbō, -āre, -āvī, -ātus, throw into confusion

perveniō, -īre, -vēnī, -ventus, arrive

pēs, pedis (*m.*), foot

pestis, -is (*f.*), plague, destruction, ruin

petō, -ere, -īvī, -ītus, seek, ask

placeō, -ēre, -uī, -itus, please

plēbs, plēbis (*f.*), common people

plēnus, -a, -um, full, abounding in

plērīque, -aeque, -aque, very many, most

poena, -ae (*f.*), punishment

poēta, -ae (*m.*), poet

polliceor, -ērī, -icitus sum, promise

pōnō, -ere, posuī, positus, put, place

pōns, pontis (*m.*), bridge

pontifex, -ficis (*m.*), priest

populārēs, -ium (*m. pl.*), popular party

populus, -ī (*m.*), people

porta, -ae (*f.*), gate

portō, -āre, -āvī, -ātus, carry

portus, -ūs (*m.*), harbor, port

possum, posse, potuī, be able, can

post (*with acc.*), after, behind

posteā, afterwards

posteritās, -ātis (*f.*), posterity, future

posterus, -a, -um, following, next

postquam, after

postrīdiē, the next day

postulō, -āre, -āvī, -ātus, demand

potēns, powerful

potestās, -ātis (*f.*), power

potior, -īrī, -ītus sum, take possession of

potius, rather

praecipiō, -ere, -cēpī, -ceptus, direct, instruct

praeclārus, -a, -um, very famous, brilliant

praeditus, -a, -um, endowed, gifted

praeficiō, -ere, -fēcī, -fectus, put in charge of

praemittō, -ere, -mīsī, -missus, send ahead

praemium, -ī (*n.*), reward, prize

praenōmen, -inis (*n.*), first name

praesēns, present, at hand, favorable

praesertim, especially

praesidium, -ī (*n.*), protection, guard

praestō, -āre, -stitī, -stitūrus, excel

praesum, -esse, -fuī, -futūrus, be in command

praeter, beyond, except, besides

praetereā, besides

praetereō, -īre, -iī, -itus, pass over, omit

praetermittō, -ere, -mīsī, -missus, pass over, omit

praetor, -ōris (*m.*), praetor, judge

prehendō, -ere, -ī, -hēnsus, seize, grasp

premō, -ere, pressī, pressus, press, oppress

pretium, -ī (*n.*), price

prīdem, long ago

prīdiē, the day before

prīmō, at first

prīmum, first

prīmus, -a, -um, first

prīnceps, -ipis (*m.*), chief, leader

prīncipātus, -ūs (*m.*), leadership

prior, prius, former, previous

priusquam, before

prīvātus, -a, -um, private, personal

prīvātus, -ī (m.), private citizen

prō (with abl.), before, for

probō, -āre, -āvī, -ātus, prove, approve

prōcēdō, -ere, -cessī, -cessūrus, advance

prōcurrō, -ere, -currī, -cursūrus, run forward

prōdūcō, -ere, -dūxī, -ductus, lead forth

proelium, -ī (n.), battle

profectō, certainly, indeed

proficīscor, -ficīscī, -fectus sum, set out

profiteor, -ērī, -fessus sum, confess, declare, register

prōgredior, -gredī, -gressus sum, proceed, advance

prohibeō, -ēre, -uī, -itus, hold back, prevent

prope, near

properō, -āre, -āvī, -ātus, hurry

propinquus, -a, -um, near, neighboring

prōpōnō, -ere, -posuī, -positus, set forth, offer

propter (with acc.), because of, on account of

propereā, for this reason

prōvideō, -ēre, -vīdī, -vīsus, foresee, provide, take care

prōvincia, -ae (f.), province

proximus, -a, -um, nearest, next, last

prūdēns, foreseeing, wise

pūblicus, -a, -um, public

puella, -ae (f.), girl

puer, puerī (m.), boy

pugna, -ae (f.), fight, battle

pugnō, -āre, -āvī, -ātus, fight

pulcher, -chra, -chrum, beautiful

putō, -āre, -āvī, -ātus, think

quaerō, quaerere, -sīvī, -sītus, seek, ask

quaestor, -ōris (m.), quaestor

quālis, -e, of what kind, such as

quam, how, as, than

quamquam, although, and yet

quandō, when, at any time

quantus, -a, -um, how great

quārē, for what reason, why

quārtus, -a, -um, fourth

quasi, as if, so to speak

quattuor, four

-que, and

queror, -ī, questus sum, complain

quī, quae, quod, who, which, that

quīdam, quaedam, quoddam, a certain

quidem, indeed, in fact

quiēs, -ētis (f.), quiet, rest

quiēscō, -ere, quiēvī, quiētus, be quiet, rest

quīn, that not, but that, from

quīnque, five

quīntus, -a, -um, fifth

Quirītēs, -ium (m. pl.), fellow citizens

quis, quid, who, what

quisquam, quicquam, anyone, anything

quisque, quidque, each one, each thing

quō, where

quod, because

quod sī, but if

quondam, once, formerly

quoniam, since

quoque, also, even

quot, how many, as many as

quotiēns, how often, as often as

ratiō, -ōnis (f.), method, plan,

reason

recēns, recent, fresh

recipiō, -ere, -cēpī, -ceptus, take back, receive; sē recipiō, retreat

recordor, -ārī, -ātus sum, call to mind

reddō, -ere, -didī, -ditus, give back, return

redeō, -īre, -iī, -itūrus, go back, return

reditus, -ūs (m.), return

redūcō, -ere, -dūxī, -ductus, lead back

rēgīna, -ae (f.), queen

regiō, -ōnis (f.), region, district

rēgius, -a, -um, royal

rēgnō, -āre, -āvī, -ātus, reign

rēgnum, -ī (n.), kingdom, rule

regō, -ere, rēxī, rēctus, rule, guide

religiō, -ōnis (f.), religious scruples, sacredness

relinquō, -ere, -līquī, -lictus, leave, abandon

reliquus, -a, -um, remaining, rest (of)

remaneō, -ēre, -mānsī, -mānsūrus, remain

remittō, -ere, -mīsī, -missus, send back

removeō, -ēre, -mōvī, -mōtus, move back, withdraw

renūntiō, -āre, -āvī, -ātus, bring back word, report

repellō, -ere, reppulī, repulsus, drive back

reperiō, -īre, repperī, repertus, find, discover

repudiō, -āre, -āvī, -ātus, reject, scorn

requīrō, -ere, -quīsīvī, -quīsītus, seek, miss

rēs, reī (f.), thing, matter

rēs pūblica, reī pūblicae (f.), republic, government

resistō, -ere, -stitī, resist, oppose

respondeō, -ēre, -spondī, -spōnsus, reply, answer

retardō, -āre, -āvī, -ātus, check, hinder

retineō, -ēre, -tinuī, -tentus, hold back, keep

revertō, -ere, -tī, -sus, return

revocō, -āre, -āvī, -ātus, call back, recall

rēx, rēgis (m.), king

rīdeō, -ēre, rīsī, rīsus, laugh

rīpa, -ae (f.), bank of a river

rogō, -āre, -āvī, -ātus, ask, beg

rostrum, -i (n.), beak of a ship; (pl.), rostrum, platform

rūrsus, again

rūs, rūris, (n.), country

sacer, -cra, -crum, sacred

sacrificium, -ī (n.), sacrifice

saepe, often

sagitta, -ae (f.), arrow

salūs, -ūtis (f.), safety, welfare, health

salvus, -a, -um, safe, sound

sānctus, -a, -um, sacred

sapiēns, wise

sapiēns, -entis (m.), philosopher

satis, enough

saxum, -ī (n.), rock, stone

scelus, -eris (n.), crime

scientia, -ae (f.), knowledge

sciō, -īre, -īvī, -ītus, know

scrībō, -ere, scrīpsī, scrīptus, write

scrīptor, -ōris (m.), writer

scūtum, -ī (n.), shield

sēcernō, -ere, -crēvī, -crētus, separate, distinguish

secundus, -a, -um, second
sed, but
sedeō, -ēre, sēdī, sessūrus, sit
sēdēs, -is (f.), seat, abode
semper, always
senātor, -ōris (m.), senator
senātus, -ūs (m.), senate
senectūs, -ūtis (f.), old age
senex, senis (m.), old man
sēnsus, -ūs (m.), feeling
sententia, -ae (f.), feeling, opinion
sentiō, -īre, sēnsī, sēnsus, feel, perceive
septem, seven
septimus, -a, -um, seventh
sequor, sequī, secūtus sum, follow
sermō, -ōnis (m.), talk, conversation
serviō, -īre, -īvī, -ītus, be a slave, serve
servō, -āre, -āvī, -ātus, save, keep
servus, -ī (m.), slave
sevēritās, -ātis (f.), severity, harshness
sex, six
sextus, -a, -um, sixth
sī, if
sīc, thus, so
sīca, -ae (f.), dagger
sīcut, just as, as
signum, -ī (n.), signal, standard, sign
silentium, -ī (n.), silence
silva, -ae (f.), forest
similis, -e, similar, like
simul, at the same time; simul atque (ac), as soon as
simulācrum, -ī (n.), image, likeness
sīn, but if
sine (with abl.), without

singulāris, -e, unique, remarkable, unusual
singulī, -ae, -a, one at a time
sinister, -tra, -trum, left
sīve (seu), or if, or
societās, -ātis (f.), alliance
socius, -ī (m.), ally, comrade
sōl, sōlis (m.), sun
soleō, -ēre, solitus sum, be accustomed
sōlum, only
sōlus, -a, -um, alone, only
solvō, -ere, solvī, solūtus, loosen, set sail
somnium, -ī (n.), dream
somnus, -ī (m.), sleep
soror, -ōris (f.), sister
spatium, -ī (n.), space, distance
speciēs, -ēī (f.), appearance, sight
spectō, -āre, -āvī, -ātus, look at
spērō, -āre, -āvī, -ātus, hope
spēs, speī (f.), hope
spīritus, -ūs (m.), spirit, breath
statim, immediately, at once
statuō, -ere, statuī, statūtus, station, decide
stō, -āre, stetī, stātūrus, stand
studeō, -ēre, studuī, be eager for, desire
studium, -ī (n.), eagerness, enthusiasm, zeal
stultus, -a, -um, foolish, stupid
sub (with acc. and abl.), under
subitō, suddenly
subsequor, -sequī, -secūtus sum, follow closely
subsidium, -ī (n.), aid, support
suēscō, -ere, suēvī, suētus, become accustomed
suī, of himself, herself, itself, themselves
sum, esse, fuī, futūrus, be

summus, -a, -um, highest, top of

sūmō, -ere, sūmpsī, sūmptus, take

super, above

superbus, -a, -um, haughty, proud

superior, -ius, higher, upper

superō, -āre, -āvī, -ātus, defeat, surpass

superus, -a, -um, upper, above

supplex, suppliant, begging

supplicātiō, -ōnis (f.), thanksgiving

supplicium, -ī (n.), punishment, torture

suprā, above

suscipiō, -ere, -cēpī, -ceptus, undertake

suspīciō, -ōnis (f.), suspicion

sustineō, -ēre, -tinuī, -tentus, hold up, withstand

suus, -a, -um, his (her, its, their) own

tabula, -ae (f.), tablet, record

taceō, -ēre, -uī, -itus, be silent

tālis, -e, such

tam, so

tamen, however, still, yet, nevertheless

tandem, at last, finally

tangō, -ere, tetigī, tāctus, touch

tantus, -a, -um, so great, so much

tardō, -āre, -āvī, -ātus, slow up, stop

tardus, -a, -um, slow, late

tēctum, -ī (n.), roof, home

tegō, -ere, tēxī, tēctus, cover, protect

tēlum, -ī (n.), weapon

temere, rashly, without reason

temeritās, -ātis (f.), rashness

temperantia, -ae (f.), self-control

tempestās, -ātis (f.), weather, storm

templum, -ī (n.), temple

temptō, -āre, -āvī, -ātus, try

tempus, -oris (n.), time

teneō, -ēre -uī, hold, keep

tenuis, -e, thin, humble

tergum, -ī (n.), back

terra, -ae (f.), land

terreō, -ēre, -uī, -itus, frighten

terror, -ōris (m.), fright

tertius, -a, -um, third

testāmentum, -ī (n.), will

testis, -is (m.), witness

timeō, -ēre, -uī, fear, be afraid of

timor, -ōris (m.), fear

toga, -ae (f.), toga

togātus, -a, -um, wearing the toga

tollō, -ere, sustulī, sublātus, raise

tot, so many

tōtus, -a, -um, whole, entire

trādō, -ere, -didī, -ditus, surrender, hand over

trādūcō, -ere, -dūxī, -ductus, lead across

trahō, -ere, trāxī, trāctus, draw, drag

trāns (with acc.), across

trānseō, -īre, -iī, -itūrus, go across

trānsportō, -āre, -āvī, -ātus, carry across

trēs, tria, three

tribūnus, -ī (m.), tribune

tribuō, -ere, -uī, -ūtus, assign, bestow

!rīstis, -e, sad

triumphō, -āre, -āvī, -ātus, celebrate a triumph

triumphus, -ī (m.), triumph

tū, you

tuba, -ae (f.), trumpet

tum, then, at that time
turpis, -e, disgraceful
turris, -is (f.), tower
tūtus, -a, ·um, safe, secure
tuus, -a, -um, your, yours

ubi, where
ūllus, -a, -um, any
ulterior, -ius, farther
ultimus, -a, -um, farthest, last
umquam, ever
ūnā, together
unde, whence, from which
undique, from everywhere
ūniversus, -a, -um, all, whole
ūnus, -a, -um, one
urbs, urbis (f.), city
ūsque, up to, as far as
ūsus, -ūs (m.), use, experience, practice
ut, utī, in order to, that, as
uter, -tra, -trum, which (of two)
uterque, utraque, utrumque, each (of two), both
ūtilis, -e, useful
ūtilitās, -ātis (f.), usefulness, advantage
ūtor, ūtī, ūsus sum, use
uxor, -ōris (f.), wife

vacuus, -a, -um, empty, free
vādō, -ere, go
vagor, -ārī, -ātus sum, wander
valeō, -ēre, -uī, -itūrus, be well, be strong
validus, -a, -um, strong, vigorous
vallēs, -is (f.), valley
vāllum, -ī (n.), wall, rampart
varietās, -ātis (f.), variety
varius, -a, -um, various, different
vāstō, -āre, -āvī, -ātus, destroy, lay waste
vehemēns, violent, vigorous, strong

vehō, -ere, vexī, vectus, carry
vel, or, even
veniō, -īre, vēnī, ventus, come
ventus, -ī (m.), wind
verbum, -ī (n.), word
vereor, -ērī, -itus sum, fear, respect
vēritās, -ātis (f.), truth
vērō, in truth, indeed
versor, -ārī, -ātus sum, be engaged in, remain
versus, -ūs (m.), verse
vertō, -ere, -tī, -sus, turn
vērum, but
vērus, -a, -um, true, real
vesper, -erī (m.), evening, dusk
vester, -tra, -trum, your, yours
vēstīgium, -ī (n.), footprint, trace
vetus, old, former
via, -ae (f.), way, road, street
vīcīnus, -a, -um, neighboring
vīcīnus, -ī (m.), neighbor
victor, -ōris (m.), conqueror, victor
victōria, -ae (f.), victory
vīcus, -ī (m.), village
videō, -ēre, vīdī, vīsus, see
videor, -ērī, vīsus sum, seem
vigilia, -ae (f.), watch, guard
vigilō, -āre, -āvī, -ātus, keep awake, watch
vīgintī, twenty
vīlla, -ae (f.), country house, farm
vincō, -ere, vīcī, victus, conquer
vinculum, -ī (n.), chain
vīnum, -ī (n.), wine
violō, -āre, -āvī, -ātus, wrong, dishonor
vir, virī (m.), man
virtūs, -ūtis (f.), courage, valor

vīs, vīs (*f.*), force, violence, strength

vīta, -ae (*f.*), life

vītō, -āre, -āvī, -ātus, avoid, escape

vīvō, -ere, vīxī, vīctūrus, live

vīvus, -a, -um, alive, living

vix, hardly, with difficulty

vocō, -āre, -āvī, -ātus, call

volō, velle, voluī, want, wish

voluntās, -ātis (*f.*), will, wish

voluptās, -ātis (*f.*), pleasure

vōx, vōcis (*f.*), voice, word

vulnerō, -āre, -āvī, -ātus, wound

vulnus, -eris (*n.*), wound

EXERCISES

A. Match each word in column *A* with its nearest equivalent in column *B*.

Column A	Column B
1. coniūrātiō	*a.* once
2. fīdus	*b.* treaty
3. perdō	*c.* witness
4. quondam	*d.* conspirators
5. sīcut	*e.* attack
6. tenuis	*f.* perish
7. coniūrātī	*g.* but if
8. vītō	*h.* lose
9. foedus	*i.* conspiracy
10. sīn	*j.* since
11. adorior	*k.* live
12. testis	*l.* faithful
13. vīvō	*m.* avoid
14. pereō	*n.* thin
15. quoniam	*o.* just as

B. Which word in each group does *not* belong? Explain why.

1. timeō	taceō	vereor	metuō
2. adversārius	hostis	adventus	inimīcus
3. ēgregius	īnsignis	praeclārus	perniciōsus
4. accidō	accēdō	adeō	appropinquō
5. hinc	hūc	inde	iste
6. adulēscēns	ingēns	iuvenis	puer
7. comitium	cūria	cōntiō	orbis
8. audācia	clēmentia	mūnicipium	cupiditās
9. frūctus	dēlūbrum	pontifex	sacrificium
10. ferrum	scelus	gladius	sīca

C. Select the Latin word that best completes each of the following sentences:

1. A weary person would long for (a) odium (b) onus (c) ōtium (d) culpa.
2. To pass a measure, the Senate would have to (a) dēcernere (b) aperīre (c) augēre (d) aggredī.
3. A person could easily be injured by a thrown (a) ōmen (b) ops (c) iūdicium (d) lapis.
4. Cicero would have been relieved if Catiline had been (a) cōnscrīptus (b) excitātus (c) necātus (d) requīsītus.
5. A doctor would be called in if a patient had a (an) (a) ōra (b) morbus (c) quiēs (d) sēdēs.
6. A moral person would avoid being (a) improbus (b) manifestus (c) mātūrus (d) perītus.
7. In order to bind a prisoner, a guard would need a (a) comes (b) cūstōs (c) doctrīna (d) vinculum.
8. It is normal to want to be happy (a) ferē (b) quasi (c) aliquandō (d) quālis.
9. At a funeral, most people are (a) turpis (b) trīstis (c) occultus (d) locuplēs.
10. It is unpleasant to be in a (a) tēctum (b) carcer (c) āra (d) lūmen.

D. Choose the word that is most nearly equivalent in meaning to the capitalized word.

1. PERPETUUS — apertus, aeternus, necessārius, clārus
2. OMITTŌ — praetereō, nōscō, occurrō, probō
3. FERĒ — tot, num, sīn, paene
4. PERNICIĒS — voluptās, mōtus, exitium, invidia
5. DĒFICIŌ — discēdō, timeō, dēsum, dēserō
6. METUS — aedēs, aeger, timor, onus
7. LŪMEN — ops, quiēs, sēdēs, lūx
8. DĒLŪBRUM — templum, rūs, triumphus, vīcīnus
9. QUOQUE — quasi, etiam, sīcut, sīve
10. VĀDŌ — vehō, tangō, eō, soleō

E. Choose the English word that best translates the Latin word.

1. TŪTUS — whole, your, safe, tower
2. AURIS — ear, gold, silver, iron
3. IACEŌ — throw, lie, injure, be silent
4. PLĒNUS — plane, plain, most, full

5.	POTIUS	powerful, rather, able, long ago
6.	TANGŌ	touch, dance, cover, assign
7.	VETUS	soldier, verse, old, various
8.	QUONIAM	once, that not, also, since
9.	ĀRA	shore, altar, art, anger
10.	IUVŌ	help, swear, order, join
11.	FACILITĀS	luck, crime, ease, fate
12.	INDICIUM	judgment, testimony, ability, envy
13.	COMPERIŌ	compare, seize, compete, discover
14.	SOLEŌ	lonely, alone, be accustomed, be lacking
15.	INGENIUM	talent, huge, race, family
16.	SERVIŌ	save, be a slave, severe, talk
17.	QUEROR	seek, for what reason, rest, complain
18.	OMNĪNŌ	altogether, every, omen, burden
19.	MĀLŌ	evil, evil deed, prefer, want
20.	MEMINĪ	no one, remember, deserve, walls
21.	ŪSQUE	whence, up to, ever, which
22.	RĪDEŌ	laugh, give back, go back, lead back
23.	NŪPER	wife, above, recently, whether
24.	VEHŌ	go, wander, harm, carry
25.	ŌRNŌ	beg, know, adorn, wish
26.	SIMULĀCRUM	free town, image, will, decoration
27.	NUM	for, none, whether, no
28.	SUPPLEX	punishment, thanksgiving, begging, haughty
29.	PRAECIPIŌ	perceive, omit, put in charge, direct
30.	CRĀS	tomorrow, today, always, never
31.	VĒSTĪGIUM	garment, evening, footprint, truth
32.	POTIOR	be able, place, harbor, take possession of
33.	STULTUS	safe, foolish, upper, useful
34.	INVIDIA	watch, envy, neighbor, unseen
35.	ĪRĀSCOR	be jealous, enjoy, be angry, enclose
36.	CARCER	around, senate house, altar, prison
37.	IŪCUNDUS	young, just, pleasant, cruel
38.	TEGŌ	cover, rule, read, touch
39.	PENDEŌ	lose, perish, hang, pay
40.	TEMERE	fear, rashly, timid, thin

Lesson 43. ENGLISH-LATIN VOCABULARY

abandon, relinquō, -ere, -līquī, -lictus

ability, facultās, -ātis (*f.*)

able (be), possum, posse, potuī

about, dē (*with abl.*)

absent (be), absum, -esse, āfuī, āfutūrus

abundance, cōpia, -ae (*f.*)

across, trāns (*with acc.*)

advance, prōgredior, -gredī, -gressus sum

advice, cōnsilium, -ī (*n.*)

advise, moneō, -ēre, -uī, -itus

afraid of (be), timeō, -ēre, -uī

after, post (*with acc.*)

after, postquam

afterwards, posteā

against, contrā (*with acc.*)

age, aetās, -ātis (*f.*)

aid, auxilium, -ī (*n.*)

alarm, commoveō, -ēre, -mōvī, -mōtus

all, omnis, -e

allow, permittō, -ere, -mīsī, -missus

ally, socius, -ī (*m.*)

alone, sōlus, -a, -um

already, iam

also, etiam, quoque

although, cum

always, semper

among, apud (*with acc.*)

and, et

and not, neque (nec)

and so, itaque

announce, nūntiō, -āre, -āvī, -ātus

another, alius, -a, -ud

answer, respondeō, -ēre, -spondī, -spōnsus

any, ūllus, -a, -um

anyone, quisquam

approach, appropinquō, -āre, -āvī, -ātus

Archias, Archiās, -ae (*m.*)

arms, arma, -ōrum (*n. pl.*)

army, exercitus, -ūs (*m.*)

around, circum (*with acc.*)

arouse, permoveō, -ēre, -mōvī, -mōtus

arrival, adventus, -ūs (*m.*)

arrive, perveniō, -īre, -vēnī, -ventus

arrow, sagitta, -ae (*f.*)

art, ars, artis (*f.*)

as, ut, utī

as if, quasi

as soon as, simul atque (ac)

ask, rogō, -āre, -āvī, -ātus

assemble, conveniō, -īre, -vēnī, -ventus

at last, tandem

at once, statim

at the same time, simul

Athens, Athēnae, -ārum (*f. pl.*)

attack, impetus, -ūs (*m.*)

attack, oppugnō, -āre, -āvī, -ātus

authority, auctōritās, -ātis (*f.*)

away (be), absum, -esse, āfuī, āfutūrus

bad, malus, -a, -um

baggage, impedīmenta, -ōrum (*n. pl.*)

bank, rīpa, -ae (*f.*)

barbarian, barbarus, -ī (*m.*)
battle, proelium, -ī (*n.*)
be, sum, esse, fuī, futūrus
be able, possum, posse, potuī
be in command, praesum, -esse,
-fuī, -futūrus
be near, adsum, -esse, -fuī, -futū-
rus
be present, same as be near
bear, ferō, ferre, tulī, lātus
because, quod
because of, propter (*with acc.*)
become, fīō, fierī, factus sum
before, ante (*with acc.*)
beg, ōrō, -āre, -āvī, -ātus
begin, incipiō, -ere, -cēpī, -ceptus
behind, post (*with acc.*)
believe, crēdō, -ere, -idī, -itus
benefit, beneficium, -ī (*n.*)
between, inter (*with acc.*)
body, corpus, -oris (*n.*)
bold, audāx
book, liber, -brī (*m.*)
born (be), nāscor, nāscī, nātus
sum
both . . . and, et . . . et
boundary, fīnis, -is (*m.*)
boy, puer, puerī (*m.*)
brave, fortis, -e
bravely, fortiter
bridge, pōns, pontis (*m.*)
bring, ferō, ferre, tulī, lātus
bring in, īnferō, -ferre, -tulī, illātus
brother, frāter, -tris (*m.*)
build, aedificō, -āre, -āvī, -ātus
burn, incendō, -ere, -cendī, -cēn-
sus
business, negōtium, -ī (*n.*)
but, sed
by, ā, ab (*with abl.*)

Caesar, Caesar, -aris (*m.*)

call, vocō, -āre, -āvī, -ātus
call together, convocō, -āre, -āvī,
-ātus
camp, castra, -ōrum (*n. pl.*)
can, possum, posse, potuī
capture, capiō, -ere, cēpī, captus
carry, portō, -āre, -āvī, -ātus
carry on, gerō, -ere, gessī, gestus
Catiline, Catilīna, -ae (*m.*)
cause, causa, -ae (*f.*)
cavalry, equitātus, -ūs (*m.*)
certain, certus, -a, -um
certain (a), quīdam, quaedam,
quoddam
chance, cāsus, -ūs (*m.*)
chief, prīnceps, -ipis (*m.*)
children, līberī, -ōrum (*m. pl.*)
choose, dēligō, -ere, -lēgī, -lēctus
Cicero, Cicerō, -ōnis (*m.*)
citizen, cīvis, -is (*m.*)
city, urbs, urbis (*f.*)
clear, clārus, -a, -um
cohort, cohors, -tis (*f.*)
collect, cōgō, -ere, coēgī, coāctus
come, veniō, -īre, vēnī, ventus
come together, conveniō, -īre,
-vēnī, -ventus
command, imperium, -ī (*n.*)
command, imperō, -āre, -āvī,
-ātus
commander, imperātor, -ōris
(*m.*)
common, commūnis, -e
common people, plēbs, plēbis
(*f.*)
companion, comes, -itis (*m.*)
compel, cōgō, -ere, coēgī, coāctus
comrade, socius, -ī (*m.*)
concerning, dē (*with abl.*)
confess, cōnfiteor, -ērī, -fessus
sum
conquer, vincō, -ere, vīcī, victus
conqueror, victor, -ōris (*m.*)

conspiracy, coniūrātiō, -ōnis (f.)
conspirators, coniūrātī, -ōrum (m. pl.)
consul, cōnsul, -ulis (m.)
conversation, sermō, -ōnis (m.)
country, patria, -ae (f.)
country house, vīlla, -ae (f.)
courage, virtūs, -ūtis (f.)
crime, scelus, -eris (n.)
crowd, multitūdō, -inis (f.)
crush, opprimō, -ere, -pressī, -pressus
custom, cōnsuētūdō, -inis (f.)

danger, perīculum, -ī (n.)
daughter, fīlia, -ae (f.)
day, diēs, -ēī (m.)
death, mors, mortis (f.)
decide, cōnstituō, -ere, -stituī, -stitūtus
decree, cōnsultum, -ī (n.)
decree, dēcernō, -ere, dēcrēvī, dēcrētus
deed, factum, -ī (n.)
deep, altus, -a, -um
defeat, superō, -āre, -āvī, -ātus
defend, dēfendō, -ere, -fendī, -fēnsus
delay, mora, -ae (f.)
delay, moror, -ārī, -ātus sum
demand, postulō, -āre, -āvī, -ātus
depart, discēdō, -ere, -cessī, -cessūrus
depth, altitūdō, -inis (f.)
desire, cupiditās, -ātis (f.)
desire, cupiō, -ere, -īvī, -ītus
desirous, cupidus, -a, -um
destroy, dēleō, -ēre, -ēvī, -ētus
die, morior, morī, mortuus sum
difficult, difficilis, -e
difficulty, difficultās, -ātis (f.)
display, ostendō, -ere, -dī, -tus

distance, spatium, -ī (n.)
distant (be), absum, -esse, āfuī, āfutūrus
do, faciō, -ere, fēcī, factus
doubt, dubitō, -āre, -āvī, -ātus
down from, dē (with abl.)
drag, trahō, -ere, trāxī, trāctus
draw, same as drag
draw up, īnstruō, -ere, -strūxī, -strūctus
drive, agō, -ere, ēgī, āctus
duty, officium, -ī (n.)

each one, each thing, quisque, quidque
eager for (be), studeō, -ēre, studuī
eagerness, studium, -ī (n.)
ease, facilitās, -ātis (f.)
easily, facile
easy, facilis, -e
eight, octō
eighth, octāvus, -a, -um
either ... or, aut ... aut
encourage, cōnfīrmō, -āre, -āvī, -ātus
end, fīnis, -is (m.)
enemy, hostis, -is (m.)
enlist, cōnscrībō, -ere, -scrīpsī, -scrīptus
enough, satis
enroll, same as enlist
enthusiasm, studium, -ī (n.)
entrust, permittō, -ere, -mīsī, -missus
envoy, lēgātus, -ī (m.)
equal, aequus, -a, -um
especially, maximē
even, etiam; not even, nē ... quidem
every, omnis, -e
evil, malus, -a, -um
example, exemplum, -ī (n.)

exile, exsilium, -ī (n.)
extend, pertineō, -ēre, -tinuī
eye, oculus, -ī (m.)

fair, aequus, -a, -um
faith, fidēs, -eī (f.)
faithful, fīdus, -a, -um
fame, glōria, -ae (f.)
famous, nōbilis, -e
farm, vīlla, -ae (f.)
farmer, agricola, -ae (m.)
father, pater, -tris (m.)
favor, beneficium, -ī (n.)
fear, timor, -ōris (m.)
fear, timeō, -ēre, -uī
feel, sentiō, -īre, sēnsī, sēnsus
feeling, sententia, -ae (f.)
few, paucī, -ae, -a
field, ager, agrī (m.)
fierce, ācer, ācris, ācre
fiercely, ācriter
fifth, quīntus, -a, -um
fight, pugna, -ae (f.)
fight, pugnō, -āre, -āvī, -ātus
finally, tandem
find, inveniō, -īre, -vēnī, -ventus
find out, cognōscō, -ere, -nōvī, -nitus
finish, cōnficiō, -ere, -fēcī, -fectus
fire, ignis, -is (m.)
first, prīmus, -a, -um
five, quīnque
flee, fugiō, -ere, fūgī, fugitūrus
flight, fuga, -ae (f.)
follow, sequor, sequī, secūtus sum
foot, pēs, pedis (m.)
for, enim
for, prō (with abl.)
for a long time, diū
for the sake of, causā
force, vīs, vīs (f.)
forces, cōpiae, -ārum (f. pl.)

foresee, prōvideō, -ēre, -vīdī, -vīsus
forest, silva, -ae (f.)
formerly, anteā
fortify, mūniō, -īre, -īvī, -ītus
fortune, fortūna, -ae (f.)
forum, forum, -ī (n.)
four, quattuor
fourth, quārtus, -a, -um
free, līber, -era, -erum
free, līberō, -āre, -āvī, -ātus
freedom, lībertās, -ātis (f.)
friend, amīcus, -ī (m.)
friendly, amīcus, -a, -um
friendship, amīcitia, -ae (f.)
frighten, terreō, -ēre, -uī, -itus
from, ā, ab (with abl.)
full, plēnus, -a, -um

gate, porta, -ae (f.)
general, imperātor, -ōris (m.)
get together, comparō, -āre, -āvī, -ātus
girl, puella, -ae (f.)
give, dō, dare, dedī, datus
give back, reddō, -ere, -didī, -ditus
glory, glōria, -ae (f.)
go, eō, īre, īvī (iī), itūrus
go back, redeō, -īre, -iī, -itūrus
go out, excēdō, -ere, -cessī, -cessūrus
god, deus, -ī (m.)
good, bonus, -a, -um
good luck, fēlīcitās, -ātis (f.)
government, rēs pūblica, reī pūblicae (f.)
grain, frūmentum, -ī (n.)
Grattius, Grattius, -ī (m.)
great, magnus, -a, -um
greatly, magnopere
greatness, magnitūdō, -inis (f.)
guard, praesidium, -ī (n.)

hand, manus, -ūs (*f.*)
hand over, trādō, -ere, -didī, -ditus
happen, fīō, fierī, factus sum
happy, fēlīx
harbor, portus, -ūs (*m.*)
hard, difficilis, -e
harm, noceō, -ēre, -uī, -itūrus
hasten, contendō, -ere, -tendī, -tentus
have, habeō, -ēre, -uī, -itus
he (she, it), is, ea, id
head, caput, -itis (*n.*)
health, salūs, -ūtis (*f.*)
hear, audiō, -īre, -īvī, -ītus
heavy, gravis, -e
height, altitūdō, -inis (*f.*)
help, auxilium, -ī (*n.*)
hem in, contineō, -ēre, -tinuī, -tentus
hesitate, dubitō, -āre, -āvī, -ātus
high, altus, -a, -um
hill, collis, -is (*m.*)
hindrance, impedīmentum, -ī (*n.*)
his (her, its, their) own, suus, -a, -um
hold, teneō, -ēre, -uī
hold back, prohibeō, -ēre, -uī, -itus
hold together, contineō, -ēre, -tinuī, -tentus
hold up, sustineō, -ēre, -tinuī, -tentus
home, domus, -ūs (*f.*)
honor, honor, -ōris (*m.*)
hope, spēs, speī (*f.*)
hope, spērō, -āre, -āvī, -ātus
horn, cornū, -ūs (*n.*)
horse, equus, -ī (*m.*)
horseman, eques, -itis (*m.*)
hostage, obses, obsidis (*m.*)
hour, hōra, -ae (*f.*)

house, domus, -ūs (*f.*)
how, quam
how great, quantus, -a, -um
how many, quot
however, tamen
human, hūmānus, -a, -um
hundred, centum
hurl, iaciō, -ere, iēcī, iactus
hurry, properō, -āre, -āvī, -ātus

I, ego, meī
if, sī
if not, nisi
immediately, statim
immortal, immortālis, -e
in, in (*with abl.*)
in fact, quidem
in front of, ante (*with acc.*)
in order not, nē
in order to, ut, utī
in the presence of, apud (*with acc.*)
in truth, vērō
indeed, vērō
inflict, īnferō, -ferre, -tulī, illātus
influence, auctōritās, -ātis (*f.*)
influence, addūcō, -ere, -dūxī, -ductus
injury, iniūria, -ae (*f.*)
injustice, iniūria, -ae (*f.*)
into, in (*with acc.*)
island, īnsula, -ae (*f.*)

join, committō, -ere, -mīsī, -missus; iungō, -ere, iūnxī, iūnctus
journey, iter, itineris (*n.*)
judge, iūdex, -icis (*m.*)
judge, iūdicō, -āre, -āvī, -ātus
judgment, iūdicium, -ī (*n.*)
juror, iūdex, -icis (*m.*)

keep, teneō, -ēre, -uī
kill, interficiō, -ere, -fēcī, -fectus

kind, genus, -eris (*n.*)
kindness, beneficium, -ī (*n.*)
king, rēx, rēgis (*m.*)
kingdom, rēgnum, -ī (*n.*)
know, sciō, -īre, -īvī, -ītus
known, nōtus, -a, -um

lack, inopia, -ae (*f.*)
land, terra, -ae (*f.*)
language, lingua, -ae (*f.*)
large, magnus, -a, -um
law, lēx, lēgis (*f.*)
lay waste, vāstō, -āre, -āvī, -ātus
lead, dūcō, -ere, dūxī, ductus
lead forth, prōdūcō, -ere, -dūxī,
    -ductus
lead to, addūcō, -ere, -dūxī,
    -ductus
leader, dux, ducis (*m.*)
learn, cognōscō, -ere, -nōvī, -nitus
leave, discēdō, -ere, -cessī, -cessū-
    rus
leave behind, relinquō, -ere,
    -līquī, -lictus
left, sinister, -tra, -trum
legion, legiō, -ōnis (*f.*)
let go, dīmittō, -ere, -mīsī,
    -missus
letter (*of alphabet*), littera, -ae
    (*f.*); (*communication*), lit-
    terae, -ārum (*f. pl.*)
level, aequus, -a, -um
liberty, lībertās, -ātis (*f.*)
lieutenant, lēgātus, -ī (*m.*)
life, vīta, -ae (*f.*)
light, levis, -e
light, lūx, lūcis (*f.*)
like, similis, -e
like, amō, -āre, -āvī, -ātus
line of battle, aciēs, -ēī (*f.*)
little, parvus, -a, -um
live, vīvō, -ere, vīxī, vīctūrus
long, longus, -a, -um

long time, diū
look at, spectō, -āre, -āvī, -ātus
lose, āmittō, -ere, -mīsī, -missus
lost, perditus, -a, -um
love, amō, -āre, -āvī, -ātus
luck, fortūna, -ae (*f.*)

make, faciō, -ere, fēcī, factus
man, vir, virī (*m.*)
manner, modus, -ī (*m.*)
many, multī, -ae, -a
march, iter, itineris (*n.*)
march, iter facere
maritime, maritimus, -a, -um
master, dominus, -ī (*m.*)
matter, rēs, reī (*f.*)
meanwhile, interim
memory, memoria, -ae (*f.*)
merchant, mercātor, -ōris (*m.*)
message, nūntius, -ī (*m.*)
messenger, nūntius, -ī (*m.*)
method, ratiō, -ōnis (*f.*)
middle (**of**), medius, -a, -um
mile, mīlle passūs (*m.*)
mind, animus, -ī (*m.*)
mine, meus, -a, -um
money, pecūnia, -ae (*f.*)
month, mēnsis, -is (*m.*)
moon, lūna, -ae (*f.*)
more, magis
moreover, autem
most of all, maximē
mother, māter, -tris (*f.*)
mountain, mōns, montis (*m.*)
move, moveō, -ēre, mōvī, mōtus
move back, removeō, -ēre, -mōvī,
    -mōtus
move deeply, permoveō, -ēre,
    -mōvī, -mōtus
much, multus, -a, -um
multitude, multitūdō, -inis (*f.*)
murder, caedēs, -is (*f.*)
my, meus, -a, -um

name, nōmen, -inis (*n.*)
name, appellō, -āre, -āvī, -ātus
nation, nātiō, -ōnis (*f.*)
native land, patria, -ae (*f.*)
nature, nātūra, -ae (*f.*)
near, prope
near, propinquus, -a, -um
nearest, proximus, -a, -um
necessary, necessārius, -a, -um
neighboring, fīnitimus, -a, -um
neither ... nor, neque ... neque
never, numquam
nevertheless, tamen
new, novus, -a, -um
next, proximus, -a, -um
night, nox, noctis (*f.*)
nine, novem
ninth, nōnus, -a, -um
no, none, nūllus, -a, -um
no one, nēmō, nūllīus
noble, nōbilis, -e
noon, merīdiēs, -ēī (*m.*)
nor, neque (nec)
not, nōn
not even, nē ... quidem
nothing, nihil
now, nunc
number, numerus, -ī (*m.*)

offer, prōpōnō, -ere, -posuī, -positus
often, saepe
old man, senex, senis (*m.*)
on, in (*with abl.*)
on account of, propter (*with acc.*)
once, ōlim
one, ūnus, -a, -um
only, sōlus, -a, -um
open, aperiō, -īre, aperuī, apertus
opinion, opīniō, -ōnis (*f.*)
opportunity, facultās, -ātis (*f.*)

oppress, premō, -ere, pressī, pressus
or, aut
orator, ōrātor, -ōris (*m.*)
order, ōrdō, -inis (*m.*)
order, iubeō, -ēre, iussī, iussus
other, alius, -a, -ud
other (the), alter, -era, -erum
ought, dēbeō, -ēre, -uī, -itus
our, ours, noster, -tra, -trum
out of, ē, ex (*with abl.*)
outstanding, ēgregius, -a, -um
owe, dēbeō, -ēre, -uī, -itus

pace, passus, -ūs (*m.*)
pain, dolor, -ōris (*m.*)
part, pars, partis (*f.*)
peace, pāx, pācis (*f.*)
people, populus, -ī (*m.*)
perceive, sentiō, -īre, sēnsī, sēnsus
permitted (it is), licet, licēre, licuit
persuade, persuādeō, -ēre, -suāsī, -suāsūrus
pertain, pertineō, -ēre, -tinuī
place, locus, -ī (*m.*) ; (*pl.*), loca, -ōrum (*n.*)
place, pōnō, -ere, posuī, positus
plain, campus, -ī (*m.*)
plan, cōnsilium, -ī (*n.*)
play, lūdō, -ere, lūsī, lūsus
pleasing, grātus, -a, -um
poet, poēta, -ae (*m.*)
point out, dēmōnstrō, -āre, -āvī, -ātus
Pompey, Pompeius, -ī (*m.*)
poor, miser, -era, -erum
port, portus, -ūs (*m.*)
possess, obtineō, -ēre, -tinuī, -tentus
power, potestās, -ātis (*f.*)
powerful, potēns

praetor, praetor, -ōris (*m.*)
praise, laus, laudis (*f.*)
praise, laudō, -āre, -āvī, -ātus
prefer, mālō, mālle, māluī
prepare, parō, -āre, -āvī, -ātus
prepared, parātus, -a, -um
present (be), adsum, -esse, -fuī,
    -futūrus
preserve, cōnservō, -āre, -āvī,
    -ātus
press, premō, -ere, pressī, pres-
    sus
prestige, dignitās, -ātis (*f.*)
prevent, prohibeō, -ēre, -uī, -itus
previously, anteā
private, prīvātus, -a, -um
prize, praemium, -ī (*n.*)
proceed, prōgredior,   -gredī,
    -gressus sum
promise, polliceor, -ērī, -icitus
    sum
protect, dēfendō, -ere, -fendī,
    -fēnsus
protection, praesidium, -ī (*n.*)
province, prōvincia, -ae (*f.*)
public, pūblicus, -a, -um
punishment, poena, -ae (*f.*)
put, pōnō, -ere, posuī, positus
put in charge of, praeficiō, -ere,
    -fēcī, -fectus
put out, expōnō, -ere, -posuī,
    -positus

queen, rēgīna, -ae (*f.*)
quickly, celeriter

race, genus, -eris (*n.*)
rank, ōrdō, -inis (*m.*)
reach, pertineō, -ēre, -tinuī
read, legō, -ere, lēgī, lēctus
ready, parātus, -a, -um
realize, intellegō, -ere, -lēxī, -lēc-
    tus

reason, causa, -ae (*f.*)
receive, accipiō, -ere, -cēpī, -cep-
    tus
recent, recēns
region, regiō, -ōnis (*f.*)
remain, maneō, -ēre, mānsī,
    mānsūrus
remaining, reliquus, -a, -um
remarkable, ēgregius, -a, -um
reply, respondeō, -ēre, -spondī,
    spōnsus
report, renūntiō, -āre, -āvī, -ātus
republic, rēs pūblica, reī pūblicae
    (*f.*)
rescue, ēripiō, -ere, -uī, -reptus
resist, resistō, -ere, -stitī
rest (of), reliquus, -a, -um
retreat, sē recipiō, -ere, -cēpī,
    -ceptus
return (*give back*), reddō, -ere,
    -didī, -ditus
return (*go back*), redeō, -īre, -iī,
    -itūrus
revolt, dēficiō, -ere, -fēcī, -fectus
reward, praemium, -ī (*n.*)
right, dexter, -tra, -trum
right, iūs, iūris (*n.*)
rise, orior, orīrī, ortus sum
river, flūmen, -inis (*n.*)
road, via, -ae (*f.*)
Roman, Rōmānus, -a, -um
Roman, Rōmānus, -ī (*m.*)
Rome, Rōma, -ae (*f.*)
route, iter, itineris (*n.*)
rule, rēgnum, -ī (*n.*)
rule, regō, -ere, rēxī, rēctus

safe, tūtus, -a, -um
safety, salūs, -ūtis (*f.*)
sail, nāvigō, -āre, -āvī, -ātus
sailor, nauta, -ae (*m.*)
same, īdem, eadem, idem
savage, barbarus, -a, -um

save, servō, -āre, -āvī, -ātus
say, dīcō, -ere, dīxī, dictus
scarcity, inopia, -ae (f.)
sea, mare, -is (n.)
second, secundus, -a, -um
see, videō, -ēre, vīdī, vīsus
seek, petō, -ere, -īvī, -ītus
seem, videor, -ērī, vīsus sum
seize, occupō, -āre, -āvī, -ātus
-self, ipse, ipsa, ipsum
self (reflexive), sē
senate, senātus, -ūs (m.)
senate house, cūria, -ae (f.)
senator, senātor, -ōris (m.)
send, mittō, -ere, -mīsī, missus
send ahead, praemittō, -ere, -mīsī, -missus
send away, dīmittō, -ere, -mīsī, -missus
send back, remittō, -ere, -mīsī, -missus
serious, gravis, -e
set forth, prōpōnō, -ere, -posuī, -positus
set out, proficīscor, -ficīscī, -fectus sum
setting, occāsus, -ūs (m.)
seven, septem
seventh, septimus, -a, -um
several, complūrēs, -a
severe, gravis, -e
sharp, ācer, ācris, ācre
sharply, ācriter
she, ea
ship, nāvis, -is (f.)
short, brevis, -e
show, dēmōnstrō, -āre, -āvī, -ātus
sign, signum, -ī (n.)
signal, signum, -ī (n.)
silent (be), taceō, -ēre, -uī, -itus
similar, similis, -e
since, cum

sister, soror, -ōris (f.)
six, sex
sixth, sextus, -a, -um
size, magnitūdō, -inis (f.)
skill, ars, artis (f.)
slaughter, caedēs, -is (f.)
slave, servus, -ī (m.)
small, parvus, -a, -um
so, ita, tam
so great, so much, tantus, -a, -um
soldier, mīles, -itis (m.)
someone, something, aliquis, -quid
son, fīlius, -ī (m.)
soon, iam, mox
sorrow, dolor, -ōris (m.)
space, spatium, -ī (n.)
speak, dīcō, -ere, dīxī, dictus
speech, ōrātiō, -ōnis (f.)
speed, celeritās, -ātis (f.)
spirit, animus, -ī (m.)
stand, stō, -āre, stetī, stātūrus
standard, signum, -ī (n.)
state, cīvitās, -ātis (f.)
station, cōnstituō, -ere, -stituī, -stitūtus
stay, maneō, -ēre, mānsī, mānsūrus
step, passus, -ūs (m.)
still, tamen
stop, intermittō, -ere, -mīsī, -missus
strange, novus, -a, -um
street, via, -ae (f.)
strength, vīs, vīs (f.)
strengthen, cōnfīrmō, -āre, -āvī, -ātus
strong, fortis, -e
suffer, patior, patī, passus sum
suitable, idōneus, -a, -um
summer, aestās, -ātis (f.)
summon, convocō, -āre, -āvī, -ātus

sun, sōl, sōlis (*m.*)
supply, cōpia, -ae (*f.*)
sure, certus, -a, -um
surpass, superō, -āre, -āvī, -ātus
surrender, trādō, -ere, -didī, -ditus
surround, circumveniō, -īre, -vēnī, -ventus
swift, celer, -eris, -ere
swiftness, celeritās, -ātis (*f.*)
sword, gladius, -ī (*m.*)

take, capiō, -ere, cēpī, captus
talent, ingenium, -ī (*n.*)
task, negōtium, -ī (*n.*)
teach, doceō, -ēre, -uī, -tus
teacher, magister, -trī (*m.*)
tell, dīcō, -ere, dīxī, dictus
temple, templum, -ī (*n.*)
ten, decem
tenth, decimus, -a, -um
terms, condiciō, -ōnis (*f.*)
terrify, perterreō, -ēre, -uī, -itus
territory, fīnēs, -ium (*m. pl.*)
than, quam
that, ille, illa, illud
that, quī, quae, quod
that, ut, utī
then, tum, deinde
there, ibi
therefore, itaque
thing, rēs, reī (*f.*)
think, putō, -āre, -āvī, -ātus
third, tertius, -a, -um
this, hic, haec, hoc
thousand, mīlle
three, trēs, tria
through, per (*with acc.*)
throw, iaciō, -ere, iēcī, iactus
throw out, ēiciō, -ere, -iēcī, -iectus
thus, ita, sīc
time, tempus, -oris (*n.*)

to, toward, ad (*with acc.*)
today, hodiē
toga, toga, -ae (*f.*)
tongue, lingua, -ae (*f.*)
town, oppidum, -ī (*n.*)
trader, mercātor, -ōris (*m.*)
tree, arbor, -oris (*f.*)
trial, iūdicium, -ī (*n.*)
tribe, nātiō, -ōnis (*f.*)
troops, cōpiae, -ārum (*f. pl.*)
true, vērus, -a, -um
trumpet, tuba, -ae (*f.*)
trust, fidēs, -eī (*f.*)
try, temptō, -āre, -āvī, -ātus; cōnor, -ārī, -ātus sum
turn, vertō, -ere, -tī, -sus
twenty, vīgintī
two, duo, duae, duo

unbelievable, incrēdibilis, -e
under, sub (*with acc. and abl.*)
understand, intellegō, -ere, -lēxī, -lēctus
undertake, suscipiō, -ere, -cēpī, -ceptus
unequal, inīquus, -a, -um
uneven, inīquus, -a, -um
unfavorable, inīquus, -a, -um
unfriendly, inimīcus, -a, -um
unusual, singulāris, -e
unless, nisi
until, dum
unusual, singulāris, -e
unwilling (be), nōlō, nōlle, nōluī
upper, superus, -a, -um
urge, hortor, -ārī, -ātus sum
use, ūsus, -ūs (*m.*)
use, ūtor, ūtī, ūsus sum

valor, virtūs, -ūtis (*f.*)
very, ipse, ipsa, ipsum
victor, victor, -ōris (*m.*)
victory, victōria, -ae (*f.*)

village, vīcus, -ī (m.)
violence, vīs, vīs (f.)
violent, vehemēns
voice, vōx, vōcis (f.)

wage, gerō, -ere, gessī, gestus
wait (for), exspectō, -āre, -āvī, -ātus
wall, mūrus, -ī (m.)
want, volō, velle, voluī
war, bellum, -ī (n.)
warn, moneō, -ēre, -uī, -itus
watch, vigilia, -ae (f.)
watch, vigilō, -āre, -āvī, -ātus
water, aqua, -ae (f.)
way, modus, -ī (m.)
we, nōs
weapon, tēlum, -ī (n.)
welfare, salūs, -ūtis (f.)
well, bene
well (be), valeō, -ēre, -uī, -itūrus
what, quid
when, cum
where, ubi
which, quī, quae, quod
while, dum
who, quī, quae, quod; quis
whole, tōtus, -a, -um
why, cūr
wicked, nefārius, -a, -um
wide, lātus, -a, -um
width, lātitūdō, -inis (f.)
wing, cornū, -ūs (n.)

winter, hiems, -emis (f.)
wise, prūdēns
wish, cupiō, -ere, -īvī, -ītus
with, cum (with abl.)
withdraw, removeō, -ēre, -mōvī, -mōtus
without, sine (with abl.)
withstand, sustineō, -ēre, -tinuī, -tentus
witness, testis, -is (m.)
woman, fēmina, -ae (f.)
word, verbum, -ī (n.)
work, labor, -ōris (m.)
work, labōrō, -āre, -āvī, -ātus
worthy, dignus, -a, -um
wound, vulnus, -eris (n.)
wound, vulnerō, -āre, -āvī, -ātus
wretched, miser, -era, -erum
write, scrībō, -ere, scrīpsī, scrīptus
wrong, iniūria, -ae (f.)

year, annus, -ī (m.)
yet, tamen
yield, cēdō, -ere, cessī, cessūrus
you, tū; (pl.), vōs
young man, adulēscēns, -entis (m.)
your, tuus, -a, -um; vester, -tra, -trum
youth, adulēscentia, -ae (f.)

zeal, studium, -ī (n.)

EXERCISES

A. Select the Latin word that best translates the English word.

1. EACH ONE   quisquam, quoque, quisque, quīdam
2. DELAY   moror, morior, mūtō, nāscor
3. HARBOR   porta, pōns, metus, portus
4. EASE   facultās, facilitās, factum, facilis
5. TRY   hortor, sequor, ūtor, cōnor

6. THUS   sī, vel, sīc, tamen
7. TALENT   genus, ingenium, gēns, ingēns
8. DEMAND   pōnō, ostendō, premō, postulō
9. JOIN   iūdicō, iungō, iubeō, incendō
10. THAN   tum, quod, quam, nisi
11. BOLD   fēlīx, audāx, iūcundus, salvus
12. ZEAL   subsidium, auxilium, ōtium, studium
13. FULL   plēnus, tantus, perditus, tālis
14. NEXT   reliquus, dignus, proximus, mox
15. READ   regō, pellō, legō, sentiō

B. Choose the correct Latin word to be used in translating each sentence.

1. (levis, lūx)   The *light* was poor.
2. (labor, labōrō)   He decided *to work* hard.
3. (tum, deinde)   First he was silent, *then* he spoke up.
4. (alius, alter)   *The other* person failed to arrive.
5. (certus, quīdam)   She was *certain* she would pass.
6. (cōnsultum, dēcernō)   The senate's *decree* was final.
7. (moror, mora)   The *delay* was six hours.
8. (quisque, quidque)   *Each one* had a chance to talk.
9. (iniūria, noceō)   They promised not *to harm* him.
10. (quō modō, quam)   I wonder *how* tall she is.

C. Match each word in column *A* with its nearest equivalent in column *B*.

Column A		*Column B*
1. nothing		*a.* nōlō
2. conspiracy		*b.* oculus
3. prefer		*c.* nēmō
4. pain		*d.* polliceor
5. unless		*e.* satis
6. be unwilling		*f.* nihil
7. no one		*g.* coniūrātī
8. eye		*h.* patior
9. rescue		*i.* mālō
10. conspirators		*j.* nisi
11. suitable		*k.* testis
12. promise		*l.* coniūrātiō
13. witness		*m.* ēripiō
14. suffer		*n.* idōneus
15. enough		*o.* dolor

A GUIDE TO THE COLLEGE BOARD ACHIEVEMENT TEST IN LATIN (LEVEL III)

The College Board Achievement Test in Latin is intended for students who have had two, three, or four years of high school Latin. It is not surprising, therefore, that this single test contains questions of varying degrees of difficulty. Only a superior student with four years of high school Latin is equipped to answer *all* the questions on the examination.

Although the types of questions used may vary somewhat from year to year, the following types illustrate what the candidate may generally expect. All the questions below are intended for students who have completed *three* years of high school Latin.

VOCABULARY QUESTIONS

Knowledge of vocabulary is basic and is tested implicitly throughout the examination. The following type of question, however, tests mastery of vocabulary directly.

Select the best English meaning for each of the following Latin words:

1. *scelus*
   (A) ladder   (B) crime   (C) weight   (D) earth

2. *mōs*
   (A) custom   (B) death   (C) soon   (D) delay

3. *quoque*
   (A) each one   (B) certain   (C) someone   (D) also

The following are sample questions reprinted from the editions indicated of *A Description of the College Board Achievement Tests*, published by the College Entrance Examination Board, New York: 1963—q. 22 (p. 226); 1966—qq. 1-7 (pp. 229-230) and q. 4 (p. 232, III). This booklet, which contains many illustrative examples of the different kinds of questions that are used in the Achievement Tests, is revised annually and is supplied without cost to high schools for distribution to students before they take the test. The booklet may also be obtained on request by writing to College Entrance Examination Board Publications Order Office, Box 592, Princeton, New Jersey 08540, or Box 1025, Berkeley, California 94701.

4. *tūtus*
   (A) whole   (B) your   (C) safe   (D) witness

5. *patior*
   (A) take possession of   (B) promise   (C) suffer
   (D) extend

6. *dignus*
   (A) worthy   (B) finger   (C) dignity   (D) careful

7. *morior*
   (A) delay   (B) die   (C) deserve   (D) wonder

8. *ingenium*
   (A) huge   (B) family   (C) race   (D) ability

9. *plēnus*
   (A) full   (B) almost   (C) most   (D) a little

10. *quasi*
    (A) for what reason   (B) but if   (C) as if   (D) such as

11. *metus*
    (A) month   (B) mind   (C) table   (D) fear

12. *tandem*
    (A) however   (B) at once   (C) so   (D) at last

13. *perditus*
    (A) skilled   (B) lost   (C) terrified   (D) powerful

14. *aetās*
    (A) summer   (B) age   (C) art   (D) temple

15. *trahō*
    (A) draw   (B) surrender   (C) go across   (D) carry

16. *vīvō*
    (A) watch   (B) be well   (C) live   (D) conquer

17. *comes*
    (A) assembly   (B) meeting place   (C) companion
    (D) murder

18. *vertō*
    (A) turn   (B) destroy   (C) go   (D) avoid

19. *facultās*
    (A) ease   (B) deed   (C) crime   (D) opportunity

20. *iūcundus*
    (A) judgment   (B) pleasant   (C) yoke   (D) just

21. *nancīscor*
    (A) obtain   (B) be born   (C) not know   (D) neglect

22. *dēlīctum*
    (A) fault   (B) choice   (C) remainder   (D) delight

23. *tangō*
    (A) break   (B) dance   (C) stop   (D) touch

24. *mūtō*
    (A) fear   (B) think   (C) change   (D) move

25. *occultō*
    (A) hide   (B) kill   (C) run against   (D) seize

READING COMPREHENSION QUESTIONS

Reading comprehension questions are based on connected passages of about a hundred words each. The questions aim to test the student's ability to understand the meaning of a passage and to extract information from it. In addition, some questions test knowledge of vocabulary in context, while others deal with grammatical constructions.

Read the following passages carefully to get the meaning. Below each passage you will find a series of incomplete statements. Select the answer that best completes each statement.

I

The city of Alba is captured by the Romans.

Legiōnēs deinde ad vāstandam urbem Albam ductae sunt. Ubi iērunt intrā portās, nōn fuit tumultus nec metus; sed silentium trīste ac tacitus dolor ita dēfīxit omnium Albānōrum animōs ut incertī essent quid relinquerent, quid sēcum ferrent;
(5) aliī ante domōs stetērunt, aliī per domōs vagābantur. Ut fragor tectōrum audiēbātur pulvisque ex locīs omnibus oriēbātur, quisque id quod poterat rapuit. Iam agmen fugientium complēverat viās et cōnspectus aliōrum īnfēlīcium integrābat lacrimās, vōcēsque etiam miserārum mulierum audiēbantur cum templa
(10) sacra praeterīrent ac deōs captōs relinquerent.

Ēgressīs ex urbe Albānīs, Rōmānī undique pūblica prīvātaque omnia tecta dēlēvērunt ūnāque hōrā quadringentōrum annōrum opus ruīnīs dedērunt.

1. *ad vāstandam urbem* (line 1) is best translated:
   - (A) to capture the city
   - (B) to destroy the city
   - (C) to surrender the city
   - (D) to visit the city

2. *intrā* (line 2) is best translated:
   - (A) within
   - (B) among
   - (C) between
   - (D) outside

3. From *nōn . . . animōs* (lines 2–4) we are informed that the Albans were
   - (A) fearful
   - (B) excited
   - (C) provoked
   - (D) sadly subdued

4. *ut . . . ferrent* (line 4) states that the Albans were uncertain as to
   - (A) whether to remain or take themselves off
   - (B) whether to leave or endure their fate
   - (C) what to leave behind and what to endure
   - (D) what to salvage and what to leave behind

5. *aliī . . . aliī* (line 5) is best translated:
   - (A) others . . . others
   - (B) one . . . another
   - (C) some . . . others
   - (D) the one . . . the other

6. From *Ut . . . rapuit* (lines 5–7) we learn that the Albans carried off what they could
   - (A) as soon as the dawn arose
   - (B) when they heard noise inside the houses
   - (C) as soon as the Romans started their destruction
   - (D) when they were surrounded on all sides

7. *agmen fugientium* (line 7) is best translated:
   - (A) the column of fugitives
   - (B) the fleeing line of battle
   - (C) the battle line of those fleeing
   - (D) the marching column in pursuit

8. *praeterīrent* (line 10) is best translated:
   - (A) destroyed
   - (B) passed by
   - (C) entered
   - (D) deserted

9. From *Rōmānī . . . dedērunt* (lines 11–13) we are informed that the Romans
   - (A) examined the ruins of 400 years
   - (B) left the city of Alba in ruins
   - (C) restored both the public and private buildings
   - (D) in one hour destroyed 400 dwellings

II

A philosopher justifies his conduct.

Mare vāstum et violentum ā Cassiopā Brundisium nāvigā-
bāmus. Tōtam noctem prīmam ventus ā latere nāvem aquā
complēverat et omnia nōbīs impendēre vidēbantur. In nāve
fuit philosophus clārus nōn parvā auctōritāte. Eum in tantīs
(5) perīculīs et in tantā maris tempestāte ego oculīs quaerēbam,
scīre cupiēns in quō animō esset. Atque illum hominem cōn-
speximus timidum et perterritum, colōre et speciē nōn multum
dissimilem cēterīs. Ubi mare factum est quiētum, quīdam
Graecus eum rogāvit: "Cūr, Ō Philosophe, timuistī et palluistī?
(10) Ego neque timuī neque palluī." Philosophus respondit, "Ego
sēnsī vītam meam esse magnō pretiō."

1. *ā Cassiopā Brundisium* (line 1) is best translated:
    (A) from Cassiopa to Brundisium
    (B) to Cassiopa Brundisium
    (C) from Cassiopa Brundisium
    (D) to Cassiopa from Brundisium

2. From *Tōtam . . . complēverat* (lines 2–3) we gather that the ship
    (A) ran short of water
    (B) weathered the storm surprisingly well
    (C) was kept from sailing the entire first night
    (D) was in great danger of sinking

3. *In . . . auctōritāte* (lines 3–4) tells of a philosopher on board
    (A) of small stature   (C) of no mean influence
    (B) of little authority   (D) not particularly famous

4. *in quō animō esset* (line 6) is best translated:
    (A) whether he had a soul
    (B) what his feelings were
    (C) if he was in his right mind
    (D) why his spirits were high

5. *nōn . . . cēterīs* (lines 7–8) is best translated:
    (A) not similar to the others
    (B) not much different from the rest
    (C) very unlike the others
    (D) not very sure of himself

6. *Ubi ... quiētum* (line 8) is best translated:
   (A) When the sea made us quiet
   (B) When the quiet sea receded
   (C) Where the sea in fact was quiet
   (D) When the sea became calm

7. *Ego ... pretiō* (lines 10–11) states that the philosopher
   (A) considered his life of great value
   (B) felt a great price had been placed on his life
   (C) sensed that life was worth the effort
   (D) perceived his life as a great event

III

*On receipt of certain information, Sulla
takes action against the enemy.*

Interim certior factus P. Sulla, quem discēdēns castrīs prae-
fēcerat Caesar, auxiliō cohortī vēnit cum legiōnibus duābus;
cuius adventū facile sunt repulsī Pompeiānī. Neque vērō cōn-
spectum aut impetum nostrōrum tulērunt, prīmīsque dēiectīs
(5) reliquī sē vertērunt et locō cessērunt. Sed īnsequentēs nostrōs,
nē longius prōsequerentur, Sulla revocāvit. At plērīque exīsti-
mant, sī acrius īnsequī voluisset, bellum eō diē potuisse fīnīre.
Cuius cōnsilium reprehendendum nōn vidētur. Aliae enim sunt
lēgātī partēs atque imperātōris: alter omnia agere ad prae-
(10) scrīptum, alter līberē ad summam rērum cōnsulere dēbet.

1. *auxiliō cohortī* (line 2) is best translated:
   (A) after helping the cohort
   (B) to help the cohort
   (C) with the help of the cohort
   (D) by encouraging the auxiliaries

2. From *Interim ... Pompeiānī* (lines 1–3), we learn that
   (A) Sulla came with two legions and defeated Pompey's
       men
   (B) Caesar had ordered Sulla to help the cohort
   (C) Sulla heard that at Caesar's arrival Pompey's men had
       fled
   (D) Sulla had put Caesar in command of the cohort that
       had defeated Pompey's men

3. *Neque . . . cessērunt* (lines 3–5) states that

(A) Pompey's men turned around and attacked from a different place

(B) Pompey's men all ran away when our men appeared on the scene

(C) after the men in Pompey's front ranks were defeated, the others fled

(D) the sight of our men encouraged the dejected men in the first ranks

4. *īnsequentēs* (line 5) implies that when the men were recalled, they

(A) were following the enemy

(B) were about to follow the enemy

(C) had finished following the enemy

(D) were being followed by the enemy

5. In *Cuius . . . vidētur* (line 8) it is implied that Sulla's

(A) plan did not seem to be understood

(B) questionable decision was not understood

(C) wisdom was above reproach

(D) decision should not be criticized

6. *Aliae* (line 8) is best translated:

(A) The other   (C) Others

(B) Another   (D) Different

7. *partēs* (line 9) is best translated:

(A) duties   (C) privileges

(B) parts   (D) shares

GRAMMAR QUESTIONS

Grammar questions usually appear together with questions on reading comprehension. The following questions are based on the previous passages.

Select the answer that best completes each statement.

I

1. *vāstandam* (line 1) is a
    (A) gerund
    (B) gerundive
    (C) present participle
    (D) future active participle

2. *ferrent* (line 4) is subjunctive in
    (A) a result clause
    (B) a purpose clause
    (C) an indirect question
    (D) a subordinate verb in indirect statement

3. The subject of *integrābat* (line 8) is
    (A) cōnspectus
    (B) agmen
    (C) he (understood)
    (D) *agmen* and *cōnspectus*

4. *relinquerent* (line 10) is subjunctive in a
    (A) relative clause of characteristic
    (B) relative clause of purpose
    (C) condition contrary to fact
    (D) cum circumstantial clause

5. *ūnā hōrā* (line 12) is ablative of
    (A) time within which
    (B) cause
    (C) means
    (D) manner

II

1. *noctem* (line 2) is accusative
    (A) of place to which
    (B) of duration of time
    (C) used as direct object
    (D) used as subject of an infinitive

2. *Eum* (line 4) is direct object of
    (A) *quaerēbam*
    (B) *scīre*
    (C) *cupiēns*
    (D) *esset*

3. *esset* (line 6) is subjunctive in
    (A) a relative clause of description
    (B) a clause after an expression of doubt
    (C) a result clause
    (D) an indirect question

4. *specie* (line 7) is an ablative
    (A) of means   (C) of description
    (B) of manner   (D) absolute

5. *esse* (line 11) is infinitive used as
    (A) main verb in indirect statement   (C) object infinitive
    (B) complementary infinitive   (D) subject infinitive

III

1. *discēdēns* (line 1) modifies
    (A) *Sulla*   (C) *castrīs*
    (B) *quem*   (D) *Caesar*

2. *castrīs* (line 1) is
    (A) dative with a compound verb
    (B) dative of purpose
    (C) ablative of place from which
    (D) ablative of separation

3. *adventū* (line 3) is ablative of
    (A) time within which   (C) time when
    (B) means   (D) respect

4. *prōsequerentur* (line 6) is subjunctive in
    (A) a result clause
    (B) an indirect command
    (C) a clause after a verb of fearing
    (D) a purpose clause

5. *fīnīre* (line 7) depends upon
    (A) *existimant*   (C) *voluisset*
    (B) *potuisse*   (D) *īnsequī*

DERIVATION QUESTIONS

In each of the following sentences, there is an italicized word of Latin derivation. Select the letter of the word or expression below each sentence that best expresses the meaning of the italicized word.

1. The furnishings of the house were *ornate.*

   (A) elaborate   (B) unpleasant   (C) old-fashioned
   (D) antique

2. The president gave *tacit* approval to the plan.
   (A) unwilling   (B) silent   (C) temporary
   (D) unjustified

3. The student had a *morbid* desire to read tragedy.
   (A) frequent   (B) profound   (C) secret
   (D) very unhealthy

4. His life was *sanctified* by his deeds.
   (A) made difficult   (B) made holy   (C) made famous
   (D) enriched

5. There was *dissension* among the committee members.
   (A) disagreement   (B) discussion   (C) disloyalty
   (D) dismay

6. The visitor made *odious* remarks.
   (A) pleasant   (B) untruthful   (C) hateful
   (D) flattering

7. His action is *detrimental* to this organization.
   (A) harmful   (B) helpful   (C) costly   (D) deceiving

8. A *prudent* man will have few regrets.
   (A) happy   (B) generous   (C) brave   (D) wise

9. His life was *exemplary.*
   (A) scandalous   (B) full of adventure   (C) reckless
   (D) worthy of imitation

10. This mark is *indelible.*
    (A) counterfeited   (B) blurred   (C) irremovable
    (D) symbolic

11. The patient is now *rational.*
    (A) reasonable   (B) hungry   (C) submissive
    (D) cheerful

12. The government may not *legislate* in this matter.
(A) use force   (B) offer advice   (C) make laws
(D) show disapproval

13. Physics *postulates* a good foundation in mathematics.
(A) trains for   (B) insures   (C) is equivalent to
(D) requires

14. She was greatly *incensed* by the news.
(A) puzzled   (B) reassured   (C) delighted
(D) provoked

15. The *utility* of this action is uncertain.
(A) purpose   (B) usefulness   (C) advantage
(D) result

16. This was his *ultimate* conclusion.
(A) earliest   (B) simplest   (C) only   (D) last

17. This *indignity* was received quietly.
(A) reaction   (B) demotion   (C) insult   (D) report

18. He knew no one more *vivacious*.
(A) sensible   (B) lively   (C) polite   (D) attractive

19. There are symptoms of *incipient* cancer.
(A) beginning   (B) arrested   (C) malignant
(D) advanced

20. The *advocates* of the plan are confident.
(A) enemies   (B) supporters   (C) receivers
(D) defamers

21. Can federal laws *ameliorate* substandard wages?
(A) improve   (B) remove   (C) aggravate   (D) affect

22. The inexperienced officer accepted the assignment with *diffidence*.
(A) courage   (B) eagerness   (C) uncertainty   (D) joy

23. The Greeks transmitted these principles to *posterity*.
(A) backward peoples   (B) later generations   (C) the West
(D) their neighbors

24. The mayor promises to *accelerate* housing reforms.
(A) hasten   (B) defer   (C) demand   (D) explain

25. The hot, damp weather of the jungle was extremely *oppressive*.
(A) objectionable   (B) hateful   (C) unpleasant
(D) overpowering

LATIN FOUR YEARS

POETRY

(*Vergil, Ovid*)

Unit XIV—*Forms*

Lesson 44. FORMS PECULIAR TO POETRY

It is customary for poets to take liberties with language. This custom is popularly called poetic license. Vergil, like other Roman poets, makes use of two types of license rarely used in classical prose: *archaisms* and *Grecisms*.

An archaism is a form or expression that was once in use, but is no longer current. A Grecism is an imitation of Greek usage. These variations from classical prose serve several purposes: to attract attention by their startling effect, to lend an air of distinction to the verses, and (occasionally) to solve metrical problems.

Following is a list of the more important archaisms and Grecisms. Some rare forms are also included.

NOUNS

1. *Genitive singular* ending in **-āī,** instead of **-ae,** in first declension nouns.

    Example: **aurāī** for **aurae**

2. *Genitive plural* ending in **-um,** instead of **-ārum, -ōrum, -uum.**

    Examples: <u>**Aeneadum**</u> for **Aeneadārum**
    1st declension

    <u>**deum**</u> for **deōrum**
    2nd declension

    <u>**currum**</u> for **curruum**
    4th declension

3. *Dative singular* ending in **-ū,** instead of **-uī,** in fourth declension nouns.

    Example: **metū** for **metuī**

237

4. Nouns of *Greek origin* that retain some Greek case endings:

    a. first declension proper nouns ending in the nominative singular in **-ē, -ās, -ēs**, instead of **-a**.

    Examples: **Andromachē, Aenēās, Anchīsēs**

    b. third declension nouns ending in the accusative singular in **-a**, instead of **-em**.

    Example: **āera**

5. *Contracted* or shortened forms.

    Example: **perīclum** for **perīculum**

PRONOUNS

1. **Ollī** and **ollīs** instead of **illī** and **illīs**.
2. **Quīs** instead of **quibus**.
3. **Mī** instead of **mihi**.

VERBS

1. *Imperfect indicative* active of the fourth conjugation ending in **-ībat, -ībant**, instead of **-iēbat, -iēbant**.

    Examples: **lēnībat** for **lēniēbat**
                   lēnībant for **lēniēbant**

2. *Perfect indicative* active third person plural ending in **-ēre**, instead of **-ērunt**.

    Example: **tenuēre** for **tenuērunt**

3. *Contracted* or shortened forms in the perfect and pluperfect.

    Examples: **accestis** for **accessistis**
                exstīnxem for **exstīnxissem**
                trāxe for **trāxisse**

4. *Present infinitive* passive ending in **-ier**, instead of **-ī**.

    Example: **accingier** for **accingī**

5. The use of the *future imperative*.

The future imperative is used in commands where there is a distinct reference to future time. It exists in the second and third person, singular and plural, and is formed by adding to the present stem the following endings:

	SINGULAR	PLURAL
2nd person	-tō	-tōte
3rd person	-tō	-ntō
Examples:	amātō	amātōte
	amātō	amantō

6. The use of the *supine*.

The supine, resembling a fourth declension noun, exists in two forms: the accusative singular with its ending in **-um**; and the ablative singular with its ending in **-ū**. The former is used with verbs of motion to express *purpose*; the latter is used mainly with adjectives as an ablative of *respect* or *specification*.

Examples: Vēnērunt **vīsum**. They came to see.
                    <u>purpose</u>

        Mīrābile **dictū**.   Wonderful to tell.
                <u>respect</u>

Note: The future infinitive passive (a rare form) is made up of the supine in **-um** plus the present passive infinitive of **īre** (**īrī**).

Example: **datum īrī**

EXERCISES

A. Each of the following verses contains a poetic form. Find this form; then rewrite the form as it would appear in classical prose.

1. vī superum, saevae memorem Iūnōnis ob īram
2. ō virgō, nova mī faciēs inopīnave surgit
3. rūrsus ad ōrāclum Ortygiae Phoebumque remēnsō
4. nec latuēre dolī frātrem Iūnōnis et īrae
5. partibus ex īsdem, et summā dominārier arce
6. Dardana quī Paridis dīrēxtī tēla manūsque
7. Classe vehō mēcum, fāmā super aethera nōtus
8. ollī subrīdēns hominum sator atque deōrum

9. parce metū, Cytherēa : manent immōta tuōrum
10. cum genere exstīnxem, mēmet super ipsa dedissem

B. Identify the following forms :

1. aulāī
2. tenuēre
3. Peliās
4. ollīs
5. petitō

6. quīs
7. audītū
8. Alētēs
9. pārentō
10. amātum īrī

C. Complete the following English phrases by translating the italicized words.

1. fūmidus amnis *aquāī*   a steaming torrent _____
2. classis *Argīvum*   the fleet _____
3. nōn vult *capier*   he doesn't want _____
4. miserābile *vīsū*   pitiful _____
5. *portū* subīmus   we go up _____
6. urbem *occupāvēre*   _____ the city
7. *ollī* Venus respondit   _____ Venus replied
8. eunt pācem *petītum*   they are going _____ peace
9. ipse *venītō*, Aenēās   _____ yourself, Aeneas
10. vincula *quīs* innexa   the chains _____ it was bound

Unit XV—*Grammatical Structures*

***Lesson 45.* GRAMMATICAL STRUCTURES AND IRREGULARITIES PECULIAR TO POETRY**

When dealing with grammatical structures, poets take liberties uncommon with writers of prose.

Following is a list of the more important poetical structures found in the works of Vergil.

NOUNS

1. **Genitive**

    a. of *respect* or *specification,* instead of the ablative.

    Example: fessī **rērum,** *weary of hardships*

    b. of *separation,* instead of the ablative.

    Example: **operum** solūti, *free from labors*

2. **Dative**

    a. of *agency* with any passive form, instead of the ablative.

    Example: vetor **fātīs,** *I am forbidden by the fates*

    b. of *place to which,* instead of the accusative with **in** or **ad.**

    Example: īnferret deōs **Latiō,** *he should bring the gods to Latium*

3. **Accusative**

    a. of *respect* or *specification,* instead of the ablative (a Greek construction usually limited to parts of the body).

    Example: nūda **genū,** *with knee bare* (bare in respect to the knee)

    b. of *place to which* without a preposition, where prose requires **in** or **ad.**

    Example: **Ītaliam** vēnit, *he came to Italy*

c. as the *object* of a verb in the *passive* voice (an imitation of the Greek middle voice).

> *Example:* inūtile **ferrum cingitur,** *he girds* (on himself) *his useless sword*

4. Ablative

a. of *place where* without a preposition, where prose requires **in.**

> *Example:* celsā sedet **arce,** *he sits in his lofty citadel*

b. of *place from which* without a preposition, where prose requires **ab, dē,** or **ex.**

> *Example:* dētrūdunt nāvīs **scopulō,** *they shove the ships off from the rock*

c. of *manner* with no adjective and no preposition, where prose requires **cum.**

> *Example:* **turbine** perflant, *they blow in a whirlwind*

5. Locative

The locative is used with names of countries and large islands, instead of the ablative with **in** (in prose, the locative is restricted to names of towns and small islands).

> *Examples:* nōn **Libyae,** *not in Libya*
> **Crētae,** *in Crete*

VERBS

1. Imperative

The imperative is used with **nē** to express a negative command, instead of **nōlī** with the infinitive.

> *Example:* equō **nē crēdite,** *don't trust the horse*

2. Infinitive

a. to express *purpose,* instead of the subjunctive with **ut.**

> *Example:* nōn **populāre** vēnimus, *we have not come to destroy*

b. to express an *exclamation* with subject accusative.

Example: **mēne** inceptō **dēsistere!**, *what! I desist from my purpose!*

OTHER IRREGULARITIES

1. Plural for Singular

In poetry we often find nouns in the plural where prose would use the singular. This practice is followed sometimes for metrical reasons, and sometimes to indicate repeated instances of the quality denoted by an abstract noun.

Examples: **montīs** instead of **montem**
īrae instead of **īra**

2. Passive Form with Active Meaning

The passive voice is sometimes used in an active sense with reflexive force (equivalent to the Greek middle voice).

Example: **vertuntur** ad ōrās, *they turn toward the shores* (instead of *sē vertunt* ad ōrās)

3. Deponent Verb with Passive Meaning

The perfect participle of a deponent verb (whose meaning is normally active) is occasionally used in a passive sense.

Example: pelagō **remēnsō,** *having recrossed the sea* (the sea having been recrossed)

4. Past Participle with Present Force

The perfect participle of a regular verb is sometimes used with the force of a present participle.

Example: caelō **invectus** apertō, *riding under a clear sky*

5. Adjectives and Participles as Nouns

Adjectives and participles, especially in the neuter gender, are used as nouns more commonly in poetry than in prose.

Examples: **altō,** on the sea
commissa, misdeeds

6. Simple Verb for Compound

Vergil often uses a simple verb where prose prefers a compound. This device serves to avoid a precise, prosaic expression, and allows the reader to use his imagination.

Example: artūs **pōnunt** (instead of artūs *dēpōnunt*)

7. Variety of Words

To secure variety and to avoid monotony, Vergil uses different words for the same thing.

Example: The *sea* is variously called **mare, altum, aequor, aestus, pelagus, pontus,** etc., all with essentially the same meaning.

8. Patronymics

A patronymic is a noun indicating descent or relationship. It is recognized generally by the ending **-adēs** or **-īdēs** for the masculine, and **-is** for the feminine.

Examples: Scīpiadēs, *son of Scipio*
Tȳdīdēs, *son of Tydeus*
Tyndaris, *daughter of Tyndareus*

EXERCISES

A. Each of the following verses contains a grammatical structure peculiar to poetry. Identify the type of each structure (in italics) ; then rewrite the structure as it would appear in classical prose.

1. lītora, multum ille et *terrīs* iactātus et altō
2. Trīnacriā *fīnīs* Italōs mittēre relictā
3. arcēbat longē *Latiō*, multōsqué per annōs
4. Dēïphobus contrā : *"Nē saevī*, magna sacerdōs"
5. ōstia, dīves *opum*, studiīsque asperrima bellī
6. per mediōs, miscetque virīs, neque cernitur *ūllī*
7. forte suā Libycīs tempestās appulit *ōrīs*
8. vēnimus, aut raptās ad lītora *vertere* praedās
9. Hīs *animum* arrēctī dictīs, et fortis Achātēs
10. et capita ante ārās Phrygiō *vēlāmur* amictū

B. Match each word in column *A* with its prosaic synonym in column *B*.

Column A	Column B
1. aequor	*a.* Trōiānī
2. Dardanī	*b.* frūmentum
3. tēctum	*c.* ventus
4. Danaī	*d.* mare
5. ēnsis	*e.* flūmen
6. Cerēs	*f.* Graecī
7. amnis	*g.* domus
8. lympha	*h.* vīnum
9. Auster	*i.* aqua
10. Bacchus	*j.* gladius

C. Translate the following expressions into English; identify each peculiarity.

1. remēnsō marī
2. Anchīsiadēs
3. tum facta silentia
4. implentur veteris Bacchī
5. timōrem mittite
6. dictō citius
7. comitātus (ab) Achātē
8. tūnsae pectora palmīs
9. tū mihi scēptra conciliās
10. cingor fulgentibus armīs

Unit XVI—Versification

Lesson 46. VERSIFICATION OR PROSODY

Latin poetry (which was meant to be read aloud) differs from English poetry in one important respect: Whereas English poetry depends for its rhythm or meter upon *accent* and *rhyme,* Latin poetry depends on *quantity,* i.e., a regularized succession of long and short syllables.

Quantity of Syllables

A syllable is long by *nature* or by *position* as follows:

1. By nature, if it contains a long vowel or a diphthong.

   Examples: lītora, *cae*dem

2. By position, if it contains a short vowel followed by two consonants in one or two words.

   Examples: *cond*eret, *et s*oror

If it is not long by nature or by position, a syllable is short. A long syllable is marked thus ___; a short syllable thus ◡ . In marking syllables, place the symbols for long or short below the syllables.

Note. A syllable containing a short vowel followed by a mute (p, b, t, d, c, g) and a liquid (l, r) may be either long or short, according to the needs of the verse. In the word **patrem,** for example, the vowel **a** is short. However, the syllable, since it is followed by a mute **t** and a liquid **r,** may be short or long.

Elision

Sometimes, for ease of pronunciation, part of a word is elided or omitted in reading. This is called *elision.* There are three common types of elision (indicated by parentheses and a curved line).

1. Eliding a vowel at the end of a word when the next word begins with a vowel, a diphthong, or h.

Examples: vād (e) age

Jūn (ō) aeternum

ignār (ī) hominum

2. Eliding a diphthong under the same conditions as type 1.

Example: caus (ae) īrārum

3. Eliding the final **m** of a word with its preceding vowel under the same conditions as type 1.

Examples: omnī (um) et

terr (am) hērōs

Note. Elision is sometimes omitted when we might normally expect it. This omission, called *hiatus,* occurs when a word ending in a vowel has a special emphasis, or is followed by a natural pause. For example, in the verse

et vēra incessū patuit dea. Ille ubi mātrem

hiatus occurs between the words **dea** and **Ille.**

Terms of Prosody

Poetry is composed of lines, called *verses,* divided into certain regular units, called *feet.* A *foot* is a combination of syllables. The feet in the *Aeneid* are either *dactyls* or *spondees.*

A *dactyl* consists of one long and two short syllables.

Examples: dīceret

praemia

sanguine

A *spondee* consists of two long syllables.

Examples: fātīs

aequās

montēs

The first syllable of the dactyl and the spondee always receives the accent or beat, called the *ictus,* represented thus /. The rhythmic repetition of this beat forms the *meter,* or measure, of the verse. The accented part of a foot is called the *thesis;* the unaccented part, the *arsis.*

Examples:	*Foot*	*Thesis*	*Arsis*
	ultrō	ul	trō
	crēdita	crē	dita

Scansion

To scan a verse means to read it metrically. Close attention must be paid to long and short syllables. Scansion can also be written out by employing certain markings.

The meter regularly found in Vergil and Ovid is called the *dactylic hexameter*—dactylic because most of the feet are dactyls, hexameter because each verse contains six feet. The first four feet may be either dactyls or spondees. The fifth foot is practically always a dactyl, and the sixth foot is always a spondee. The last syllable of the sixth foot, called the **syllaba anceps** (doubtful syllable), is always treated long by poetic license, even though it may actually be a short syllable.

Note. In general, a poet will use mostly dactyls if he wants to convey rapid movement; excitement; joy. A preponderance of spondees, on the other hand, conveys slow, labored movement; solemnity; sadness.

Caesura

In reading Latin poetry there is usually a pause near the middle of the verse. This pause, called **caesura,** comes at the end of a word, usually in the third foot, and is indicated by two short parallel lines ‖ .

Hints on Scanning

The following five steps are suggested to facilitate scanning a verse. The same verse will be repeated at each step with the proper markings.

1. Mark all elisions.

Albānīque patrēs atqu(e) altae moenia Rōmae

2. Proceed to the end of the verse, marking the last foot a spondee and the fifth foot a dactyl. Separate the feet by a perpendicular line.

Albānīque patrēs atqu(e) altae | moenia | Rōmae

3. Now mark as long all syllables which are long by nature or by position.

Albānīque patrēs atqu(e) altae | moenia | Rōmae

4. Next mark as short the remaining syllables, and indicate the ictus over the first syllable of each foot.

Albānīque patrēs atqu(e) altae | moenia | Rōmae

5. Finally indicate the caesura, and the verse is completely scanned.

Albānīque patrēs ‖ atqu(e) altae | moenia | Rōmae

EXERCISES

A. Select five dactyls and five spondees from the following list of words:

sēdibus	portae	cernimus	terrent	nostrīs
sociīs	caput	silvā	ingentem	resēdit
vērō	reddite	hominum	lambere	alterum

B. Indicate all the long syllables in each of the following verses by putting long marks below them.

1. dēlēgī comitēs nunc illās prōmite vīrīs
2. fert pictūrātās aurī subtēmine vestīs
3. cūra deum bis Pergameīs ērepte ruīnīs
4. turba sonāns praedam pedibus circumvolat uncīs
5. Sergestus capit ante locum scopulōque propinquat

C. Indicate all the short syllables in each of the following verses by putting short marks below them.

1. tum satus Anchīsā caestūs pater extulit aequōs
2. dispiciunt clausae tenebrīs et carcere caecō
3. vōs quoque Pergameae iam fās est parcere gentī
4. hic membrīs et mōle valēns sed tarda trementī
5. fīxerit aeripedem cervam licet aut Erymanthī

D. In the following list there are ten words containing syllables that may be considered long or short, depending on the needs of the verse. Indicate these syllables by putting both a long and short mark below each.

sacram	cupressus	patribus	macrēscō	Cyclōpas
tablīnum	Trīnacria	capra	probrum	Atrīdae
temptāmus	alterque	pōcula	intereā	vīscera

E. Each of the following verses contains at least one instance of elision. Rewrite each verse, putting parentheses around the elided letters. Indicate the elision by a curved line.

1. multa quoque et bellō passus dum conderet urbem
2. quō rēs cumque cadent ūnum et commūne perīclum
3. nec posse Argolicīs exscindī Pergama tēlīs
4. corripuēre sacram effigiem manibusque cruentīs
5. lītora multum ille et terrīs iactātus et altō

F. Hiatus occurs at least once in each of the following verses. Indicate the words in each verse between which hiatus occurs.

1. posthabitā coluisse Samō : hīc illius arma
2. tūne ille Aenēās quem Dardaniō Anchīsae
3. lāmentīs gemitūque et fēmineō ululātū
4. quid struit? aut quā spē inimīcā in gente morātur
5. Nēreidum mātrī et Neptūnō Aegaeō

G. In the following statements, if the italicized term is incorrect, write the correct term. If the italicized term is correct, write *true*.

1. A verse with many *spondees* would be used to describe a solemn procession.
2. Latin poetry depends for its meter on *accent*.
3. A syllable is long by *position* if it contains a short vowel followed by two consonants.
4. *Ictus* is the name given to the syllable of a foot that receives the accent.
5. *Arsis* is a pause near the middle of a verse.
6. The syllaba anceps is the last syllable of the *fifth* foot.
7. The *accented* part of a foot is called the thesis.
8. The meter generally used by Vergil and Ovid is called the dactylic *pentameter*.
9. A syllable containing a *long* vowel followed by the letters *tr* may be considered long or short at the discretion of the poet.
10. *Hiatus* is the failure to elide when we would normally expect to.

H. Scan each of the following verses: mark the feet, elisions, ictus, and caesura.

1. vēnimus aut raptās ad lītora vertere praedās
2. nī dare coniugium et dictō pārēre fatētur
3. et mē quem dūdum nōn ūlla iniecta movēbant
4. ut terrae utque novae pateant Karthāginis arcēs
5. concilium horrendum quālēs cum vertice celsō

Unit XVII—*Figures of Speech*

Lesson 47. GRAMMATICAL AND RHETORICAL FIGURES

One of the main differences between prose and poetry is the more frequent use in the latter of grammatical and rhetorical figures. These figures serve to lend beauty and charm to a poem. Without them, poetry would be prosaic. Following is a list of the more important figures, arranged in alphabetical order.

1. **Alliteration:** the repetition of the same letter at the beginning of successive words or syllables.

   Example: **m**agnō cum **m**ur**m**ure **m**ontis

2. **Anaphora:** the repetition of a word, for emphasis, at the beginning of successive phrases or clauses.

   Example: **nunc** augur Apollō, **nunc** Lyciae sortēs, **nunc** et Jove missus

3. **Anastrophe:** inversion of the usual order of words, such as placing a preposition after, instead of before, the word it governs.

   Example: **Ītaliam contrā** (instead of the normal **contrā Ītaliam**)

4. **Aposiopesis:** an abrupt pause in a sentence for rhetorical effect.

   Example: **quōs ego — ! sed mōtōs praestat**

5. **Asyndeton:** the omission of conjunctions where one would normally expect them.

   Example: **urbe, domō sociās** (instead of **urbe et domō sociās**)

6. **Chiasmus:** the arrangement of pairs of words in reverse, or crisscross, order.

   Example: <u>luctantīs</u> <u>ventōs</u> <u>tempestātēsque</u> <u>sonōrās</u>
            adjective   noun   noun   adjective

7. **Ellipsis:** the omission of words necessary to the grammatical structure of the sentence and easily supplied from the context.

   Example: **haec sēcum: "Mēne inceptō dēsistere . . .** (After **sēcum,** some verb of saying such as **dīcit** or **ait** is understood.)

8. **Hendiadys:** the use of two nouns connected by **et** instead of a single modified noun.

   Example: **vī et armīs** (instead of **vī armōrum,** *by force of arms*)

9. **Hyperbole:** an exaggeration for rhetorical effect.

   Example: **praeruptus aquae mōns,** a towering mountain of water (referring merely to a large wave)

10. **Hysteron Proteron:** a reversal of the natural or logical order of ideas; literally "putting last things first."

    Example: **moriāmur et in media arma ruāmus,** let us die and rush into the midst of arms (Obviously the rushing into arms must take place before the dying.)

11. **Litotes:** the affirming of something by denying its opposite; a double negative.

    Example: ***nōn indecōrō* pulvere sordidī,** soiled with *not unbecoming* (*i.e., becoming* or *glorious*) dust

12. **Metaphor:** an implied simile or comparison, without the use of some word meaning "as" or "like."

    Example: **lūce sedet *cūstōs*,** by day she (Rumor) sits a sentinel (*i.e.,* like a sentinel)

13. **Metonymy:** the substitution of one word for another that it suggests.

    Example: implentur veteris **Bacchī** (**Bacchus,** the *god* of wine, is used instead of **vīnum,** wine.)

14. **Onomatopoeia:** the use of a word whose sound suggests its meaning.

    Example: ***clāmor*que virum *clangor*que** tubārum (**Clāmor** and **clangor** suggest noise.)

15. **Oxymoron:** the use in combination of apparently contradictory words.

   Example: **via** dīvidit **invia**

16. **Personification:** attributing human characteristics to inanimate or impersonal things.

   Example: **Lūctus et ultrīcēs posuēre cubīlia Cūrae,** Grief and avenging Cares have made their bed. (*Grief* and *Cares* are treated as persons.)

17. **Pleonasm:** the use of superfluous words.

   Example: **sīc ōre locūta est,** thus she spoke with her mouth (**Ōre** is superfluous.)

18. **Polysyndeton:** the use of unnecessary conjunctions.

   Example: **ūnā Eurus*que* Notus*que* ruunt crēber*que* procellīs Āfricus**

19. **Prolepsis (Anticipation):** the use of a word sooner than is logically appropriate.

   Example: **submersās obrue puppīs,** overwhelm the sunken ships (*i.e.,* overwhelm and sink the ships)

20. **Simile:** an expressed comparison introduced by some word meaning "as" or "like," such as **similis, qualis,** or **velut (velutī).**

   Example: **migrantīs cernās . . . ac *velut ingentem formīcae farris acervum cum populant*,** one could see them moving away, just as when ants plunder a huge heap of corn

21. **Synecdoche:** the use of a part of an object to represent the entire object.

   Example: **natat ūncta carīna (Carīna,** the *keel* of a ship, is used instead of **nāvis,** the *entire* ship.)

22. **Tmesis:** the separation of a compound word by one or more intervening words.

   Example: **quae mē cumque vocant terrae** (instead of **quaecumque mē vocant terrae**)

23. Zeugma: the use of a word in two connections, though strictly applicable only to one.

Example: victōsque **deōs** parvumque **nepōtem** ipse **trahit**

The verb **trahit** is used both with **deōs** and **nepōtem**, though it strictly applies only to **nepōtem** (he *drags* his *grandson*, but *bears* the *gods*).

EXERCISES

A. Each of the following verses contains a grammatical or rhetorical figure. Identify and explain the figure.

1. ac velutī magnō in populō cum saepe coorta est sēditiō
2. mīrantur dōna Aenēae, mīrantur Iūlum
3. tum Cererem corruptam undīs Cereāliaque arma
4. intereā magnō miscērī murmure pontum
5. Īlionēa petit dextrā laevāque Serestum
6. quōs inter medius vēnit furor. Ille Sychaeum
7. et multō nebulae circum dea fūdit amictū
8. fertque refertque soror. Sed nūllīs ille movētur
9. nōta tibi, et nostrō doluistī saepe dolōre
10. imperiō premit ac vinclīs et carcere frēnat

B. Complete the following statements:

1. An exaggeration for rhetorical effect is a figure known as _____.
2. Oxymoron is the use of _____.
3. The words **magnō cum murmure montis** illustrate two rhetorical figures, alliteration and _____.
4. An implied simile, or comparison, is known as a _____.
5. The double negative **nec nōn** is an example of a rhetorical figure called _____.
6. Aposiopesis is a rhetorical figure that indicates _____.
7. The omission of conjunctions where they would normally be expected is a grammatical figure called _____.
8. The expression **Aeolus haec contrā: "Tuus . . .** is an example of a grammatical figure known as _____.
9. Hysteron proteron is a grammatical figure in which _____.
10. In the expression **pallentēsque habitant Morbī** there is a rhetorical figure called _____.

C. In the following statements, if the italicized term is incorrect, write the correct term. If the italicized term is correct, write *true*.

1. The use of **tēctum** (roof) for **domus** (house) is an example of *litotes*.

2. The rhetorical figure *personification* is illustrated in the verse **lūctus et ultrīcēs posuēre cubīlia Cūrae.**

3. The word **similis, quālis,** or **velut** in a verse introduces a figure called *metaphor*.

4. The substitution of **Vulcānus** for **ignis** is known as *metonymy*.

5. The order of the words **magnōrum horrentia . . . terga suum** is an illustration of the figure called *chiasmus*.

6. The omission of conjunctions is a grammatical figure known as *polysyndeton*.

7. The expression *circum maria* is an example of anastrophe.

8. The use of a word in two connections, though strictly applicable only to one, is known as *hysteron proteron*.

9. The verse **sanguine plācāstis ventōs et virgine caesā** illustrates a rhetorical figure called alliteration, and a grammatical figure called *hendiadys*.

10. *Prolepsis* is the use of a word sooner than is logically appropriate.

Unit XVIII—Quotations

Lesson 48. FAMILIAR QUOTATIONS FROM THE *AENEID*

The following verses, taken from the *Aeneid*, are quoted so frequently that they are worthy of memorization.

BOOK I

1. **Arma virumque canō.** I sing of arms and the man.
2. **Tantae mōlis erat Rōmānam condere gentem!** So great was the task of founding the Roman race!
3. **Ō terque quaterque beātī!** O three times and four times blessed!
4. **Ō passī graviōra, dabit deus hīs quoque fīnem!** O you who have suffered more grievous wrongs, some god will put an end to these too!
5. **Forsan et haec ōlim meminisse iuvābit.** Perhaps some day it will be a joy to recall even this hardship.
6. **Dux fēmina factī.** A woman is the leader of the deed.
7. **Mīrābile dictū!** Wonderful to tell!
8. **Sunt lacrimae rērum, et mentem mortālia tangunt.** There are tears for misfortune, and mortal sorrows touch the human heart.
9. **Trōs Tyriusque mihī nūllō discrīmine agētur.** Trojan and Tyrian alike I shall treat with no distinction.
10. **Nōn ignāra malī, miserīs succurrere discō.** Having suffered misfortune, I know how to help those in need.
11. **Semper honōs nōmenque tuum laudēsque manēbunt.** Ever shall your honor, your name, and your praises endure.

BOOK II

12. **Quōrum pars magna fuī.** I was a great part of all this.
13. **Equō nē crēdite.** Do not trust the horse.
14. **Timeō Danaōs et dōna ferentīs.** I fear the Greeks, even when bearing gifts.
15. **Teneor patriae nec lēgibus ūllīs.** I am bound to no country and to no laws.

16. **Vēnit summa diēs et inēluctābile tempus Dardaniae.** The last day and the inevitable hour for Troy have come.

17. **Fuimus Trōes, fuit Īlium et ingēns glōria Teucrōrum.** Trojans we were; Troy and the great fame of the Trojans are things of the past.

18. **Ūna salūs victīs nūllam spērāre salūtem.** The only safety for the conquered is not to hope for safety.

19. **Dolus an virtūs, quis in hoste requīrat?** Whether deceit or valor, who would ask in dealing with an enemy?

20. **Dīs aliter vīsum.** The gods decreed otherwise.

BOOK IV

21. **Dēgenerēs animōs timor arguit.** It is fear that proves souls ignoble.

22. **Fāma, malum quā nōn aliud vēlōcius ūllum.** Gossip, of all evils there is none more swift.

23. **Quis fallere possit amantem?** Who can deceive a lover?

24. **Improbe Amor, quid nōn mortālia pectora cōgis!** Wicked Love, to what extremes you drive mortal hearts!

25. **Horrendum dictū!** Horrible to tell!

26. **Varium et mūtābile semper fēmina.** Woman is ever a fickle and changeable thing.

BOOK V

27. **Possunt quia posse videntur.** They are strong because they are convinced they are strong.

BOOK VI

28. **Tū nē cēde malīs.** Do not yield to misfortunes.

29. **Facilis dēscēnsus Avernō.** Easy is the descent to Hades.

30. **Nunc animīs opus.** Now is there need for courage.

EXERCISES

A. From verses *a* through *j* below, select the one that would be appropriate to quote in each of the following situations:

1. Man proposes, Fate disposes.
2. Anne is always changing her mind.
3. You may be down, but you're never out.
4. You recall an event that almost cost you your life.
5. It is not difficult to get into trouble.
6. A plea for tolerance.
7. In times of emergency one must display courage.
8. A perfect stranger, in dire straits, elicits from us sorrow and tears.
9. The credo of an internationalist.
10. Deserved fame is everlasting.

      a. Facilis dēscēnsus Avernō.
      b. Forsan et haec ōlim meminisse iuvābit.
      c. Dīs aliter vīsum.
      d. Nunc animīs opus.
      e. Trōs Tyriusque mihī nūllō discrīmine agētur.
      f. Sunt lacrimae rērum, et mentem mortālia tangunt.
      g. Varium et mūtābile semper fēmina.
      h. Tū nē cēde malīs.
      i. Semper honōs nōmenque tuum laudēsque manēbunt.
      j. Teneor patriae nec lēgibus ūllīs.

B. Complete the following quotations:

1. Timeō Danaōs et _____.
2. Possunt quia _____.
3. _____ canō.
4. Dux _____.
5. _____ crēdite.

C. Give the meaning of the following quotations:

1. Mīrābile dictū!
2. Ō terque quaterque beātī!
3. Tantae mōlis erat Rōmānam condere gentem!
4. Fuimus Trōes, fuit Īlium et ingēns glōria Teucrōrum.
5. Ūna salūs victīs nūllam spērāre salūtem.
6. Quis fallere possit amantem?
7. Quōrum pars magna fuī.
8. Nōn ignāra malī, miserīs succurrere discō.
9. Fāma, malum quā nōn aliud vēlōcius ūllum.
10. Vēnit summa diēs et inēluctābile tempus Dardaniae.

Unit XIX—Word Study and Derivation

Lesson 49. PREFIXES, SUFFIXES, AND ROOTS

For a review of prefixes, suffixes, and roots, see pages 131 to 142. The following exercises are based on the vocabulary of Vergil.

EXERCISES

A. Separate the following English words into their component parts (prefix and Latin root), and give the meaning of each part.

1. prelude
2. insult
3. refulgent
4. ambivalent
5. coeval
6. progeny
7. perfervid
8. subliminal
9. exhume
10. infant

B. Each italicized word (of Latin derivation) is followed by four words, one of which furnishes a clue to the meaning of the derivative. Select the correct clue.

1. *ferrous* (*a*) game (*b*) vehicle (*c*) steel (*d*) iron
2. *sidereal* (*a*) star (*b*) sun (*c*) moon (*d*) giant
3. *telluric* (*a*) dish (*b*) earth (*c*) sky (*d*) fire
4. *capillary* (*a*) disease (*b*) hat (*c*) hair (*d*) map
5. *nubilous* (*a*) cloud (*b*) rain (*c*) marriage (*d*) comfort
6. *cincture* (*a*) cavity (*b*) belt (*c*) medicine (*d*) cough
7. *pelagic* (*a*) land (*b*) germ (*c*) skin (*d*) sea
8. *frondose* (*a*) noise (*b*) weight (*c*) leaf (*d*) forehead
9. *graminaceous* (*a*) vegetable (*b*) measure (*c*) grass (*d*) orphan
10. *ossicle* (*a*) mouth (*b*) bone (*c*) ship (*d*) reptile

C. Separate the following English words into their component parts (Latin root and suffix), and give the meaning of each part.

1. velocity
2. stellar
3. sepulchral
4. edible
5. fluency
6. lupine
7. aviary
8. libation
9. spumous
10. tremor

D. For each of the following sentences, (1) write a Latin word with which the italicized word is associated by derivation, and (2) choose the word in the accompanying list that best expresses the meaning of the italicized word.

1. There issued from the organ strange, *lacrimose* tones.
   (*a*) joyful   (*b*) tearful   (*c*) bass   (*d*) deafening
2. She begged for *succor*, to no avail.
   (*a*) company   (*b*) food   (*c*) help   (*d*) drink
3. The senator was accused of *nepotism*.
   (*a*) favoritism   (*b*) bribery   (*c*) slander   (*d*) libel
4. The king chided Hamlet for his "obstinate *condolement*."
   (*a*) seclusion   (*b*) anger   (*c*) stubbornness   (*d*) grief
5. The animal displayed a strange, *gradient* motion.
   (*a*) halting   (*b*) clumsy   (*c*) convulsive   (*d*) walking
6. Swift *coruscations* flashed through the skies.
   (*a*) sparkles   (*b*) meteors   (*c*) birds   (*d*) thunderbolts
7. The crowd gathered to watch the *lustral* ceremony.
   (*a*) brilliant   (*b*) sensual   (*c*) purification   (*d*) illegal
8. The plant was thick with large *geminate* leaves.
   (*a*) coarse   (*b*) twin   (*c*) withered   (*d*) colored
9. He practiced the art of *vaticination*.
   (*a*) oratory   (*b*) poetry   (*c*) worship   (*d*) prophecy
10. The creditor relied upon the *nexal* contract.
    (*a*) commercial   (*b*) final   (*c*) binding   (*d*) signed

E. Each of the following English words is derived from two Latin words. Give the Latin words and their meanings.

1. tercentenary	5. multiplicate	8. mitigate
2. soporific	6. penumbra	9. proliferous
3. primogeniture	7. genuflection	10. vaticide
4. juxtaposition		

F. Using your knowledge of prefixes, suffixes, and roots, give the meaning of the following Latin words:

1. lēvitās	8. mēnsūra	15. circumsecō
2. complicō	9. intrōgredior	16. sēmibōs
3. memorātor	10. fragilis	17. rubēscō
4. īnfluō	11. crepitō	18. tricuspis
5. perarduus	12. ēruptiō	19. praecerpō
6. ōminōsus	13. vēnātrīx	20. dīscindō
7. trānō	14. marmoreus	

Lesson 50. RELATED WORDS

The following list contains groups of words that are related in meaning and that resemble one another in spelling:

acuō, sharpen; **ācer,** sharp
āla, wing; **āles,** winged, bird
alternus, alternate; **alter,** the other
anima, breath, life; **animus,** mind, soul
attonitus, thunderstruck, terrified; **attonō,** thunder at
aureus, golden; **aurum,** gold
celerō, quicken; **celer,** quick
comitor, accompany; **comes,** companion
coniugium, union, marriage; **iungō,** join
cōnscius, knowing, conscious of; **īnscius,** ignorant; **scientia,** knowledge; **sciō,** know
cruentus, bloody; **cruor,** blood
cupīdō, desire; **cupiditās,** desire; **cupidus,** desirous; **cupiō,** desire
decōrus, becoming, beautiful; **decus,** ornament, beauty
dignor, deem worthy; **dignitās,** worthiness, prestige; **dignus,** worthy
dīvus, god, godlike; **dīvīnus,** godlike; **deus,** god; **dea,** goddess
doleō, suffer pain; **dolor,** pain, grief
dominor, rule, master; **dominus,** master; **domina,** mistress
duplex, double; **duo,** two
fātālis, fated; **fātum,** fate
ferreus, made of iron; **ferrum,** iron
fleō, weep; **flētus,** weeping
flō, flow; **fluō,** flow; **flūmen,** river; **fluctus,** wave; **fluvius,** river
frangō, break; **suffrāgium,** something broken off, vote
fulgeō, flash, lighten; **fulmen,** lightning
furia, rage, madness; **furor,** rage, madness
gaudeō, rejoice; **gaudium,** joy
gemitus, sigh; **gemō,** sigh
genitor, begetter, father; **gignō,** beget, bear; **prōgeniēs,** race, offspring; **genus,** race; **gēns,** family
gressus, step; **gradior,** walk
horreō, bristle, shudder; **horridus,** bristly, rough
hospes, host, guest; **hospitium,** hospitality
iaculum, missile; **iaciō,** throw
ignārus, ignorant; **ignōtus,** unknown; **ignōrō,** be ignorant, not know
iuvencus, young person; **iuvenis,** youth; **iuventa,** time of youth; **iuventūs,** time of youth

lacrimō, weep; lacrima, tear
latebra, hiding place; lateō, lie hidden
lūceō, shine; lūx, light
lūctus, mourning; lūgeō, mourn
memor, mindful; memorō, call to mind, relate; memoria, memory
minae, battlements, threats; minor, jut out, threaten; immineō,
    threaten
mīrābilis, wonderful; mīror, wonder at
misereor, pity; miseror, pity; miser, pitiable, poor
namque, for; nam, for
nefandus, unspeakable, impious; for, speak
nūbes, cloud; nūbila, clouds; nūbilus, cloudy
obvius, in the way; via, way
onerō, burden; onus, burden
ōrdior, begin; ōrdō, order
pallēns, pale; palleō, be pale
pāscō, feed; pāstor, shepherd
penna, feather; pinna, feather
pietās, dutifulness; pius, dutiful
placidus, quiet, gentle; placeō, please
praeceps, headlong; caput, head
prīncipium, beginning; prīnceps, leader
reliquiae, remains; relinquō, leave behind; reliquus, remaining;
    linquō, leave
sacerdōs, priest; sacer, sacred; sacrō, make sacred, consecrate
saeviō, rage; saevus, raging
sīdō, sit; sedeō, sit
signō, mark; signum, sign, signal; īnsignis, marked, distinguished
sileō, be silent; silentium, silence
simulācrum, likeness, statue; similis, like, similar
sistō, stand; stō, stand
sonitus, sound; sonō, sound
testor, bear witness; testis, witness; testāmentum, will
tumeō, swell; tumidus, swollen
turba, disturbance, crowd; turbidus, confused, wild; turbō, disturb;
    turbō, whirlwind
vāstus, desolate, laid waste; vāstō, lay waste
vīctus, means of living, support; vīvō, live; vīvus, living
vīsus, vision; vīsō, visit; video, see

EXERCISES

A. In each group, select the word in parentheses that is *not* related to the word in italics.

1. *nūbēs*   (nūbila, nōbilis, nūbilus)
2. *sacer*   (saeculum, sacerdōs, sacrō)
3. *dignus*   (digitus, dignor, dignitās)
4. *ignōtus*   (ignōrō, ignārus, īgnis)
5. *vīsus*   (vīsō, vīvus, videō)
6. *miser*   (misereor, miseror, missus)
7. *memor*   (memoria, membrum, memorō)
8. *testor*   (tēstūdō, testis, testāmentum)
9. *victus*   (vīvō, vīvus, vincō)
10. *flō*   (flōs, flūmen, fluō)

B. Match each word in column *A* with its related word in column *B*.

Column A	*Column B*
1. signum	*a.* furor
2. comitor	*b.* ōrdō
3. fulgeō	*c.* silentium
4. furia	*d.* palleō
5. pāscō	*e.* cruor
6. sileō	*f.* comes
7. praeceps	*g.* sonō
8. via	*h.* prīnceps
9. pallēns	*i.* īnsignis
10. ōrdior	*j.* obvius
11. coniugium	*k.* onerō
12. cruentus	*l.* fulmen
13. sonitus	*m.* caput
14. onus	*n.* pāstor
15. prīncipium	*o.* iungō

C. In each group, complete the second pair of words to make them bear the same relationship as the first pair.

1. *deus* is to *dea* as *dominus* is to _____
2. *dolor* is to *doleō* as *flētus* is to _____
3. *horreō* is to *horridus* as *tumeō* is to _____
4. *sīdō* is to *sedeō* as *stō* is to _____
5. *aurum* is to *aureus* as *āla* is to _____
6. *gaudium* is to *gaudeō* as *gemitus* is to _____

7. *iaciō* is to *iaculum* as *lūgeō* is to _____
8. *pius* is to *pietās* as *similis* is to _____
9. *lūceō* is to *lūx* as *lacrimō* is to _____
10. *gressus* is to *gradior* as *suffrāgium* is to _____

D. In each group, there is *one* word related to the word in italics. Select that word and give its meaning.

1. *acuō*   (ager, ācer, accidō)
2. *decōrus*   (decus, decimus, dēcernō)
3. *saevus*   (saeculum, saeviō, salvus)
4. *celerō*   (celebrō, cēlō, celer)
5. *duplex*   (dēpellō, duo, dēpendeō)
6. *lateō*   (latebra, latus, lātus)
7. *iuvencus* (iuvō, iuventa, iūstus)
8. *reliquiae* (religiō, relūceō, linquō)
9. *vāstus*   (vāstō, vātēs, vestis)
10. *prōgeniēs* (prōgredior, prōgressus, gignō)

Lesson 51. SYNONYMS

VERBS

arceō, contineō, inclūdō, confine, enclose
bibō, hauriō, drink
caleō, tepeō, be warm
candeō, ferveō, lūceō, micō, niteō, shine, glow
carpō, vellō, pluck
celerō, contendō, properō, ruō, hasten, rush
cessō, cūnctor, moror, retardō, delay
cieō, moveō, move
cingō, circumdō, circumveniō, surround
concutiō, afflīgō, feriō, pulsō, strike, beat
domō, pācō, superō, vincō, subdue
ēvādō, fugiō, escape
fleō, lacrimō, weep
for, dīcō, loquor, nārrō, speak
foveō, amō, love, cherish
frangō, rumpō, break
gaudeō, ovō, rejoice
immineō, minor, threaten
intrō, ineō, enter
invādō, adorior, aggredior, oppugnō, attack
laedō, noceō, violō, hurt
luctor, contendō, nītor, struggle, strive
mergō, tingō, wet, immerse
nectō, stringō, vinciō, bind
ōrdior, incipiō, begin
pandō, sternō, spread out
paveō, metuō, timeō, vereor, fear
precor, rogō, ask, beg
prōmittō, polliceor, promise
rapiō, capiō, occupō, prehendō, seize
reor, arbitror, exīstimō, putō, think
secō, caedō, cut
sileō, quiēscō, taceō, be silent
struō, aedificō, build
succurrō, iuvō, help
surgō, orior, rise
urgeō, hortor, impellō, urge
ūrō, incendō, burn

vēlō, tegō, cover
veneror, colō, worship
vetō, prohibeō, forbid
vīsō, spectō, look at

NOUNS

aequor, mare, pelagus, pontus, sea
āēr, aura, air
aethēr, caelum, polus, sky
aevum, saeculum, lifetime
āles, avis, bird
altāria, āra, altar
amnis, flūmen, fluvius, river
anima, vīta, life
antrum, spēlunca, cave
armentum, pecus, cattle
artus, membrum, limb
arvum, ager, campus, field
astrum, sīdus, stella, star
capillus, coma, crīnis, hair
caterva, multitūdō, turba, crowd
cervīx, collum, neck
clipeus, scūtum, shield
coniugium, cōnūbium, marriage
corōna, sertum, wreath
cruor, sanguis, blood
cupīdō, cupiditās, studium, desire
daps, epulae, feast, banquet
decus, ōrnāmentum, ornament, distinction
dolus, fraus, īnsidiae, deceit, trickery
ēnsis, gladius, sword
faciēs, cōnspectus, fōrma, speciēs, vīsus, appearance, sight
famulus, servus, slave, servant
fās, nūmen, divine will
fax, taeda, torch
flūctus, unda, wave
folium, frōns, leaf
foris, porta, door
furia, furor, rabiēs, madness
gaudium, fēlīcitās, joy

genitor, pater, father
germānus, frāter, brother
grāmen, herba, grass
gressus, passus, step
harundō, sagitta, arrow
hasta, tēlum, spear
humus, solum, ground
iaculum, pīlum, spīculum, javelin
iuventa, iuventūs, pūbēs, youth
lētum, mors, death
lūctus, dolor, grief
lūcus, nemus, silva, grove, forest
mōnstrum, ōmen, warning, omen
nimbus, nūbēs, cloud
penna, pinna, feather
pondus, onus, weight, burden
prōgeniēs, prōlēs, offspring
rādīx, stirps, root
ratis, nāvigium, nāvis, ship
ruīna, exitium, interitus, perniciēs, pestis, destruction
rūpēs, saxum, scopulus, rock
sonitus, clāmor, sound, noise
sopor, somnus, sleep
superī, deī, gods
tellūs, terra, earth
vīctus, cibus, food

ADJECTIVES

albus, cānus, white
āles, volucer, winged
āmēns, ferōx, saevus, mad, wild
arduus, altus, celsus, sublīmis, superus, high, lofty
asper, dūrus, harsh
āter, niger, black
caecus, occultus, hidden
citus, celer, rapidus, vēlōx, swift
curvus, uncus, bent, crooked
dīrus, nefandus, nefārius, cursed, impious
dīvus, dīvīnus, godlike
ignārus, īnscius, not knowing, ignorant

immānis, ingēns, huge
inānis, vacuus, empty
laevus, sinister, left
lēvis, lēnis, smooth
maestus, trīstis, sad
mītis, placidus, gentle, kind
saucius, vulnerātus, wounded
serēnus, clārus, clear, bright
sērus, tardus, late

ADVERBS

dēmum, dēnique, tandem, at last
dūdum, diū, for a long time
equidem, quidem, profectō, vērō, indeed
extemplō, statim, prōtinus, immediately
haud, nōn, not
intus, intrā, inside

CONJUNCTIONS

namque, nam, for
nēquīquam, frūstrā, in vain
nī, nisi, if not, unless
-ve, aut, vel, sive (seu), or

EXERCISES

A. In each group, select the word in parentheses that is *not* a synonym of the italicized word.

1.	*ruīna*	(pestis, exitium, rūs, perniciēs)
2.	*lūceō*	(micō, cieō, candeō, ferveō)
3.	*faciēs*	(foris, speciēs, vīsus, cōnspectus)
4.	*celsus*	(arduus, dūrus, sublīmis, superus)
5.	*feriō*	(concutiō, pulsō, afflīgō, portō)
6.	*equidem*	(quidem, vērō, quīdam, profectō)
7.	*pontus*	(pōns, pelagus, mare, aequor)
8.	*paveō*	(timeō, polliceor, metuō, vereor)
9.	*citus*	(rapidus, celer, citerior, vēlōx)
10.	*rapiō*	(occupō, capiō, prehendō, noceō)

B. In each group, select the synonym of the italicized word.

1. *carpō:*   vellō, rapiō, solvō
2. *spēlunca:*   rūpēs, folium, antrum
3. *laevus:*   placidus, sinister, dūrus
4. *haud:*   statim, nōn, dūdum
5. *nēquīquam:*   vel, nam, frūstrā
6. *mergō:*   tingō, vādō, pōnō
7. *succurrō:*   contendō, iuvō, cēdō
8. *ēnsis:*   scūtum, gladius, pīlum
9. *sērus:*   gravis, lēvis, tardus
10. *stirps:*   metus, rādīx, portus

C. Match each word in column *A* with its synonym in column *B*.

Column A	*Column B*
1. fleō	*a.* niger
2. pecus	*b.* albus
3. grāmen	*c.* sertum
4. āter	*d.* avis
5. gaudeō	*e.* vulnerātus
6. tegō	*f.* armentum
7. āles	*g.* frangō
8. daps	*h.* trīstis
9. immānis	*i.* ovō
10. cānus	*j.* ingēns
11. bibō	*k.* servus
12. rumpō	*l.* lacrimō
13. ōrdior	*m.* sternō
14. corōna	*n.* herba
15. famulus	*o.·* tepeō
16. lētum	*p.* incipiō
17. maestus	*q.* vēlō
18. caleō	*r.* mors
19. saucius	*s.* hauriō
20. pandō	*t.* epulae

D. In each group, supply a third synonym.

1. sīdus, stella, _____
2. dēnique, tandem, _____
3. āmēns, ferōx, _____
4. nāvigium, ratis, _____
5. arceō, inclūdō, _____

6. amnis, fluvius, _____
7. extemplō, prōtinus, _____
8. scopulus, rūpēs, _____
9. urgeō, impellō, _____
10. furia, rabiēs, _____

E. In each sentence, replace the italicized word with a correct synonym.

1. *Ovēmus* igitur.
2. Vir *clipeō* usus est.
3. Faciēs eius *aspera* vīsa est.
4. *Haud* aliter volābat ad lītus.
5. Omnēs revertere *pollicitī sunt*.
6. Hostēs aedificium *ūrent*.
7. Aenēās *humum* spectat.
8. *Mōnstrum* horridum apparuit.
9. Dolus erat *caecus*.
10. Rāmōs *secābant*.

Lesson 52. ANTONYMS

VERBS

accipiō, accept	**spernō,** reject
arceō, confine	**līberō,** set free
arrigō, raise up	**opprimō,** press down
celerō, hasten	**tardō,** slow up
dominor, be master	**serviō,** be a slave
domō, subdue	**trādō,** surrender
for, speak	**sileō,** be silent
foveō, cherish, love	**ōdī,** hate
gaudeō, rejoice	**doleō,** grieve
induō, put on	**exuō,** take off
intrō, enter	**exeō,** leave
iuvō, help	**laedō,** harm
nectō, bind	**laxō,** loosen
ōrdior, begin	**cōnficiō,** finish
palleō, be pale	**rubeō,** be red
pateō, be exposed	**lateō,** be hidden
rīdeō, laugh	**lacrimō,** cry
struō, build	**ēruō,** overthrow

NOUNS

aurōra, dawn	**vesper,** dusk
culmen, top	**solum,** bottom
dominus, master	**famulus,** servant
gaudium, joy	**dolor,** grief
iuventūs, youth	**senectūs,** old age
pietās, piety	**nefās,** impiety
prīncipium, beginning	**fīnis,** end
prōra, prow	**puppis,** stern
terra, land	**aequor,** sea
vēritās, honesty	**dolus,** deceit
vigilia, wakefulness	**sopor,** sleep
vīta, life	**lētum,** death

ADJECTIVES

albus, white

ambō, both

apertus, exposed

beātus, blessed

citus, swift

cōnscius, knowing

dexter, right

dulcis, sweet

dūrus, hard

laetus, joyful

lēvis, smooth

mītis, gentle

placidus, serene

plēnus, full

pulcher, beautiful

saucius, wounded

serēnus, clear, bright

siccus, dry

solidus, solid

validus, strong, vigorous

niger, black

neuter, neither

caecus, hidden

dīrus, cursed

tardus, slow

īnscius, not knowing

laevus, left

acerbus, bitter

mollis, soft

trīstis, sad

asper, rough

ferōx, wild

turbidus, disturbed

inānis, empty

foedus, foul, ugly

incolumis, unharmed

āter, dark

ūmidus, wet

liquidus, liquid

sēgnis, sluggish

ADVERBS

equidem, indeed, of course

intus, inside

iūxtā, nearby

prīmō, at first

usquam, anywhere

minimē, not at all

extrā, outside

longē, far off

dēmum, at last

nūsquam, nowhere

EXERCISES

A. In each group, select the antonym of the italicized word.

1. *intrō:* ineō, exuō, exeō
2. *gaudium:* dolor, sublīmis, amor
3. *laevus:* dexter, sinister, gravis
4. *intus:* inde, extrā, hinc
5. *albus:* cānus, almus, niger
6. *prīncipium:* fīnis, ōrdō, dux

7. *foveō:* horreō, ōdī, accendō
8. *laedō:* noceō, arceō, iuvō
9. *dēmum:* dēnique, anteā, prīmō
10. *lētum:* vīta, metus, mors

B. Match each word in column *A* with its antonym in column *B*

Column A

1. lacrimō
2. aequor
3. ambō
4. iūxtā
5. citus
6. prōra
7. domō
8. palleō
9. culmen
10. asper

Column B

a. longē
b. trādō
c. rīdeō
d. puppis
e. lēvis
f. solum
g. tardus
h. terra
i. rubeō
j. neuter

C. In each sentence, replace the italicized word with its antonym.

1. Fīnēs *latēbant.*
2. Terra *sicca* erat.
3. Possuntne vidērī *usquam* equī?
4. Quis *iuventūtem* māvult?
5. Omnēs fuērunt *laetī.*
6. Servōs līberārī *vetuit.*
7. Mīles praemium *spernet.*
8. Domī *famulus* sum.
9. Mare *turbidum* spectābant.
10. Ob *dolum* eius manēmus.

D. Write an antonym of each of the following Latin words; translate each answer.

1. celerō
2. aurōra
3. caecus
4. equidem
5. cōnscius
6. struō
7. saucius
8. nectō
9. pietās
10. for

Lesson 53. WORDS OFTEN CONFUSED

accendō, set on fire
accēdō, approach

aequor, sea
aequō, make level

āla, wing
āles, winged, bird·

aliter, otherwise
alter, the other

ambō, both
ambulō, walk

amictus, cloak
amīcus, friend

āra, altar
arō, plow

aura, air
auris, ear
aurum, gold

avis, bird
avus, grandfather

bōs, ox, cow
bis, twice

caleō, be warm, glow
careō, lack

canis, dog
cānus, gray, hoary
cinis, ashes

cervīx, neck
cervus, stag, deer

curvus, bent
currus, chariot

dīrus, dreadful, cursed
dūrus, hard, harsh

dīves, rich
dīvus, godlike, god

dolus, deceit, trickery
dolor, grief

exuō, take off
exeō, leave

famēs, hunger
fāma, report, reputation

fās, divine right
fax, torch

feriō, strike
ferō, bear

frēnum, bit, reins
fretum, strait

fulmen, lightning
flūmen, river

fūnis, rope
fūnus, funeral, death

geminus, twin
gemitus, sigh

habēna, rein, strap
harēna, sand

haereō, cling, adhere
hauriō, drink, drain
horreō, shudder

immānis, huge
inānis, empty

laedō, harm, hurt
laudō, praise

laetus, joyful
laevus, left

lēvis, smooth
levis, light, mild

līmen, threshold
lūmen, light, brightness

lūceō, shine
lūgeō, mourn

lūctus, mourning
lūcus, grove

mōlēs, mass, heap
mollis, soft

niteō, shine
nītor, lean on, strive

nūmen, divine will
nōmen, name

parcō, spare
pāscō, feed
pāreō, obey

pectus, breast
pecus, beast, cattle

peragō, accomplish
pergō, continue

pignus, pledge
pinguis, fat

pondus, weight
pontus, sea

rāmus, branch
rēmus, oar

rīdeō, laugh
rigeō, stiffen

secus, otherwise
sērus, late

solum, ground
sōlum, only

tingō, wet, dip
tangō, touch

torus, couch
torvus, stern, grim

unda, wave
unde, whence

vellō, pluck
vēlō, cover, veil

veneror, worship
vēnor, hunt

vinciō, bind
vincō, conquer

EXERCISES

A. Select the correct English meaning of each Latin word.

1. *auris*   (gold, ear, air)
2. *dolus*   (deceit, grief, gift)
3. *lūcus*   (grove, mourning, lake)
4. *fūnis*   (funeral, end, rope)
5. *torvus*   (couch, stern, whole)
6. *avis*   (grandfather, bird, altar)
7. *mollis*   (soft, mass, hill)
8. *gemitus*   (twin, ancestor, sigh)
9. *nītor*   (shine, lean on, delay)
10. *pondus*   (sea, bridge, weight)

11. *tingō* (touch, back, wet)
12. *rigeō* (stiffen, laugh, seize)
13. *hauriō* (cling, drink, shudder)
14. *parcō* (feed, obey, spare)
15. *fretum* (bit, strait, lightning)

B. Match each word in column *A* with its meaning in column *B*.

Column A	*Column B*
1. ambō	*a.* mourn
2. canis	*b.* pledge
3. lūceō	*c.* continue
4. vellō	*d.* dog
5. cinis	*e.* both
6. pignus	*f.* gray
7. ambulō	*g.* ashes
8. vēlō	*h.* walk
9. lūgeō	*i.* shine
10. vinciō	*j.* fat
11. peragō	*k.* conquer
12. pinguis	*l.* accomplish
13. pergō	*m.* pluck
14. vincō	*n.* bind
15. cānus	*o.* cover

C. Select the word in parentheses that you would use to translate the italicized English word or expression.

1. Aeneas decided *to leave* Troy. (exeō, exuō)
2. Midas was reputed to be extremely *rich*. (dīvus, dīves)
3. The goddess ascended the *chariot*. (curvus, currus)
4. He lets the *reins* stream freely. (habēna, harēna)
5. She walks the *ground* with head hidden. (solum, sōlum)
6. Dido seemed *joyful* in the undertaking. (laevus, laetus)
7. The mariners' shouts *strike* the heavens. (feriō, ferō)
8. He plunged the sword into his *breast*. (pecus, pectus)
9. The horse halted at the very *threshold*. (līmen, lūmen)
10. Encircle your brow with *branches*. (rāmus, rēmus)

Lesson 54. REVIEW OF WORD STUDY AND DERIVATION

A. Select the correct definition of each of the following English words; give a Latin word associated with it by derivation.

1.	mollify	(soothe, change, deceive)
2.	immaculate	(divine, proper, spotless)
3.	strident	(quick, harsh, seated)
4.	progeny	(genius, disease, offspring)
5.	venerate	(make new, avenge, worship)
6.	extort	(wrench, urge, carry out)
7.	exonerate	(honor, acquit, embitter)
8.	denigrate	(sail away, denote, blacken)
9.	viridity	(manliness, greenness, worthiness)
10.	ululation	(howl, wave, imitate)

B. Separate the following English words into their Latin component parts (prefix and root), and give the meaning of each part.

1. commemorate	5. reverberate	8. deprecate
2. translucent	6. inherent	9. extirpate
3. suspend	7. percussion	10. indecorous
4. abhor		

C. Each italicized word, of Latin derivation, is followed by three words, one of which gives a clue to the meaning of the derivative. Select the correct clue.

1. *tonsorial* (a) operate　(b) shear　(c) thunder
2. *lugubrious* (a) mourn　(b) drink　(c) shine
3. *minatory* (a) threaten　(b) lessen　(c) delay
4. *mordant* (a) die　(b) sorrow　(c) bite
5. *speluncous* (a) javelin　(b) foam　(c) cave
6. *lethal* (a) sleep　(b) death　(c) medicine
7. *lesion* (a) study　(b) hurt　(c) joy
8. *pinguid* (a) fat　(b) colorful　(c) devoted
9. *nodal* (a) cloud　(b) swim　(c) knot
10. *unciform* (a) crooked　(b) straight　(c) round

D. Separate the following English words into their Latin component parts (root and suffix), and give the meaning of each part.

1. bovine
2. agitator
3. volatile
4. candor

5. lethal
6. ovation
7. saline

8. ponderous
9. capillary
10. acuity

E. Give a synonym and an antonym for each of the following Latin words:

1. vetō
2. gaudium
3. laevus
4. intrō

5. lētum
6. intus
7. foveō

8. inānis
9. famulus
10. ōrdior

Unit XX—*Culture*

Lesson 55. THE LIFE OF VERGIL

SIGNIFICANT EVENTS

BIRTH

Publius Vergilius Marō (Vergil or Virgil) was born on October 15, 70 B.C. His birthplace was the village of Andes, near Mantua, in Cisalpine Gaul. His father was a farmer of moderate means. Vergil's early life in the country greatly influenced his future writings.

EDUCATION

Vergil attended school in Mantua, in Cremona, and in Milan. Finally, in 53 B.C., he went to Rome. His studies included grammar, rhetoric, philosophy, mathematics, and medicine.

PERSONAL CHARACTERISTICS

Vergil was very shy, physically delicate, and slow of speech. Unlike Caesar and Cicero, he was ill-fitted to take part in the political and military events of his time. Vergil lived the retiring life of a scholar; he never married.

PRIVATE LIFE

At the age of fifteen, Vergil assumed the **toga virīlis** (toga of the adult male). After his studies were completed, he settled on his father's farm and began to write poetry. In 41 B.C., after the battle of Philippi, Vergil's farm was confiscated. However, his poetry gained him powerful friends, notably Maecenas who was an adviser of Augustus and a wealthy patron of literature. Through the intervention of these friends, his farm was later restored.

LAST DAYS AND DEATH

In the year 19 B.C., Vergil met the Emperor Augustus in Athens. Augustus induced the poet to return to Rome with him, but Vergil became seriously ill on the voyage. He died on September 21, shortly after landing at Brundisium, in southern Italy, and was buried at Naples.

His tomb bore this inscription:

Mantua mē genuit; Calabrī rapuēre; tenet nunc Parthenopē; cecinī pascua, rūra, ducēs.

Mantua gave me birth; Calabria snatched my life; now Parthenope (Naples) holds me; I sang of pastures (Eclogues), fields (Georgics), and heroes (Aeneid).

VERGIL'S WRITINGS

The Minor Poems.   (The authenticity of some of these early works has been questioned.)

1. **Catalepton** (Trifles). This is a collection of epigrams and other short poems, supposedly written in his youth.

2. **Cīris** (The Sea-bird)

3. **Cōpa** (The Tavern-maid)

4. **Culex** (The Gnat)

5. **Dīrae** (Bad Omens)

6. **Morētum** (The Salad)

The Eclogues (Selections), also called **Bucolics** (Pastoral Poems). These ten short poems, published in 37 B.C., describe incidents in the life of Vergil and his friends. In the **Eclogues,** actual persons appear in the guise of shepherds. To some extent the poems imitate the *Idyls* of Theocritus, a Greek poet who lived in Sicily in the third century B.C. The **Eclogues** still retain their charm and grace.

The Georgics (Husbandry or Farming). The work consists of four books, describing life on the farm. Written at the suggestion of Maecenas, the **Georgics** were completed in 29 B.C. The poem, modeled on *Works and Days* by the ancient Greek poet Hesiod, aimed to rekindle interest in rural life, and is considered Vergil's most finished work.

The Aeneid (The Story of Aeneas). This work, an epic poem in dactylic hexameter, consists of twelve books. The first six books deal with the fall of Troy and the wanderings of Aeneas, the traditional founder of the Roman race. This section may be compared with Homer's *Odyssey*, which tells of the wanderings of Odysseus. The last six books deal with Aeneas's contest for the possession of Italy. This section corresponds to Homer's *Iliad*, which deals with battles centering around the siege of Troy.

The epic, composed at the request of Augustus, occupied the last ten years of Vergil's life. His untimely death in 19 B.C. left the poem not quite complete, as is evidenced by more than fifty unfinished verses.

Vergil's purpose in writing the **Aeneid** was to glorify Rome and the Emperor Augustus, and thus to stir the Romans to a strong feeling of patriotism and pride of race. The result was a poem of exquisite beauty and lofty purpose, whose influence has been felt through the ages.

VERGIL'S FAME AND INFLUENCE

Vergil, even in his lifetime, was recognized as a great poet; as time passed, his fame reached new heights. Here are some pertinent facts:

1. Because of his incomparable literary style and his philosophic insight, Vergil is considered to be the greatest of epic poets, next to Homer.

2. Shortly after Vergil's death, Latin writers and scholars found in the **Aeneid** a fertile source for quotations.

3. Vergil's works were imitated by many Roman poets and prose writers.

4. The **Aeneid** became the leading textbook in Roman schools.

5. Vergil was held in such high reverence during the Roman Empire that the custom arose of consulting his works at random with a view to finding omens, just as the Sibylline Books were consulted. When so used, his works were called **Sortēs Vergiliānae** (The Oracles of Vergil).

6. In the period between the 13th and 16th centuries, Vergil was regarded both as a magician and as a prophet. In the fourth **Eclogue,** he had supposedly foretold the birth of Christ. The poet's name was also associated with the word **virga** (prophetic wand) ; hence the alternate spelling **Virgil.**

7. The great medieval poets, Ariosto in Italy and Chaucer in England, acknowledged their indebtedness to Vergil. Dante, in the *Divine Comedy,* addresses Vergil as his master and guide.

8. In more recent times, Milton, in his *Paradise Lost,* pays unconscious tribute to Vergil. The works of Shakespeare, Spenser, Dryden, Tennyson, Marlowe, and Swinburne all show decided Vergilian influence.

CHRONOLOGY OF IMPORTANT EVENTS IN VERGIL'S LIFE

B.C.

70 Born near Mantua, Cisalpine Gaul, on October 15.

58 Attends school at Cremona.

55 Assumes the **toga virīlis.**

54 Attends school at Milan.

53 Goes to Rome to continue his studies.

43 Starts work on the **Eclogues** in his native town.

41 Confiscation of Vergil's farm.

40 Beginning of friendship with Maecenas. Restoration of his farm.

38 Accompanies Maecenas to Brundisium.

37 Publishes the **Eclogues** and starts work on the **Georgics.**

29 Publishes the **Georgics** and starts work on the **Aeneid.**

23 Reads a portion of the **Aeneid** to Augustus and his sister Octavia, who had just lost her son Marcellus.

19 Goes to Greece and returns with Augustus to Brundisium, where he dies on September 21.

EXERCISES

A. In the following statements, if the italicized term is incorrect write the correct term. If the italicized term is correct, write *true*.

1. Vergil was born near *Cremona* in 70 B.C.
2. On his death in 19 B.C. Vergil was buried at *Brundisium*.
3. The collection of poems called CATALEPTON may have been composed by Vergil in his *youth*.
4. In *41* B.C. Vergil's farm was confiscated.
5. The AENEID, left incomplete at Vergil's death, contains about *500* unfinished verses.
6. The AENEID consists of *ten* books.
7. At the age of 15, Vergil assumed the *toga praetexta*.
8. The word "Culex" means *The Gnat*.
9. The *Georgics* are considered Vergil's most finished work.
10. The Greek poem "Works and Days" served as a model for Vergil's *Eclogues*.

B. Match each name in column *A* with the proper item in column *B*.

Column A	*Column B*
1. Hesiod	*a. Idyls*
2. Theocritus	*b.* patron of literature
3. Milton	*c.* Roman emperor
4. Maecenas	*d. Works and Days*
5. Homer	*e.* medieval English poet
6. Dante	*f.* Marcellus
7. Chaucer	*g. Cōpa*
8. Augustus	*h. Divine Comedy*
9. Vergil	*i. Iliad*
10. Octavia	*j. Paradise Lost*

C. Complete the following statements:

1. Vergil's full name was Publius Vergilius _____.
2. The meter of the *Aeneid* is called _____.
3. The last six books of the *Aeneid* deal with Aeneas's contest for _____.
4. The *Aeneid* was composed at the request of _____.
5. Vergil is considered the greatest epic poet next to _____.
6. Vergil's name has often been associated with the Latin word _____.

7. Vergil's main purpose in writing the *Aeneid* was to _____.
8. *Sortēs Vergiliānae* means _____.
9. Part of the inscription on Vergil's tomb reads *cecinī pascua, rūra, _____*.
10. The title of Vergil's collection of poems called *Catalepton* means _____.

D. The following events are connected with the life of Vergil. Arrange them in the proper chronological sequence by lettering them from *a* to *j*:

1. publishes *Eclogues*
2. attends school at Milan
3. accompanies Maecenas to Brundisium
4. attends school at Rome
5. publishes *Georgics*

6. goes to Greece
7. attends school at Cremona
8. assumes the toga virīlis
9. confiscation of his farm
10. death of Marcellus

Lesson 56. OUTLINE OF THE *AENEID*

BOOK I

While sailing on their long voyage from Troy to Italy, the Trojans, led by Aeneas, are shipwrecked as a result of Juno's scheming. They land on the coast of Africa where they are hospitably received by Dido, the Phoenician queen, who has recently founded Carthage. At a banquet, Dido requests Aeneas to recount the story of his wanderings.

BOOK II

Aeneas begins his story (filling all of Books II and III), telling of the destruction of Troy by the Greeks. He describes his flight from the burning city, accompanied by his father Anchises, his son Ascanius, and a band of faithful followers.

BOOK III

Continuing his story, Aeneas tells of his unsuccessful attempts to settle in Thrace and Crete, and of his landing at Sicily, where Anchises died. Then follows a description of the continuation of the journey and of the storm encountered in Book I.

BOOK IV

Dido falls in love with Aeneas. The Trojan is warned by Mercury, however, not to linger in Carthage but to proceed on his divine mission to build a new home in Italy. He sets sail. Dido, in despair, kills herself.

BOOK V

Aeneas lands in Sicily on the anniversary of his father's death, and marks the occasion by conducting elaborate funeral games. The Trojans then sail for Italy.

BOOK VI

Aeneas reaches Cumae on the western coast of Italy. With the aid of the Sibyl, he visits the underworld, where Anchises prophesies the glories of Rome.

BOOK VII

Aeneas arrives at the Tiber and is welcomed by King Latinus of Latium, who offers him his daughter Lavinia in marriage. Juno, however, stirs up strife between the newly arrived Trojans and the native Latins.

BOOK VIII

Aeneas sails up the Tiber to Pallanteum (this is the origin of the word *Palatine*) and makes an alliance with King Evander who reigns there. Vulcan, at the request of Venus, forges arms for Aeneas.

BOOK IX

Turnus, king of the Rutulians and Lavinia's former suitor, attacks the Trojan camp. Taking advantage of Aeneas's absence, Turnus tries, without success, to set fire to the Trojan fleet. Casualties occur on both sides.

BOOK X

Pallas, King Evander's son and ally of Aeneas, is slain by Turnus. Mezentius, an exiled king of Etruria and ally of Turnus, is slain by Aeneas.

BOOK XI

Rites for the dead are held by order of Aeneas. A truce of twelve days is granted the Latins to perform funeral ceremonies. After the truce, the Trojans advance on Laurentum, a town on the coast of Latium. Camilla, a Volscian warrior maiden and ally of Turnus, is treacherously slain.

BOOK XII

A treaty is drawn up whereby the war would be settled by the outcome of a single combat between Aeneas and Turnus. The treaty is broken by Juturna, sister of Turnus, and both sides rush into battle. In the course of the combat, Turnus is slain by Aeneas.

EXERCISES

A. Select the Book of the *Aeneid* in which each of the following events takes place:

1. Dido commits suicide.
2. The account of the destruction of Troy.
3. Aeneas makes an alliance with King Evander.
4. Aeneas is hospitably received by Queen Dido.
5. A twelve-day truce is granted the Latins.
6. Aeneas lands in Sicily the second time.
7. Evander's son Pallas is slain.
8. The death of Anchises.
9. Aeneas is welcomed by King Latinus.
10. Anchises prophesies the glories of Rome.

B. Match each name in column *A* with its description in column *B*.

Column A	*Column B*
1. Dido	*a.* king of Latium
2. Anchises	*b.* son of Aeneas
3. Latinus	*c.* son of Evander
4. Lavinia	*d.* father of Aeneas
5. Ascanius	*e.* warrior maiden
6. Evander	*f.* queen of Carthage
7. Turnus	*g.* daughter of Latinus
8. Pallas	*h.* sister of Turnus
9. Camilla	*i.* king of the Rutulians
10. Juturna	*j.* king of Pallanteum

C. In the following statements, if the italicized term is incorrect, write the correct term. If the italicized term is correct, write *true*.

1. The Trojans were shipwrecked through the scheming of *Venus*.
2. In Book III of the AENEID, Aeneas tells of his *successful* attempts to settle in Thrace and Crete.

3. Pallas was slain by *Turnus*.
4. Aeneas visited the underworld at *Cumae*.
5. Turnus was once Lavinia's *husband*.
6. Anchises died in *Sicily*.
7. In the underworld, Anchises prophesied Rome's eventual *downfall*.
8. Aeneas was warned by *Mercury* not to linger in Carthage.
9. *Book XII* tells of the breaking of the treaty by Juturna.
10. At the request of Venus, *Pluto* forged weapons for Aeneas.

Lesson 57. IMPORTANT CHARACTERS IN THE *AENEID*

Acestes. A mythical king of Sicily.

Achates. A faithful companion of Aeneas; often associated with the adjective *fīdus*.

Achilles (also called **Pelides,** son of Peleus). Greatest of the Greek heroes at Troy. He was finally slain by an arrow aimed at his heel, his one vulnerable spot; hence the expression *Achilles' heel.*

Aeneas. Son of Venus and Anchises; hero of the *Aeneid.* Often associated with the adjective *pius.*

Ajax. (1) Son of Telamon; Greek hero who contended with Ulysses for the arms of Achilles. (2) Son of Oileus; Greek hero who abducted Cassandra from Minerva's temple. As a punishment the goddess destroyed his fleet.

Anchises. Father of Aeneas.

Andromache. Wife of Hector, the Trojan hero.

Anna. Sister of Queen Dido.

Antenor. A Trojan who, after the capture of Troy, went to Italy and founded Patavium, later called Padua.

Ascanius (also called **Iulus**). Son of Aeneas; King of Lavinium; founder of Alba Longa.

Atrides. Son of Atreus, King of Mycenae, referring either to Agamemnon or Menelaus, the leaders of the Greeks at Troy. In the plural, Atrides refers to both sons of Atreus.

Augustus Caesar (formerly **Octavianus**). Emperor of Rome from 30 B.C. to 14 A.D. This period is known, in history, as the Augustan Age; in literature, as the Golden Age.

Calchas. A priest and prophet of the Greeks at Troy.

Camilla. A Volscian warrior maiden; ally of Turnus.

Cassandra. Daughter of Priam, King of Troy; loved by Apollo and endowed by him with the gift of prophecy. Later, since she did not return his love, Apollo decreed that no one should ever believe her prophecies, even though they were true.

Cerberus. The three-headed dog that guarded the entrance to the underworld.

Charon. The ferryman of the underworld, who conveyed the souls of the dead across the river Styx.

Creusa. Daughter of Priam; wife of Aeneas.

Cyclops. A member of a race of one-eyed giants who lived in Sicily.

Daedalus. An Athenian artisan who built the famous Labyrinth for King Minos of Crete. He was later imprisoned in the Labyrinth, from which he escaped to Cumae with the aid of wings fastened on with wax.

Dardanus. Ancestor of the Trojans; hence the word *Dardanī*, the Trojans.

Dido (also called **Elissa**). Founder and Queen of Carthage.

Diomedes (also called **Tydides**, son of Tydeus). A famous Greek warrior at Troy.

Evander. King of Pallanteum; ally of Aeneas.

Ganymedes (**Ganymede**). A Trojan youth, known for his beauty, who was carried off by an eagle to be the cupbearer of Jupiter.

Hector. The eldest son of Priam; the most valiant warrior of the Trojans. He was slain by Achilles, who dragged his body three times around the walls of Troy.

Hecuba. Wife of Priam.

Helena (**Helen of Troy**). Daughter of Jupiter and Leda; wife of the Spartan king, Menelaus. Her abduction by Paris, son of Priam, brought on the Trojan War.

Juturna. Sister of Turnus.

Laocoön. Son of Priam; priest of Apollo. He opposed dragging the Wooden Horse into Troy, and drove a spear into it. These actions offended Juno, who sent two serpents to kill Laocoön and his two sons.

Latinus. King of Latium who befriended Aeneas.

Lavinia. Daughter of King Latinus; second wife of Aeneas.

Marcellus. Son of Augustus' sister Octavia. His untimely death prompted the well-known passage in Book VI of the *Aeneid*.

Menelaus. King of Sparta; husband of Helen of Troy.

Mezentius. An exiled king of Etruria; ally of Turnus. He was slain by Aeneas.

Minos. King of Crete. After his death, a judge in the underworld.

Orestes. Son of Agamemnon. He killed his mother, Clytemnestra, for having murdered his father.

Palinurus. Pilot of Aeneas's ship and of the entire Trojan fleet.

Pallas. King Evander's son; ally of Aeneas. He was slain by Turnus.

Paris. Son of Priam. Juno, Minerva, and Venus selected him to judge which of the three was the "fairest." Paris awarded the prize, the Golden Apple of Discord, to Venus. In return, he received Helen, the most beautiful woman in the world.

Priamus (Priam). The last king of Troy, slain by Pyrrhus.

Pygmalion. Brother of Dido. He killed Dido's husband, Sychaeus.

Pyrrhus (also called **Neoptolemus**). Son of Achilles. After the Trojan War, he founded a kingdom in Epirus. He was slain by Orestes.

Romulus. Son of Mars, twin brother of Remus; the mythical founder of Rome.

Sibylla (Sibyl). A prophetess; refers especially to the Sibyl at Cumae, priestess of Apollo, who conducted Aeneas through the underworld.

Sinon. A Greek spy who induced the Trojans to drag the Wooden Horse into Troy.

Sychaeus. The husband of Dido; treacherously slain by Dido's brother, Pygmalion.

Teucer. Founder of the Trojan line; hence the word *Teucrī*, the Trojans.

Tithonus. Brother of Priam; husband of Aurora, goddess of the dawn.

Turnus. King of the Rutulians; slain by Aeneas in single combat.

EXERCISES

A. In the following statements, if the italicized term is incorrect, write the correct term. If the italicized term is correct, write *true*.

1. Paris awarded the prize of the Golden Apple to *Juno*.
2. Minos was king of *Sicily*.
3. The prophecies of *Cassandra* were believed by no one.
4. *Pygmalion* was the brother of Dido.
5. *Dardanus* built the famous Labyrinth.
6. *Turnus* was slain by Aeneas in single combat.

7. *Ganymede* became the cupbearer of Jupiter.
8. Charon ferried the souls of the dead across the river *Tiber*.
9. Calchas was a prophet of the *Greeks* at Troy.
10. Andromache was the wife of *Menelaus*.

B. Match each name in column *A* with its description in column *B*.

Column A	Column B
1. Creusa	*a.* king of Latium
2. Laocoön	*b.* founder of the Trojan line
3. Latinus	*c.* three-headed dog
4. Sinon	*d.* son of Aeneas
5. Teucer	*e.* wife of Priam
6. Anna	*f.* Greek spy
7. Ascanius	*g.* faithful friend of Aeneas
8. Cerberus	*h.* sister of Queen Dido
9. Hecuba	*i.* wife of Aeneas
10. Achates	*j.* priest of Apollo, slain by serpents

C. Select the word or expression that best completes each of the following statements:

1. Queen Dido was also known as (*a*) Anna (*b*) Elissa (*c*) Sibylla (*d*) Lavinia.
2. Alba Longa was founded by (*a*) Ascanius (*b*) Aeneas (*c*) Augustus (*d*) Tydides.
3. Achilles was invulnerable except in his (*a*) toe (*b*) hand (*c*) knee (*d*) heel.
4. A member of a race of one-eyed giants was called (*a*) Cerberus (*b*) Pyrrhus (*c*) Cyclops (*d*) Oileus.
5. Sychaeus was slain by (*a*) Pygmalion (*b*) Pallas (*c*) Mezentius (*d*) Turnus.
6. The adjective most often used to describe Aeneas is (*a*) fīdus (*b*) cārus (*c*) beātus (*d*) pius.
7. The two sons of Atreus were Menelaus and (*a*) Antenor (*b*) Ajax (*c*) Acestes (*d*) Agamemnon.
8. The Emperor Augustus reigned from 30 B.C. to (*a*) 14 B.C. (*b*) 14 A.D. (*c*) 30 A.D. (*d*) 40 A.D.
9. The Greek hero who abducted Cassandra from the temple was (*a*) Achilles (*b*) Atrides (*c*) Ajax (*d*) Diomedes.
10. The famous warrior maiden of the Volscians was called (*a*) Creusa (*b*) Camilla (*c*) Cassandra (*d*) Helena.

Lesson 58. DEITIES IN THE *AENEID*

Vergil gives great prominence in the *Aeneid* to the actions of deities, both major and minor. This interest reflects not only the Roman belief in the existence of gods, but also in their intervention in human affairs. Characters in the *Aeneid* become at times mere pawns moved at the will of this or that divinity. The following is an alphabetical list of deities and their functions, and the role some of them play in the *Aeneid*.

Aeolus. God of the winds, whose home was in Aeolia.

Apollo (Greek **Phoebus Apollo**). God of the sun, of prophecy, of music (the lyre), and of medicine. It is in his association with oracles, particularly at Delphi in Greece and at Cumae in Italy, that Apollo figures most prominently in the *Aeneid*. He was the twin brother of Diana.

Aurora. Goddess of the dawn.

Bacchus (Greek **Dionysus**). God of wine, whose worship was accompanied by wild orgies.

Ceres (Greek **Demeter**). Goddess of agriculture; mother of Proserpina. A temple in her honor at Troy is mentioned in the *Aeneid*.

Cupid (Greek **Eros**, also called **Amor**). God of love; son of Venus.

Cybele. A Phrygian goddess, known as the Magna Mater of the Romans.

Diana (Greek **Artemis**). Goddess of the moon and of hunting.

Eumenides (also called **Furiae**). The three Furies, Alecto, Tisiphone, and Megaera, who dwelt in the underworld. They were subject to the will of the gods. In one instance in the *Aeneid*, Alecto aids Juno in her plan to involve the Trojans in war with the Latins.

Hercules (Greek **Heracles**, also called **Alcides**). A demigod, known for his gigantic strength and for the Twelve Labors imposed upon him by King Eurystheus. After successfully completing these tasks, he was released from the servitude of Eurystheus.

Iris. Goddess of the rainbow; messenger of Juno.

Janus. The Roman god of doorways and beginnings, represented with one head, but two faces. His temple at Rome was open during war, but closed in time of peace.

Juno (Greek **Hera**). Queen of the gods; wife and sister of Jupiter. Her love for Carthage and anger at the judgment of the Trojan Paris made her the archenemy of Troy.

Jupiter (Greek **Zeus**). King of the Olympian gods; son of Saturn. He was all-powerful, influencing the affairs of gods and of men with tremendous effect. His weapons were the lightning and the thunderbolt, forged by Vulcan. His armor-bearer was the eagle. In the events leading up to the Trojan War, Jupiter discreetly refused to act as judge in the famous beauty contest; he delegated that office to Paris.

Lar (plural **Lares**). Household god who, with the Penates, presided over the fortunes of the house.

Mars (Greek **Ares**). God of war; father of the twins Romulus and Remus.

Mercury (Greek **Hermes**). Messenger of the gods; represented with wings and winged sandals.

Minerva (Greek **Pallas Athena**). Goddess of wisdom, the household arts, and warfare. Partial to the Greeks, she helped them build the Wooden Horse, by means of which they captured Troy.

Neptune (Greek **Poseidon**). God of the sea; brother of Jupiter. He could calm the sea or ride over its waves in his chariot. The symbol of his power was the trident.

Parcae. The three Fates, personified as sisters: Clotho, who spun the thread of human life; Lachesis, who measured out each mortal's portion; and Atropos, who cut the thread.

Penates. Household gods who, with the Lares, presided over the fortunes of the house.

Pluto (Greek **Hades**). King of the underworld; husband of Proserpina.

Proserpina (Greek **Persephone**). Carried off by Pluto, she became his wife and queen of the underworld. She was the daughter of Jupiter and Ceres.

Saturn (Greek **Cronus**). A very ancient ruling divinity; father of Jupiter, by whom he was dethroned. Saturn was also regarded as the god of the harvest.

Titan. Any one of the twelve children of Uranus and Ge (Heaven and Earth), who warred unsuccessfully against Jupiter.

Venus (Greek **Aphrodite**). Goddess of love and beauty. As mother of Aeneas and as the goddess favored by the Trojan Paris in the famous beauty contest, she was friendly toward the Trojans. In the *Aeneid,* Venus often appears, sometimes in disguise, to aid Aeneas.

Vesta (Greek **Hestia**). Goddess of the hearth. In the *Aeneid,* Aeneas carries her statue and her worship from Troy. A temple in her honor at Troy is also mentioned in Book II.

Vulcan (Greek **Hephaestus**). God of fire; husband of Venus. In the *Aeneid,* he forges the thunderbolts of Jupiter and the shield of Aeneas.

EXERCISES

A. In the following statements, if the italicized term is incorrect, write the correct term. If the italicized term is correct, write *true.*

1. Ceres was the mother of *Proserpina.*
2. *Mars* was the father of the twins Romulus and Remus.
3. Juno was a *friend* of Troy.
4. The Lares and the *Parcae* were household gods.
5. Bacchus was called by the Greeks *Hephaestus.*
6. Apollo was the twin brother of *Diana.*
7. Hercules succeeded in accomplishing the *Ten* Labors.
8. The temple of Janus was *open* during time of war.
9. Jupiter's armor-bearer was the *dolphin.*
10. *Cybele* was known as the **Magna Mater** of the Romans.

B. Complete the following statements:

1. Mercury is represented with wings and winged _____.
2. Cupid was the son of the goddess _____.
3. The god represented with one head but two faces was _____.
4. Neptune's symbol was the _____.
5. The Eumenides were also called _____.
6. Apollo's most famous oracles were at Cumae and at _____.
7. Minerva, partial to the Greeks, helped them build the _____.

8. Demeter was the Greek name for the Roman _____.
9. Jupiter's father was called _____.
10. The three Fates were Clotho, Lachesis, and _____.

C. Match each deity in column *A* with the proper description in column *B*.

Column A	*Column B*
1. Mercury	*a.* goddess of the rainbow
2. Vulcan	*b.* goddess of the dawn
3. Neptune	*c.* god of the winds
4. Iris	*d.* god of fire
5. Vesta	*e.* queen of the underworld
6. Aeolus	*f.* goddess of the hearth
7. Aurora	*g.* goddess of the moon
8. Saturn	*h.* messenger of the gods
9. Diana	*i.* god of the harvest
10. Proserpina	*j.* god of the sea

D. The italicized word in each of the following sentences is derived from some deity. Identify the deity, and give the meaning of the italicized word.

1. *Herculean* strength was required to lift the vehicle.
2. The band played a medley of *martial* airs.
3. The guests were in a *jovial* mood.
4. The bird was conspicuous by its *iridescent* plumage.
5. The hostess displayed a *saturnine* disposition.
6. The carnival was marked by *bacchanalian* festivities.
7. The ship was of *titanic* proportions.
8. The glow of the *auroral* light could be seen at a great distance.
9. The tube was *hermetically* sealed.
10. Her *mercurial* temperament showed itself on every occasion.

Lesson 59. GEOGRAPHICAL TERMS IN THE *AENEID*

Acheron. A river of the underworld. Sometimes refers to the underworld itself.

Argos (also written **Argi**). The capital city of Argolis in Greece, favored by Juno.

Avernus. A lake near Cumae, Italy, considered the entrance to the underworld.

Carthage. A city in northern Africa, founded by Queen Dido. Carthage was a rival of Rome.

Cocytus. A river of the underworld.

Cumae. A city on the coast of Campania, in Italy; famous as the home of the Sibyl.

Cynthus. A mountain on the island of Delos, the birthplace of Apollo and Diana.

Cyprus. A large island in the Mediterranean.

Cythera. An island in the Aegean Sea, near which Venus was born from the foam of the sea.

Delos. A small island in the Aegean Sea, on whose mountain Apollo and Diana were born.

Delphi. A city in Greece, seat of a famous oracle of Apollo.

Elysium. That part of the underworld inhabited by the souls of the good.

Erebus. The underworld. Sometimes refers to the king of the underworld.

Hesperia. Another name for Italy; literally, the western land.

Ithaca. An island in the Ionian Sea, the home of Ulysses.

Libya. Another name for Africa; strictly, a region of northern Africa.

Mycenae. A famous city of Argolis in Greece, ruled by Agamemnon.

Oceanus. The ocean. Sometimes thought of as a river flowing around the earth.

Olympus. A famous mountain in Thessaly, Greece; dwelling place of the gods.

Orcus. The underworld. Sometimes refers to the king of the underworld, Pluto.

Pergama (sometimes written **Pergamum**). The citadel of Troy. Occasionally it refers to Troy itself.

Phlegethon. A fiery river in the underworld.

Phthia. A city in Thessaly, Greece; the home of Achilles.

Samos. A large island off the coast of Asia Minor; sacred to Juno, who had a famous temple there.

Sidon. A very ancient city of Phoenicia.

Simois. A river near Troy.

Sparta (also called **Lacedaemon**). The famous capital of Laconia, Greece.

Styx. The principal river in the underworld, over which Charon ferried the souls of the dead.

Tartarus. That part of the underworld inhabited by the souls of the wicked. Sometimes refers to the underworld itself.

Tenedos. A small island in the Aegean Sea, near Troy. The Greeks sailed to Tenedos, pretending to have left for home.

Troia (**Troy,** also called **Ilium**). A famous city in the western part of Asia Minor, captured by the Greeks after a siege of ten years.

Tyrus (**Tyre**). A city in Phoenicia, Asia Minor, birthplace of Dido.

Xanthus. A river near Troy.

EXERCISES

A. Complete the following statements:

1. Another name for Troy was _____.
2. A famous oracle of Apollo in Greece was located at _____.
3. The home of the gods was on Mount _____.
4. The main river in the underworld was the _____.
5. The entrance to the underworld was Lake _____.

6. The goddess associated with the island of Cythera was _____.
7. Hesperia was another name for _____.
8. The Phoenician city from which Dido came was called _____.
9. The island of Ithaca was the home of the Greek hero _____.
10. The two principal parts of the underworld were Tartarus for the wicked and _____ for the good.

B. In the following statements, if the italicized term is incorrect, write the correct term. If the italicized term is correct, write *true*.

1. Acheron was a *lake* in the underworld.
2. Cumae was famous as the home of the *Sibyl*.
3. Apollo and Diana were born on the island of *Delos*.
4. Argos was a favorite city of *Minerva*.
5. Libya was another name for *Asia*.
6. Juno had a temple on the island of *Samos*.
7. Phthia was the home of *Ajax*.
8. Agamemnon was king of *Mycenae*.
9. Pergama was the citadel of *Troy*.
10. Lacedaemon was another name for *Athens*.

C. Match each geographical term in column *A* with its description in column *B*.

Column A	*Column B*
1. Carthage	*a.* a lake near Cumae
2. Cyprus	*b.* an ancient Phoenician city
3. Avernus	*c.* a small island in the Aegean
4. Orcus	*d.* a large island in the Mediterranean
5. Sidon	*e.* a river of fire in the underworld
6. Tenedos	*f.* a mountain on the island of Delos
7. Xanthus	*g.* a river in the underworld
8. Cynthus	*h.* a rival of Rome
9. Cocytus	*i.* a river near Troy
10. Phlegethon	*j.* the underworld

Lesson 60. OVID — HIS LIFE AND WORKS

The Augustan Age produced several poets of prominence, among them Ovid. Like Vergil, Ovid was master of the dactylic hexameter; but there the similarity ends. Whereas Vergil wrote verses of great dignity and grandeur, most of Ovid's poetry is light, delicate, and fluent. Vergil wrote to glorify Rome and the Emperor Augustus; Ovid's purpose, in general, was to entertain.

Ovid, in some of his poems, makes use of the elegiac stanza (also called distich or couplet). This meter consists of a verse of hexameter (six feet), followed by a verse of pentameter (five feet), the two verses generally making complete sense.

OVID'S LIFE

BIRTH

Publius Ovidius Naso (Ovid) was born in 43 B.C. at Sulmo, in central Italy, about ninety miles from Rome. His father was fairly wealthy, belonging to the Equestrian Order. Ovid was a contemporary of Vergil and Horace.

EDUCATION

For his education, Ovid was sent to Rome. There he received a thorough training in rhetoric and oratory in preparation for a career in law. Subsequently, to complete his education, he traveled to Athens, to Asia Minor, and to Sicily.

PRIVATE LIFE

On his return to Rome, Ovid practised law and held a number of judicial offices. He soon tired of the courts, however, and his intense love for poetry led to a literary career. Ovid lived a life of ease and pleasure at this time. His first two marriages ended in divorce, but his third marriage lasted until his death.

BANISHMENT

After living at Rome for many years, and enjoying the favor of Augustus, Ovid was suddenly banished by the Emperor to Tomi, an insignificant port on the Black Sea. However, he was permitted to retain his property and his citizenship. The cause of his banishment is somewhat of a mystery. Ostensibly, it was the publication of Ovid's poem the *Ars Amātōria* (Art of Love), which was regarded by some as immoral. However, the poem had been published some ten years earlier. The more probable reason was a scandal involving Ovid and the Emperor's granddaughter, Julia, who was banished the same year as he was. Whatever the cause, Ovid suffered miserably in exile, as is evidenced by the many pathetic letters he wrote begging to return to Rome; but his pleadings were all in vain.

DEATH

Ovid had lived in banishment for about five years when Augustus died, in 14 A.D. Four years later (18 A.D.), at the age of sixty-one, Ovid died at Tomi. He was buried nearby.

OVID'S WORKS

Ovid's literary activity extended over forty years; it is generally divided into three groups: the early years, the middle years, and the final years of his life.

EARLY YEARS

Produced in his youth, these poems, in elegiac verse, dealt mainly with the subject of love.

1. **Amōrēs** (Loves). Three books consisting of forty-nine short poems.

2. **Hērōidēs** (Heroines). A collection of fictitious love letters, supposedly written by famous women of mythology to their absent husbands or lovers.

3. **Ars Amātōria** (Art of Love). A treatise in three books on the art of winning and keeping one's love.

4. **Remedia Amōris** (Remedies for Love). A treatise on how to control love's passion.

MIDDLE YEARS

In this period, Ovid produced his most famous works.

1. **Metamorphōsēs** (Transformations). This is Ovid's masterpiece, consisting of fifteen books in dactylic hexameter. In nearly every story (about 250 in all), some character is changed into another form of existence, such as an animal, a tree, a star, etc. The range of subjects is vast, starting with the creation of the world and ending with the deification of Julius Caesar. For sheer entertainment, the work remains even today one of the world's great collections of stories. It has been a valuable source book on classical mythology for writers in modern languages.

2. **Fāstī** (Calendar). A work in six books written in the elegiac stanza. The poem is an account of legends and incidents associated with Roman religious festivals of the first six months of the year (one book devoted to each month). Apparently Ovid had originally planned twelve books, one for each month, but never finished the work.

LATER YEARS

Ovid's works of this period were written in exile in Tomi, and reflect his despondency.

1. **Trīstia** (Laments). A work in five books written in the elegiac stanza. The poem describes Ovid's life during his banishment; it also contains an appeal to Augustus for clemency.

2. **Epistulae Ex Pontō** (Letters From Pontus). A collection of letters from Ovid, comprising four books. The letters are written to his family and friends in Rome, imploring them to intercede in his behalf.
Ovid also wrote other works, including a tragic drama **Medea,** which is no longer extant.

EXERCISES

A. In the following statements, if the italicized term is incorrect, write the correct term. If the italicized term is correct, write *true*.

1. Ovid was born in Sulmo in *53* B.C.
2. Ovid's education prepared him for a career in *law*.
3. Ovid's father belonged to the *Equestrian Order*.
4. The elegiac distich consists of one six-foot verse followed by one *four*-foot verse.
5. In general, Ovid's purpose in writing was to *entertain*.
6. Ovid's literary activity lasted over *forty* years.
7. The METAMORPHŌSĒS consists of *twenty* books.
8. The HĒRŌIDĒS is a collection of fictitious *essays*.
9. The *Fāstī* deals with Roman religious festivals.
10. The cause of Ovid's exile was probably a scandal involving the *wife* of Augustus.

B. Complete the following statements:

1. Ovid's full name is Publius Ovidius _____.
2. To complete his education, Ovid traveled to Asia Minor, Sicily, and _____.
3. The *Metamorphōsēs* contains approximately _____ stories.
4. Ovid was married _____ times.
5. Ovid is known to have written a tragedy called _____.
6. Ovid was exiled to an obscure port on the Black Sea called _____.
7. Ovid died at the age of _____.
8. Ovid's early poems dealt mainly with the subject of _____.
9. Ovid's book of laments written in exile is called _____.
10. Ovid's letters from exile are called *Epistulae Ex* _____.

Unit XXI—Vocabulary

Lesson 61. LATIN-ENGLISH VOCABULARY

accendō, -ere, -cendī, -cēnsus, kindle, set on fire

acerbus, -a, -um, bitter, sour

acuō, -ere, -uī, -ūtus, sharpen

aēneus (aēnus), -a, -um, of copper, bronze

aequor, -oris (n.), sea

āēr, āeris (m.), air

aethēr, -eris (m.), upper air, sky

aevum, -ī (n.), lifetime, age

agitō, -āre, -āvī, -ātus, stir up

agnōscō, -ere, -gnōvī, -gnitus, recognize

āla, -ae (f.), wing

albus, -a, -um, white

āles, -itis, winged; (as a noun), bird

aliter, otherwise

almus, -a, -um, nourishing, kindly

altāria, -ium (n. pl.), altar

alternus, -a, -um, alternating, by turns

ambō, -ae, -ō, both

amictus, -ūs (m.), cloak

amnis, -is (m.), river, stream

amplector, -ī, -plexus sum, embrace

anguis, -is (m. and f.), snake

anima, -ae (f.), breath, life, soul

antrum, -ī (n.), cave, grotto

appāreō, -ēre, -uī, -itūrus, appear

aptō, -āre, -āvī, -ātus, fit

arceō, -ēre, -uī, enclose, keep off

arcus, -ūs (m.), bow

arduus, -a, -um, steep, high

armentum, -ī (n.), cattle, herd

arō, -āre, -āvī, -ātus, plough

arrigō, -ere, -rēxī, -rēctus, raise up

artus, -ūs (m.), joint, limb

arvum, -ī (n.), field

arx, arcis (f.), citadel

asper, -era, -erum, rough, harsh

astō, -āre, -stitī, stand near

astrum, -ī (n.), star

āter, -tra, -trum, black, dark

attonitus, -a, -um, thunderstruck

attonō, -āre, -tonuī, -tonitus, thunder at

auferō, -ferre, abstulī, ablātus, carry off

augurium, -ī (n.), augury

aura, -ae (f.), air, breeze

aureus, -a, -um, golden

aurōra, -ae (f.), dawn

avis, -is (f.), bird

avus, -ī (m.), grandfather

axis, -is (m.), axle, axis

bibō, -ere, bibī, drink

bōs, bovis (m. and f.), ox, cow

bracchium, -ī (n.), arm

caecus, -a, -um, blind, hidden

caeruleus, -a, -um, dark blue

caleō, -ēre, -uī, be warm

candeō, -ēre, -uī, be white, shine

canis, -is (m. and f.), dog

canō, -ere, cecinī, sing

cānus, -a, -um, white, hoary

capillus, -ī (m.), hair

careō, -ēre, -uī, lack

carīna, -ae (f.), keel
carmen, -inis (n.), song, poem
carpō, -ere, -psī, -ptus, pluck
castus, -a, -um, pure
caterva, -ae (f.), crowd
cavus, -a, -um, hollow
celerō, -āre, -āvī, -ātus, hasten
celsus, -a, -um, high, lofty
certāmen, -inis (n.), contest
cervīx, -īcis (f.), neck
cervus, -ī (m.), stag, deer
cessō, -āre, -āvī, -ātus, delay
ceu, as, as if
chorus, -ī (m.), dance
cieō, -ēre, cīvī, citus, stir up
cingō, -ere, cīnxī, cīnctus, gird, surround
cinis, -eris (m.), ashes
citus, -a, -um, swift
clipeus, -ī (m.), shield
cognōmen, -inis (n.), surname
collum, -ī (n.), neck
coma, -ae (f.), hair
comitor, -ārī, -ātus sum, accompany
compellō, -āre, -āvī, -ātus, address
complector, -ī, -plexus sum, embrace, surround
compōnō, -ere, -posuī, -positus, put together
concutiō, -ere, -cussī, -cussus, strike, disturb
coniugium, -ī (n.), marriage
cōnscius, -a, -um, conscious
cōnūbium, -ī (n.), marriage
convīvium, -ī (n.), feast, banquet
cor, cordis (n.), heart
corōna, -ae (f.), wreath
corripiō, -ere, -ripuī, -reptus, seize

coruscus, -a, -um, waving, flashing
crātēr, -ēris (m.), mixing bowl
crepō, -āre, -uī, -itus, creak, rattle
crēscō, -ere, crēvī, crētus, grow
crīmen, -inis (n.), accusation
crīnis, -is (m.), hair
crista, -ae (f.), crest
cruentus, -a, -um, bloodstained
cruor, -ōris (m.), blood
crūs, crūris (n.), leg
culmen, -inis (n.), top, summit
cūnctor, -ārī, -ātus sum, delay
cupīdō, -inis (f.), desire
curvus, -a, -um, crooked
cuspis, -idis (f.), spear point

daps, dapis (f.), feast, banquet
decōrus, -a, -um, becoming
decus, -oris (n.), beauty, ornament
dēmittō, -ere, -mīsī, -missus, let down, lower
dēmum, at last
dēnsus, -a, -um, thick
dignor, -ārī, -ātus sum, deem worthy
dīrus, -a, -um, dreadful
dīves, dīvitis, rich
dīvus, -a, -um, godlike; (as a noun), god
doleō, -ēre, -uī, -itūrus, grieve
dolus, -ī (m.), deceit, trickery
dominor, -ārī, -ātus sum, rule, be master
domō, -āre, -uī, -itus, tame, subdue
dōnec, until
dūdum, lately
dulcis, -e, sweet
duplex, -icis, twofold
dūrus, -a, -um, hard, harsh

ebur, -oris (*n.*), ivory

ecce, lo!, behold!

edō, -ere, ēdī, ēsus, eat

ēn, lo!, behold!

ēnsis, -is (*m.*), sword

epulae, -ārum (*f. pl.*), banquet

equidem, indeed

ērigō, -ere, -rēxī, -rēctus, raise up

ēruō, -ere, ēruī, ērutus, dig up, throw out

ēvādō, -ere, -vāsī, -vāsus, go out, escape

exanimus, -a, -um, breathless, lifeless

excutiō, -ere, -cussī, -cussus, shake out

exsequor, -ī, -secūtus sum, follow out, perform

exsultō, -āre, -āvī, -ātus, leap, exult

extemplō, immediately

exuō, -ere, -uī, -ūtus, take off, lay aside

exuviae, -ārum (*f. pl.*), spoils

faciēs, -ēī (*f.*), form, appearance, face

famēs, -is (*f.*), hunger

famulus, -ī (*m.*), servant

fās (*indecl. n.*), divine right, law

fātālis, -e, destined, fated

fatīgō, -āre, -āvī, -ātus, wear out, tire

faucēs, -ium (*f. pl.*), throat

fax, facis (*f.*), torch

feriō, -īre, strike

ferōx, -ōcis, wild, fierce

ferreus, -a, -um, of iron

ferveō, -ēre, -buī, boil, glow

fessus, -a, -um, tired out

fīgō, -ere, fīxī, fīxus, fasten

flāvus, -a, -um, yellow

flectō, -ere, flexī, flexus, bend, turn

fleō, -ēre, flēvī, flētus, weep

flētus, -ūs (*m.*), weeping

flō, flāre, flāvī, flātus, blow

flōs, flōris (*m.*), flower

flūctus, -ūs (*m.*), flood, wave

fluō, -ere, flūxī, flūxus, flow

fluvius, -ī (*m.*), river

fodiō, -ere, fōdī, fossus, dig

foedus, -a, -um, foul

folium, -ī (*n.*), leaf

fōns, fontis (*m.*), spring, fountain

for, fārī, fātus sum, speak

foris, -is (*f.*), door

fortasse, perhaps

foveō, -ēre, fōvī, fōtus, warm, cherish

frangō, -ere, frēgī, frāctus, break

fraus, fraudis (*f.*), fraud, deceit

fremō, -ere, -uī, -itus, roar, murmur

frēnum, -ī (*n.*), bit, bridle

fretum, -ī (*n.*), strait

frōns, frondis (*f.*), leaf, foliage

fulgeō, -ere, fulsī, gleam, flash

fulmen, -inis (*n.*), lightning, thunderbolt

fulvus, -a, -um, tawny

fūmus, -ī (*m.*), smoke

fundō, -ere, fūdī, fūsus, pour out

fūnis, -is (*m.*), rope

fūnus, -eris (*n.*), funeral, death, corpse

furia, -ae (*f.*), rage, madness

galea, -ae (*f.*), helmet

gaudeō, -ēre, gāvīsus sum, rejoice

gaudium, -ī (*n.*), joy

gelidus, -a, -um, ice cold

geminus, -a, -um, twin

gemitus, -ūs (*m.*), groan, sigh

gemō, -ere, -uī, -itus, groan, sigh
gener, -erī (*m.*), son-in-law
genitor, -ōris (*m.*), father
genū, -ūs (*n.*), knee
germānus, -ī (*m.*), brother
gignō, -ere, genuī, genitus, beget, bear
glomerō, -āre, -āvī, -ātus, collect
grāmen, -inis (*n.*), grass
gremium, -ī (*n.*), lap, bosom
gressus, -ūs (*m.*), step, course
grex, gregis (*m.*), flock, herd
gurges, -itis (*m.*), whirlpool

habēna, -ae (*f.*), rein
haereō, -ēre, haesī, haesūrus, stick, adhere
harēna, -ae (*f.*), sand
harundō, -inis (*f.*), reed, arrow
hasta, -ae (*f.*), spear
haud, not at all
hauriō, -īre, hausī, haustus, drink, drain
herba, -ae (*f.*), grass
hērōs, -ōis (*m.*), hero
heu, alas!
hiō, -āre, -āvī, -ātūrus, yawn, gape
horreō, -ēre, horruī, bristle, shudder
horridus, -a, -um, bristling, rough
hospes, -itis (*m.*), guest, stranger
hospitium, -ī (*n.*), hospitality
hymenaeus, -ī (*m.*), wedding song

iaculum, -ī (*n.*), javelin
ictus, -ūs (*m.*), blow
ignārus, -a, -um, ignorant
īlex, -icis (*f.*), oak
imber, -bris (*m.*), rain
immānis, -e, huge

immēnsus, -a, -um, vast, immense
immineō, -ēre, overhang, threaten
immittō, -ere, -mīsī, -missus, send into
implicō, -āre, -āvī (-uī), -ātus (-itus), enfold
inānis, -e, empty
incēdō, -ere, -cessī, -cessūrus walk, proceed
incumbō, -ere, -cubuī, -cubitūrus recline
induō, -ere, -uī, -ūtus, put on
īnferī, -ōrum (*m. pl.*), the dead
ingeminō, -āre, -āvī, -ātus, redouble
īnscius, -a, -um, ignorant
intendō, -ere, -tendī, -tentus stretch, strain
intrō, -āre, -āvī, -ātus, enter
intus, within
invādō, -ere, -vāsī, -vāsus, enter, attack
iuvencus, -ī (*m.*), bullock
iuventa, -ae (*f.*), youth
iuventūs, -ūtis (*f.*), youth
iūxtā, close by

lābor, -ī, lāpsus sum, glide, slip
lacertus, -ī (*m.*), upper arm
lacrimō, -āre, -āvī, -ātus, weep
lacus, -ūs (*m.*), lake
laedō, -ere, laesī, laesus, hurt, injure
laetus, -a, -um, joyful
laevus, -a, -um, left
latebra, -ae (*f.*), hiding place
lateō, -ēre, -uī, be hidden
laurus, -ī (-ūs) (*f.*), laurel
laxō, -āre, -āvī, -ātus, loosen
lentus, -a, -um, slow, pliant
leō, -ōnis (*m.*), lion
lētum, -ī (*n.*), death

lēvis, -e, smooth
lībō, -āre, -āvī, -ātus, taste, pour
līmen, -inis (n.), threshold
liquidus, -a, -um, flowing, clear
longaevus, -a, -um, aged, old
lōrīca, -ae (f.), coat of mail
lūceō, -ēre, lūxī, gleam, shine
luctor, -ārī, -ātus sum, struggle, wrestle
lūctus, -ūs (m.), grief, mourning
lūcus, -ī (m.), grove
lūgeō, -ēre, lūxī, lūctus, mourn
lupus, -ī (m.), wolf
lūstrō, -āre, -āvī, -ātus, purify

mactō, -āre, -āvī, -ātus, sacrifice
macula, -ae (f.), spot, stain
madeō, -ēre, -uī, be wet
maestus, -a, -um, sad
magnanimus, -a, -um, high-spirited
mānēs, -ium (m. pl.), shades of the dead
marmor, -oris (n.), marble
membrum, -ī (n.), limb
memor, -oris, mindful
memorō, -āre, -āvī, -ātus, recall, relate
mēnsa, -ae (f.), table
mergō, -ere, mersī, mersus, dip
mēta, -ae (f.), goal
mētior, -īrī, mēnsus sum, measure
micō, -āre, -uī, quiver
minae, -ārum (f. pl.), threats
minor, -ārī, -ātus sum, threaten
mīrābilis, -e, wonderful
misceō, -ēre, -uī, mixtus, mix, mingle
misereor, -ērī, -itus sum, pity
miseror, -ārī, -ātus sum, pity
mītis, -e, mild, gentle
mōlēs, -is (f.), mass, heap

mollis, -e, soft
mōnstrum, -ī (n.), warning, portent
morsus, -ūs (m.), bite
mūcrō, -ōnis (m.), sword point
mūgiō, -īre, -īvī (-iī), -ītus, bellow
mulceō, -ēre, mulsī, mulsus, soothe

namque, for
nectō, -ere, nexuī (nexī), nexus, bind
nefandus, -a, -um, impious
nefās (indecl. n.), impiety
nemus, -oris (n.), forest, grove
nepōs, -ōtis (m.), grandson
nēquīquam, in vain
nervus, -ī (m.), sinew
nī, if not, unless
niger, -gra, -grum, black
nimbus, -ī (m.), cloud
niteō, -ere, -uī, gleam, shine
nītor, -ī, nīsus (nīxus) sum, lean on, strive
nix, nivis (f.), snow
nō, -āre, -āvī, -ātus, swim
nōdus, -ī (m.), knot
nūbēs, -is (f.), cloud
nūbila, -ōrum (n. pl.), clouds
nūbilus, -a, -um, cloudy
nūmen, -inis (n.), divine will
nūsquam, nowhere
nympha, -ae (f.), nymph

obruō, -ere, -ruī, -rutus, overwhelm
obstipēscō, -ere, -stipuī, be amazed
obvius, -a, -um, in the way of
ōcior, -ius, swifter
ōcius, more swiftly
opācus, -a, -um, dark, shady

ōrdior, -īrī, ōrsus sum, begin
orīgō, -inis (f.), origin, source
os, ossis (n.), bone
ōsculum, -ī (n.), kiss
ostentō, -āre, -āvī, -ātus, display
ovō, -āre, -āvī, -ātus, exult

pallēns, -entis (f.), pale
palleō, -ēre, -uī, be pale
palma, -ae (f.), palm
pandō, -ere, pandī, pānsus (passus), spread out, extend
parcō, -ere, pepercī (parsī), parsūrus, spare
pāscō, -ere, pāvī, pāstus, feed
passim, here and there
pāstor, -ōris (m.), shepherd
patera, -ae (f.), bowl
paveō, -ēre, tremble, fear
pectus, -oris (n.), breast
pecus, -udis (f.), cattle
pelagus, -ī (n.), sea
pellis, -is (f.), skin, hide
penetrālis, -e, innermost
penna, -ae (f.), feather, wing
peragō, -ere, -ēgī, -āctus, accomplish
pergō, -ere, -rēxī, -rēctus, continue
pharetra, -ae (f.), quiver
pietās, -ātis (f.), devotion
pignus, -oris (n.), pledge, token
pingō, -ere, pīnxī, pictus, paint
pinguis, -e, fat, rich
pinna, -ae (f.), feather, wing
pīnus, -ūs (-ī) (f.), pine tree
pius, -a, -um, dutiful, devoted
placidus, -a, -um, quiet, serene
plausus, -ūs (m.), applause
polus, -ī (m.), pole, sky
pondus, -eris (n.), weight
pontus, -ī (m.), sea
porrigō, -ere, -rēxī, rēctus, reach

forth, extend
postis, -is (m.), doorpost
praeceps, -cipitis, headlong
precor, -ārī, -ātus sum, pray, beg
principium, -ī (n.), beginning
prōcumbō, -ere, -cubuī, -cubitus
fall forward
prōgeniēs, -ēī (f.), lineage, offspring
prōlēs, -is (f.), offspring
prōmittō, -ere, -mīsī, -missus
promise
prōnus, -a, -um, headlong
prōra, -ae (f.), prow
prōtinus, forward, at once
pūbēs, -is (f.), youth
pulsō, -āre, -āvī, -ātus, beat, strike
pulvis, -eris (m.), dust
puppis, -is (f.), stern
purpura, -ae (f.), purple

quatiō, -ere, —, quassus, shake

rabiēs, -ēī (f.), madness, frenzy
radius, -ī (m.), staff, ray
rādīx, -īcis (f.), root
rāmus, -ī (m.), branch
rapidus, -a, -um, swift
rapiō, -ere, rapuī, raptus, seize
ratis, -is (f.), raft, boat
raucus, -a, -um, hoarse
reliquiae, -ārum (f. pl.), remains
rēmus, -ī (m.), oar
reor, rērī, ratus sum, think
resīdō, -ere, -sēdī, settle back
resolvō, -ere, -solvī, -solūtus, untie, loosen
respiciō, -ere, -spexī, -spectus
look back, regard
retrō, backwards
rigeō, -ēre, -riguī, be stiff
rīte, duly
rota, -ae (f.), wheel

rubeō, -ēre, -uī, be red

ruīna, -ae (f.), downfall, destruction

rumpō, -ere, rūpī, ruptus, break

ruō, -ere, ruī, rutus, rush, fall

rūpēs, -is (f.), rock, cliff

sacerdōs, -ōtis (m. and f.), priest, priestess

sacrō, -āre, -āvī, -ātus, make holy

saeculum, -ī (n.), race, generation

saeviō, -īre, -iī, -ītus, rage

saevus, -a, -um, fierce, savage

sāl, salis (m. and n.), salt, sea

saliō, -īre, -uī, leap

sanguis, -inis (m.), blood

saucius, -a, -um, wounded

scēptrum, -ī (n.), staff, scepter

scindō, -ere, scidī, scissus, split

scopulus, -ī (m.), rock, crag

secō, -āre, secuī, sectus, cut

secūris, -is (f.), axe

secus, otherwise

sēgnis, -e, sluggish

sepulcrum, -ī (n.), tomb

serēnus, -a, -um, bright, clear, calm

serō, -ere, sēvī, satus, sow

serpō, -ere, serpsī, serptus, creep

sertum, -ī (n.), wreath, garland

sērus, -a, -um, late

siccus, -a, -um, dry

sīdō, -ere, sīdī (sēdī), sit down, settle

sīdus, -eris (n.), star

signō, -āre, -āvī, -ātus, mark

sileō, -ēre, -uī, be silent

simulācrum, -ī (n.), image, statue

sinus, -ūs (m.), bosom, bay, fold

sistō, -ere, stitī, status, stand

socer, -erī (m.), father-in-law

solidus, -a, -um, solid, firm

sōlor, -ārī, -ātus sum, comfort

solum, -ī (n.), ground, bottom

sonitus, -ūs (m.), sound

sonō, -āre, -uī, -itus, make a sound

sopor, -ōris (m.), sleep

spargō, -ere, sparsī, sparsus, scatter

spēlunca, -ae (f.), cave

spernō, -ere, sprēvī, sprētus, reject, scorn

spīculum, -ī (n.), javelin, dart

spīrō, -āre, -āvī, -ātus, breathe

spolium, -ī (n.), spoil, booty

spūma, -ae (f.), foam

stabulum, -ī (n.), stall, stable

stāgnum, -ī (n.), pool

stella, -ae (f.), star

sternō, -ere, strāvī, strātus, spread, lay low

stimulus, -ī (m.), goad, spur

stirps, stirpis (f.), root, trunk

strīdeō, -ēre, strīdī, creak

stringō, -ere, strīnxī, strictus, draw, bind

struō, -ere, strūxī, strūctus, pile up, build

stupeō, -ēre, -uī, be amazed

subitus, -a, -um, sudden

sublīmis, -e, lofty, high

succurrō, -ere, -currī, -cursūrus, run up, assist

sulcus, -ī (m.), furrow, track

superī, -ōrum (m. pl.), the gods above

surgō, -ere, surrēxī, surrēctus, rise up, raise

suspendō, -ere, -pendī, -pēnsus, hang

suspiciō, -ere, -spexī, -spectus, look up, suspect

taeda, -ae (*f.*), torch
taurus, -ī (*m.*), bull
tellūs, -ūris (*f.*), earth
tendō, -ere, tetendī, tentus (tēnsus), stretch
tepeō, -ere, -uī, be warm
ter, three times
testor, -ārī, -ātus sum, call to witness
texō, -ere, texuī, textus, weave
thalamus, -ī (*m.*), bridal chamber
tingō, -ere, tīnxī, tīnctus, wet, dip
tondeō, -ēre, totondī, tōnsus, shear
tonō, -āre, -uī, thunder
torqueō, -ēre, torsī, tortus, twist, turn
torreō, -ēre, -uī, tostus, parch, burn
torus, -ī (*m.*), couch
torvus, -a, -um, grim, stern
trabs, trabis (*f.*), beam
tremō, -ere, -uī, tremble
trepidus, -a, -um, trembling
trīstis, -e, sad
truncus, -ī (*m.*), trunk
tumeō, -ēre, -uī, swell
tumidus, -a, -um, swollen
tundō, -ere, tutudī, tūnsus, beat, strike
turba, -ae (*f.*), crowd
turbidus, -a, -um, confused
turbō, -inis (*m.*), whirlwind
turbō, -āre, -āvī, -ātus, disturb

ūber, -eris (*n.*), udder
ultor, -ōris (*m.*), avenger
ultrō, willingly
ululō, -āre, -āvī, -ātus, howl
umbra, -ae (*f.*), shade

umerus, -ī (*m.*), shoulder
ūmidus, -a, -um, moist
uncus, -a, -um, crooked, bent
unda, -ae (*f.*), wave
unguis, -is (*m.*), nail, claw
urgeō, -ēre, ursī, press on, urge
ūrō, -ere, ussī, ustus, burn
usquam, anywhere

vānus, -a, -um, vain, empty
vāstus, -a, -um, vast, desolate
vātēs, -is (*m. and f.*), seer, prophet, prophetess
-ve, or
vellō, -ere, vellī, vulsus (volsus), pluck
vēlō, -āre, -āvī, -ātus, veil, cover
vēlōx, -ōcis, swift
vēlum, -ī (*n.*), veil, sail
velut, just as
veneror, -ārī, -ātus sum, worship
vēnor, -ārī, -ātus sum, hunt
verber, -eris (*n.*), lash, whip
vertex, -icis (*m.*), whirlpool
vestis, -is (*f.*), garment
vetō, -āre, -uī, -itus, forbid
vicis (*f. gen.*), change
vīctus, -ūs (*m.*), food
vinciō, -īre, vīnxī, vīnctus, bind
virga, -ae (*f.*), twig, wand
viridis, -e, green
vīscus, -eris (*n.*), flesh; (*pl.*), entrails
vīsō, -ere, vīsī, vīsus, look at, visit
vīsus, -ūs (*m.*), sight
vitta, -ae (*f.*), ribbon, fillet
volō, -āre, -āvī, -ātus, fly
volucer, -cris, -cre, flying, swift
volvō, -ere, volvī, volūtus, roll
voveō, -ēre, vōvī, vōtus, vow

EXERCISES

A. Select the correct translation of each Latin word.

1. *haereō:* (*a*) drink   (*b*) yawn   (*c*) stick   (*d*) bristle
2. *famēs:* (*a*) hunger   (*b*) reputation   (*c*) servant
   (*d*) divine law
3. *pinguis:* (*a*) pledge   (*b*) fat   (*c*) feather   (*d*) quiet
4. *unguis:* (*a*) snake   (*b*) nail   (*c*) crooked   (*d*) moist
5. *turba:* (*a*) whirlwind   (*b*) couch   (*c*) torch   (*d*) crowd
6. *lūgeō:* (*a*) shine   (*b*) struggle   (*c*) purify   (*d*) mourn
7. *cervīx:* (*a*) deer   (*b*) hollow   (*c*) neck   (*d*) swift
8. *sōlor:* (*a*) comfort   (*b*) sister   (*c*) alone   (*d*) sound
9. *amictus:* (*a*) cloak   (*b*) friend   (*c*) friendship   (*d*) river
10. *tonō:* (*a*) shear   (*b*) wet   (*c*) thunder   (*d*) burn
11. *arvum:* (*a*) limb   (*b*) field   (*c*) bow   (*d*) air
12. *dīrus:* (*a*) hard   (*b*) godlike   (*c*) rich   (*d*) dreadful
13. *frēnum:* (*a*) strait   (*b*) bit   (*c*) leaf   (*d*) lightning
14. *maestus:* (*a*) mild   (*b*) soft   (*c*) wet   (*d*) sad
15. *mūgiō:* (*a*) soothe   (*b*) dip   (*c*) bellow   (*d*) sacrifice

B. In each group, select the word that does *not* belong with the others. Give a reason for your answer.

1. aequor, amnis, lacus, aurōra
2. carīna, caterva, puppis, prōra
3. morsus, anguis, canis, cervus
4. avus, socer, cuspis, genitor
5. collum, antrum, bracchium, genū
6. fleō, reor, gaudeō, paveō
7. foedus, flāvus, purpura, niger
8. nūbēs, imber, nōdus, nix
9. aevum, iuventa, macula, pūbēs
10. pulsō, concutiō, ferveō, feriō
11. clipeus, aeneus, ferreus, aureus
12. galea, lōrīca, vestis, fūnis
13. hasta, harundō, frōns, iaculum
14. īlex, laurus, rēmus, pīnus
15. līmen, ratis, postis, foris

C. Match each word in column *A* with its English equivalent in column *B*.

Column A	*Column B*
1. geminus	*a.* sand
2. crēscō	*b.* gleam
3. pectus	*c.* sea
4. harēna	*d.* twin
5. niteō	*e.* cattle
6. mollis	*f.* weeping
7. pelagus	*g.* grow
8. crepō	*h.* strive
9. pecus	*i.* smoke
10. mōlēs	*j.* groan
11. nītor	*k.* rein
12. gemitus	*l.* soft
13. flētus	*m.* mass
14. habēna	*n.* creak
15. fūmus	*o.* breast

D. Below is a list of fifty Latin words that fall into the following six categories: (*a*) parts of the body; (*b*) colors; (*c*) animals; (*d*) religion; (*e*) water; (*f*) natural objects other than water. Indicate the category for each word by selecting the proper letter.

1. stella	14. albus	27. pontus	39. polus
2. os	15. altāria	28. faciēs	40. nūmen
3. cor	16. āēr	29. rūpēs	41. herba
4. leō	17. taurus	30. iuvencus	42. lacertus
5. superī	18. crūs	31. viridis	43. flōs
6. membrum	19. cānus	32. astrum	44. armentum
7. sīdus	20. sāl	33. nervus	45. scopulus
8. unda	21. aethēr	34. vātēs	46. grex
9. bōs	22. avis	35. nemus	47. sacerdōs
10. aura	23. augurium	36. nimbus	48. fluvius
11. grāmen	24. lupus	37. fulvus	49. caeruleus
12. faucēs	25. artus	38. āles	50. fulmen
13. flūctus	26. nūbila		

A GUIDE TO THE COLLEGE BOARD ACHIEVEMENT TEST IN LATIN (LEVEL IV)

The College Board Achievement Test in Latin is intended for students who have had two, three, or four years of high school Latin. It is not surprising, therefore, that this single test contains questions of varying degrees of difficulty. Only a superior student with four years of high school Latin is equipped to answer *all* the questions on the examination.

Although the types of questions used may vary somewhat from year to year, the following types illustrate what the candidate may generally expect. All the questions below are intended for students who have completed *four* years of high school Latin.

VOCABULARY QUESTIONS

Knowledge of vocabulary is basic and is tested implicitly throughout the examination. The following type of question, however, tests mastery of vocabulary directly.

Select the best English meaning for each of the following Latin words:

1. *rāmus*
   (A) oar   (B) raft   (C) bough   (D) root

2. *avis*
   (A) bird   (B) grandfather   (C) ship   (D) air

3. *puppis*
   (A) youth   (B) dust   (C) prow   (D) stern

The following are sample questions reprinted from the editions indicated of *A Description of the College Board Achievement Tests*, published by the College Entrance Examination Board, New York: 1963—qq. 1-6 (pp. 319-320, II) and qq. 2, 4, and 5 (p. 322, II); 1965—qq. 3-8 (p. 318) and qq. 1-6 (pp. 321-322, I). This booklet, which contains many illustrative examples of the different kinds of questions that are used in the Achievement Tests, is revised annually and is supplied without cost to high schools for distribution to students before they take the test. The booklet may also be obtained on request by writing to College Entrance Examination Board Publications Order Office, Box 592, Princeton, New Jersey 08540, or Box 1025, Berkeley, California 94701.

4. *tumidus*
(A) fearful   (B) swollen   (C) turbulent   (D) trembling

5. *volvō*
(A) vow   (B) roll   (C) fly   (D) wish

6. *rūpēs*
(A) cloud   (B) wheel   (C) madness   (D) rock

7. *pinna*
(A) feather   (B) pine tree   (C) pledge   (D) palm

8. *saevus*
(A) wounded   (B) sluggish   (C) fierce   (D) clear

9. *līmen*
(A) divine will   (B) light   (C) threshold   (D) grove

10. *coma*
(A) hair   (B) companion   (C) neck   (D) assembly

11. *haereō*
(A) drink   (B) stick   (C) lack   (D) grieve

12. *cānus*
(A) dog   (B) song   (C) stag   (D) hoary

13. *torreō*
(A) frighten   (B) roast   (C) stretch   (D) be warm

14. *amnis*
(A) snake   (B) cloak   (C) river   (D) cave

15. *lūceō*
(A) shine   (B) mourn   (C) purify   (D) play

16. *sternō*
(A) reject   (B) spatter   (C) bind   (D) spread

17. *habēna*
(A) sand   (B) reed   (C) grass   (D) rein

18. *fūnis*
(A) funeral   (B) smoke   (C) rope   (D) leaf

19. *nūsquam*
(A) never   (B) nowhere   (C) in vain   (D) for indeed

20. *vēlō*
(A) cover   (B) pluck   (C) carry   (D) forbid

READING COMPREHENSION QUESTIONS

Reading comprehension questions are based on connected passages of about a hundred words each. The questions aim to test the student's ability to understand the meaning of a passage and to extract information from it. In addition, some questions test knowledge of vocabulary in context, while others deal with grammatical constructions.

Read the following passages carefully to get the meaning. Below each passage you will find a series of incomplete statements. Select the answer that best completes each statement.

I

A Poet's Reflections on Human Life

Quī[1] fit, Maecēnas, ut nēmō, quam sibi sortem
seu ratiō dederit seu fors obiēcerit, illā
contentus vīvat, laudet dīversa sequentēs?
"Ō fortūnātī mercātōrēs!" gravis annīs
(5)   mīles ait, multō iam fractus membra labōre.
Contrā mercātor, nāvem iactantibus Austrīs,
"Mīlitia est potior. Quid enim? Concurritur[2] hōrae
mōmentō[3] cita mors venit aut victōria laeta."
Cētera dē genere hōc, adeō sunt multa, loquācem
(10)   dēlassāre[4] valent Fabium. Nē tē morer, audī
quō rem dēdūcam. Si quis deus, "En ego," dīcat,
"iam faciam quod vultis: eris tū, quī modo mīles,
mercātor; tū, mercātor modo, mīles: et hinc vōs,
vōs hinc mūtātīs discēdite partibus"—nōlint.

[1]*Quī:* how   [2]*Concurritur:* an attack is made
[3]*hōrae mōmentō:* in an hour's time   [4]*dēlassāre:* to tire out

1. *fors obiēcerit* (line 2) is best translated:
   (A) he has objected to fate
   (B) luck has thrown in his way
   (C) he has cast away his chance
   (D) perchance he threw himself forward

2. *gravis annīs* (line 4) is best translated:
   (A) with heavy years   (C) in the grave years ahead
   (B) for heavy years   (D) advanced in years

3. In lines 7–8 a merchant expresses a preference for a soldier's
life because
   (A) death, if it comes, comes quickly
   (B) victory comes more quickly than death
   (C) hours pass quickly
   (D) joyful victory and death come concurrently

4. *Nē tē morer* (line 10) is best translated:
   (A) To make a long story short
   (B) That I may not die before you
   (C) Do not let me delay you
   (D) So that I may not be delayed by you

5. *modo* (line 12) is best translated
   (A) only   (C) provided that
   (B) just now   (D) in what way

6. The words *mūtātīs . . . partibus* (line 14) are best translated:
   (A) partly changed
   (B) in changed directions
   (C) you are changing in part
   (D) with your roles in life exchanged

7. The tone of the passage is
   (A) genially satirical   (C) frankly fatalistic
   (B) brutally cynical   (D) boldly materialistic

8. The main point of the passage is that
   (A) a soldier would gladly become a merchant, if he had the
       chance
   (B) a merchant would gladly become a soldier, if he had the
       chance
   (C) people are inclined to suppose that other people's lives
       are better than their own
   (D) the gods control human life

II

The King of Crete kept a man-eating monster in a maze. Theseus killed the monster and eloped with the king's daughter, Ariadne. He then abandoned her on the island of Naxos. Ariadne laments.

Omne latus terrae cingit mare; nāvita nūsquam,
    nūlla per ambiguās nāvis itūra viās.
Finge darī comitēsque mihi ventōsque ratemque—
    quid sequar? Accessūs terra paterna negat.
(5)   Nam pater et tellus iūstō rēgnāta parentī
    prōdita[1] sunt factō, nōmina cāra, meō,
cum tibi, nē victor tēctō morerēre recurvō,
    quae regerent passūs, prō duce fīla dedī,
cum mihi dīcēbās: "per ego ipsa perīcula iūrō
(10)   tē fore, dum nostrum vīvet uterque, meam."
Vīvimus, et nōn sum, Thēseū, tua—sī modo vīvit
    fēmina periūrī fraude sepulta virī.

[1]*prōdita:* from *prōdō, prōdere,* to betray

1. *Finge* (line 3) means
    (A) Touch
    (B) Grant
    (C) Invent
    (D) Suppose

2. *nē ... morerēre* (line 7) is best translated:
    (A) in order not to die
    (B) in order not to delay
    (C) so that you would not die
    (D) so that you would not be delayed

3. *quae regerent passūs* (line 8) is best translated:
    (A) to guide your steps
    (B) which guided your steps
    (C) who guided your steps
    (D) what steps they guided

4. Ariadne reproaches Theseus for
    (A) breaking his promise
    (B) leading her into danger
    (C) forbidding her to go home to her father
    (D) having killed his wife

5. Ariadne complains that
   - (A) the ship has lost its way
   - (B) she has nowhere to go
   - (C) her companions have seized her ship
   - (D) her daughter is being held as hostage for Theseus

6. Ariadne implies that a life without love and good faith is
   - (A) the fate of most women
   - (B) at least better than death
   - (C) no life at all
   - (D) a just punishment for their sins

III

Aeneas Makes a Vow

Tum pius Aenēās strictō sīc ēnse precātur:
"Estō nunc Sōl testis et haec mihi Terra precantī,
quam propter tantōs potuī perferre labōrēs,
et Pater omnipotēns et tū Sāturnia coniūnx,
(5) iam melior, iam, dīva, precor; tūque inclute[1] Māvors,
cūncta tuō quī bella, Pater, sub nūmine torquēs;
Fontēsque Flūviōsque vocō, quaeque aetheris altī
rēligiō et quae caeruleō sunt nūmina pontō:
cesserit Ausoniō sī fors[2] Victōria Turnō,
(10) convenit[3] Evandrī victōs discēdere ad urbem,
cēdet Iūlus agrīs, nec post arma ūlla rebellēs[4]
Aeneadae referent ferrōve haec rēgna lacessent.
Sīn nostrum adnuerit[5] nōbīs Victōria Martem
(ut potius reor et potius dī nūmine firment),
(15) nōn ego nec Teucrīs Italōs pārēre iubēbō
nec mihi rēgna petō."

[1]famous
[2]perchance, perhaps
[3]it is agreed
[4]renewing the war
[5]shall grant

1. *strictō ēnse* (line 1) is best translated:
   - (A) drawing his sword
   - (B) with intense rage
   - (C) in strict order
   - (D) by skillful means

2. *precantī* (line 2) means
   - (A) enraged
   - (B) deceiving
   - (C) praying
   - (D) relying

3. By *Sāturnia coniūnx* (line 4) is meant
   - (A) Venus
   - (B) Saturn
   - (C) Minerva
   - (D) Juno

4. *sub nūmine* (line 6) is best translated
   - (A) beneath thy name
   - (B) under thy sway
   - (C) below thy light
   - (D) close to the divinity

5. Iulus will have to leave if
   - (A) Evander withdraws to the city
   - (B) the Ausonian is defeated
   - (C) Turnus should be victorious
   - (D) Aeneas should win the battle

6. *Aeneadae* (line 12) refers to
   - (A) the sons of Aeneas
   - (B) Aeneas himself
   - (C) the ancestors of Aeneas
   - (D) Aeneas and his followers

7. If Aeneas should be victorious, he would
   - (A) order the Italians to be subject to the Trojans
   - (B) order the Italians to prepare the kingdom
   - (C) consider Mars responsible
   - (D) not seek the realm for himself

GRAMMATICAL AND METRICAL QUESTIONS

Questions on grammar and meter generally appear together with questions on reading comprehension. The following questions are based on the previous passages.

Select the answer that best completes each statement or answers each question.

I

1. *ut* (line 1)
   - (A) introduces *dederit* (line 2)
   - (B) introduces *obiēcerit* (line 2)
   - (C) introduces *vīvat* (line 3)
   - (D) does not introduce a verb

2. *illā* (line 2) refers to
   - (A) *Maecēnas* (line 1)
   - (B) *sortem* (line 1)
   - (C) *ratiō* (line 2)
   - (D) *fors* (line 2)

3. *dīversa* (line 3)
  (A) refers to *illā* (line 2)
  (B) agrees with the subject of *laudet* (line 3)
  (C) is the subject of *laudet* (line 3)
  (D) is the object of *sequentēs* (line 3)

4. *labōre* (line 5) is an ablative of
  (A) means   (C) specification (respect)
  (B) manner   (D) separation

5. *nāvem* (line 6) is
  (A) the subject of an understood infinitive
  (B) a poetic accusative of place without a preposition
  (C) the object of *Contrā* (line 6)
  (D) the object of *iactantibus* (line 6)

6. Which of the following lines has four consecutive spondees?
  (A) Line 4   (C) Line 13
  (B) Line 11   (D) Line 14

II

1. *Accessūs* (line 4) is
  (A) accusative plural   (C) nominative singular
  (B) nominative plural   (D) genitive singular

2. *factō* (line 6) is a participle
  (A) forming part of an ablative absolute
  (B) used as a noun, in the dative case
  (C) used as an adjective, in the dative case
  (D) used as a noun, in the ablative case

3. *tibi* (line 7) depends on
  (A) *morerēre*   (C) *prōdita sunt*
  (B) *regerent*   (D) *dedī*

4. *fīla* (line 8) is
  (A) ablative singular   (C) nominative singular
  (B) accusative plural   (D) nominative plural

5. Which of the following lines is identical in metrical pattern with line 1?
  (A) 3   (B) 5   (C) 7   (D) 9

III

1. *quam* (line 3) depends on
   (A) *perferre*
   (B) *precor*
   (C) *precanti*
   (D) *propter*

2. *sī* (line 9) introduces the verb
   (A) *convenit*
   (B) *cesserit*
   (C) *cēdet*
   (D) *lacessent*

3. *Turnō* (line 9) is
   (A) dative of the indirect object
   (B) dative of possession
   (C) ablative absolute with *Ausoniō*
   (D) ablative of cause

4. *victōs* (line 10) is
   (A) object of *discēdere*
   (B) object of *convenit*
   (C) subject of *discēdere*
   (D) in apposition with *rebellēs*

5. A case of elision appears in line
   (A) 1   (B) 2   (C) 13   (D) 14

DERIVATION QUESTIONS

Each of the following English words is of Latin derivation. Select the letter of the word or words below each italicized word that best expresses its meaning.

1. *stupefied*
   (A) hurt   (B) dazed   (C) delighted   (D) deceived

2. *arable*
   (A) barren   (B) steep   (C) flat   (D) fertile

3. *strident*
   (A) shrill   (B) advancing   (C) mounted   (D) heavy

4. *bovine*
   pertaining to
   (A) deer   (B) horses   (C) oxen   (D) sheep

5. *cerulean*
   (A) blue   (B) red   (C) dark   (D) light

6. *imminent*
    (A) entering   (B) famous   (C) evil   (D) threatening

7. *undulation*
    (A) praise   (B) wavy motion   (C) doubt   (D) excess

8. *lacrimose*
    (A) swift   (B) wanting   (C) dull   (D) tearful

9. *aviary*
a place for
    (A) bees   (B) flowers   (C) birds   (D) trees

10. *cincture*
    (A) a hole   (B) a solution   (C) a belt   (D) a wound

11. *acuity*
    (A) sharpness   (B) eagerness   (C) delight   (D) sadness

12. *capillary*
resembling a
    (A) tube   (B) hair   (C) stone   (D) cloud

13. *tumescent*
    (A) damp   (B) swollen   (C) lit   (D) bubbling

14. *marmoreal*
pertaining to
    (A) tombs   (B) styles   (C) woods   (D) marble

15. *coruscate*
    (A) wear away   (B) wrinkle   (C) confirm   (D) gleam

16. *arcane*
    (A) sudden   (B) bent   (C) hidden   (D) distant

17. *connubial*
relating to
    (A) marriage   (B) grammar   (C) home   (D) climate

18. *vaticination*
    (A) prophecy   (B) postponement   (C) false reasoning
        (D) hesitation

19. *sidereal*
pertaining to the
    (A) mountains   (B) heavens   (C) stars   (D) atmosphere

20. *ululate*
    (A) enjoy   (B) howl   (C) copy   (D) teach

INDEX

INDEX TO LATIN THREE YEARS

FORMS, GRAMMAR, AND WORD STUDY

INDEX

INDEX

CULTURE

4

INDEX

5

INDEX TO LATIN FOUR YEARS
FORMS, GRAMMAR, WORD STUDY, VERSIFICATION, AND FIGURES OF SPEECH

CULTURE

INDEX